May Laffan Hartley

Late Nineteenth-Century Ireland's Political and Religious Controversies in the Fiction of May Laffan Hartley

HELENA KELLEHER KAHN

ELT Press
UNIVERSITY OF NORTH CAROLINA AT GREENSBORO

ELT PRESS English Department PO Box 26170
University of North Carolina Greensboro, NC 27402–6170
e–mail: langenfeld@uncg.edu

NUMBER NINETEEN : 1880–1920 BRITISH AUTHORS SERIES

ELT Press © 2005
All Rights Reserved
Acid–Free Paper ∞
ISBN 0–944318–18–5
Library of Congress Control Number : 2005923104

Photographs Courtesy of the National Library of Ireland

Front cover
Earl Street, Dublin
(c. 1890) Photographer Unknown

Back Cover
Junction of Nassau, Grafton & Suffolk Streets, Dublin
(c. 1897) Photographer J. J. Clarke

TYPOGRAPHY & DESIGN

Display Type & Text Type : Stone Informal

TEXT
Designed by Robert Langenfeld

COVER
Designed by Toy O'Ferrall

Printer : Thomson–Shore, Inc. Dexter, Michigan

To my husband Jacob Kahn

with love and gratitude

ᘰᘰᘰ CONTENTS

ACKNOWLEDGMENTS

I owe many thanks to many people for their help with every stage of this book: first to Sister Declan Power who put the idea of it into my head; then to Professor Tom Dunne of University College Cork who enabled me to make it a reality; also to Helen Davies and the staff of the Boole Library, U.C.C., in particular the staff of the Special Collection, all of whom were extremely helpful.

Tom Donovan, a Limerick historian, gave me much valuable information about the background of the Fitzgibbon family; Mary Guinan Dermody and her staff at Tipperary County Library helped me to research the Tipperary Laffans; James Handford, of the Archive Section to Macmillans Publishers, supplied copies of May Laffan's letters to them and advised me where to find the replies; Donal and Nancy Murphy, Tipperary historians, supplied the origins of one of Laffan's stories.

I am indebted to Karen Anderton of the Irish Society for the Prevention of Cruelty to Children; to Fr. Sean Farragher of Blackrock College; Richard Fitzsimons, Secretary of Bloomfield Complex, Dublin; Sisters Dominique Horgan O.P. and Theophane O'Dwyer O.P., Archivists, of Blackrock, Co. Dublin; Ursuline Communities in Cork and Thurles, and professional researcher Patricia Moorhead, all of whom added to my knowledge about the Dublin life and times of the Laffan-Hartley family.

Further areas of knowledge were generously opened to me by Professor Harry Ferguson of Bristol University, Professor Greta Jones of the University of Ulster, Dr. Margaret Kelleher of Maynooth and her student David Walsh, Dr. Maria Luddy of Warwick University, and Dr. J. H.Murphy of All Hallows. To Dr. Patrick Maume I am particularly grateful for his constant interest, help, advice and information.

My thanks are owed to the staffs of the National Library, King's Inns Library and the Mercier Library, Dublin; Cork County and City Libraries, Limerick Central Library, and the London Library: all of whom assisted me.

My grateful thanks go to Toy O'Ferrall, Associate Editor of ELT Press, University of North Carolina at Greensboro, U.S.A., who edited this book and helped me to prepare it for publication.

Among the friends who gave me help I would like to mention especially Maighread and Ned Maume for their continual encouragement, and the generosity with which they lent me books and made constructive suggestions.

Family members were foremost in helping and I want to mention especially my cousins: the late Brian Desmond of Kilkenny, the late Michael Joseph Laffan of Rathgar, Joe and Bridie Laffan of Kilcurkee, and Pat Laffan of Glenageary, all of whom helped to put flesh on the bones of the 100-year-old family history, and whose interest put heart in me in difficult times. Above all, without the constant encouragement and interest of my husband, Jacob Kahn, I could never have started upon this book, much less completed it.

I gratefully acknowledge permission to quote from source material coming from the following: Appletree Press, Belfast; Archives Dept. University College, Dublin; Archives Dept. of Catholic Diocese of Dublin; The British Library, London; Cambridge University Library, Cambridge; Dr. Larry Geary, University College, Cork; Macmillan Trustees, London; Palgrave Macmillan, Basingstoke, England; The Royal Society, London.

KEY MAP
OF
IRELAND
Showing Railways.

English Miles

Ireland in the 1880s

JJ∩∩ INTRODUCTION

The attempt to research the life and works of a forgotten Irish Victorian writer does require some explanation and justification. My explanation is, first of all, that the identity of the writer May Laffan Hartley, although she wrote anonymously, was known to me. She was a friend and first cousin of my father's mother, who herself died before my birth. Some relatives could remember May Laffan, and spoke of her uneasily as a strange and original being. She was a writer of fiction which in its day was successful, she got into some kind of trouble because of the anti-clerical content of that fiction, and finally she married an Englishman who was an alleged atheist and a scientist employed in one of the colleges—nobody was sure which. May Laffan seemed to have left no descendants and no history—to have vanished like water poured into sand, almost without trace. Her books were by the early twentieth century no longer in print, and the family's copies had long gone—none of her cousins being readers or savers of fiction. The last of the people who could remember her had died in the 1950s. May Laffan was therefore to me a mystery to which I had no key.

Ten years ago, a copy of Laffan's second novel, *The Honourable Miss Ferrard* (1877), was given to me as a present. It proved to be not only readable but also interesting and valuable for its vivid evocation of late-nineteenth-century Ireland, and particularly the light it shed on the lives, opinions and aspirations of the Irish middle classes. It led me to search for and eventually find the other novels by Laffan. They were witty and entertaining, presenting contentious issues of the day in a more objective and realistic manner than did other Irish novels of the time. By comparison with contemporary novels, the Laffan books seemed not only better written and more deserving of republication, but also of being analysed and explored.

Laffan's work forms part of a progression of late-nineteenth-century Irish novels which includes the works of George Moore, Edith Somerville and Violet Martyn ("Martin Ross"), fiction influenced less by English than by French models, and often overlooked because so closely followed by more famous and more influential works. The Laffan novels add a missing

1

dimension to the Irish world of Shaw and Joyce. That is why they are now, with their author, the subject of this book.

It has not been easy to research. The trail, so far as Laffan publications were concerned, was very cold and all the colder because of anonymity, a practice natural to the Victorians but perhaps less comprehensible to us. Laffan did not even use a pseudonym, as did most women writers of her time. She simply did not want to be identified publicly as a novelist.

Allibone's Dictionary and the *British Library Catalogue* supplied lists of Laffan's publications; the former also quoted excerpts from some reviews of her books. Full texts of these reviews can be read in the London Library's magazine collection. Walter Houghton's *Wesley Index of Victorian Publications* supplied further details of Laffan's writing for magazines. American and English reference books on Victorian Literature, listed in the bibliography, added details not all of which were accurate. Macmillan and Co., Laffan's chief publishers, had kept a considerable part of her letters to them, and copies of these were made available to me by the Macmillan archivist Dr. John Handford, who also told me of the location of the other half of the correspondence in the British Library's Macmillan archive.

Most antique and second-hand booksellers had never heard of May Laffan. A few specialist libraries identified and possessed copies of her books, but because of their age and condition would neither lend them out, nor permit copying. Trying to read and take notes on a three-volume novel *in situ* in a library reading-room over a number of days is not to be recommended—the memory seizes up. My only solution was to enlist help from all quarters to find and buy those of Laffan's books which it was not possible to photocopy. Eventually, after about three years, this aim was fulfilled.

Laffan was most widely known during her lifetime for her very popular "sketch" or short story, "Flitters, Tatters and the Counsellor," first published in 1879 and reprinted several times. But she also produced, in the eight years between 1874 and 1882, a controversial magazine article, four three-volume novels, three more "sketches," a two-volume children's novel translated from the French, and a "moral tale" of novella length. All these differ noticeably from each other in theme and in form, to the extent of giving an impression of strong desire to experiment on the part of the writer.

Her themes mainly concern early deprivation, search for identity, and growth towards maturity. Her characters are to begin with at the mercy of circumstances that they learn to control or to overcome. Women are depicted as strong and stable beings, men as more impulsive, emotional and vulnerable. As a writer, May Laffan is very strong on atmosphere, dialogue and characterization, less strong on plot construction. Contemporary criticisms of her writing concentrated on its pervasive political dimension, which reviewers saw as excessive—unfairly according to Professor Robert Lee Wolff who considered the political aspects of her novels to be appropriate.[1] Other criticisms found fault with her introduction of marginalised and "difficult" characters, rather than the idealised, heroic and stereotypical figures favoured by many of her writing contemporaries. But the actual quality of Laffan's writing generally drew praise, typified by this description from an unnamed reviewer who described her work as "[m]arked to a singular extent by a combination of qualities rare in female writers—strength, breadth of humour, and impartiality. . . ."[2]

Humour she certainly possessed, though her style is on the whole more witty than humorous, but it is not absolutely clear what the reviewer meant by "strength" in this connection. Did it mean having a sense of confidence, of mastery of her subject; or did it rather mean a readiness to confront the unknown and tread on dangerous and unfamiliar ground? Probably the latter, bearing in mind that very few *female* novelists of that time introduced important social and political themes, such as education, extensively and persistently, and apart from Laffan none of them appears to have used a satirical approach.

Laffan's preoccupation with secondary education can be seen as excessive, almost an obsession. References to it appear in one way or another in almost all her writings. But in reality it *was* one of the major political and social issues of the time, and it would have been strange if she had not contributed to the discussion of a matter so important, both as regards the rights of women, and the need to educate the whole Irish population to make use of coming opportunities for local self-government. Although Laffan was to some degree obsessed by the shortcomings of the Catholic education system, she did not allow herself to lose the impartiality which was one of the main characteristics of her writing. She continued, for example, to be equally critical of Catholic and Protestant social behavior. This even-handedness was very unusual for the time. Novelists tended then to be uncompromisingly partisan in their approach to controversial issues. It was all right to declare oneself openly a Unionist or a nationalist, but it was not at all considered right to point out, as Laffan persistently did, the limitations and vagaries of both stances.

In her first novel *Hogan MP* (now available in e-book format on the ELT Press website: www.uncg.edu/eng/elt), her last novel *Ismay's Children,* and still more in her short story "Weeds," Laffan comments in passing on the political importance of control and ownership of land, the corrosive effects of political extremism on ordinary life, and the immense gap in political understanding between English and Irish people, between the rulers and the ruled. At the time of publication of *Hogan MP* (1876), the abortive Fenian rising of 1867 was still fresh in people's minds, its memory perpetuated by the successful Amnesty campaign to achieve early release of Fenian prisoners.[3] Also in 1867, the execution of the "Manchester Martyrs" Allen, Larkin and O'Brien on dubious grounds raised not for the first time the question of how far the British government was prepared to go in order to please English public opinion.[4]

Demonstrated in Laffan's novels is the underlying disagreement between separatists, who wanted an Irish state independent of England, and Unionists who wanted a minimum of change so as to keep the ties with England and the Empire intact.[5] These divisions were not necessarily on class or religious lines, and they shaded into a "centre party" of those who would certainly support *some* form of devolution of power, but were not prepared to fight for it, and wanted to stay within the British Empire because they saw no valid economic alternative to doing so.[6] Most of the members of the Catholic middle class to which Laffan belonged, and of which she wrote, occupied the centre ground. Other contemporary novels and stories of Irish life did not as a rule concern themselves much with *bourgeois* lives, or with issues such as higher education and social welfare, which were seen as having limited interest for the reading public.

Members of the Home Government (or Home Rule) movement founded in 1870 by Isaac Butt are shown in Laffan's third novel *Christy Carew* to be well aware that known or suspected members of the Irish Republican Brotherhood (IRB) were presenting themselves for election to Parliament, though in most cases without the active support of the Catholic clergy which had been an important factor in the past.[7]

There were several reasons for the lack of support. By the 1870s most Irish Catholic bishops agreed with Paul Cullen, newly appointed Cardinal Archbishop of Dublin, regarding the need for clergy to keep out of active politics, now that lay people no longer depended on them to organize meetings. Also, membership of the IRB was thought incompatible with Catholic belief and practice, because it was a secret organization supporting physical force and demanding unquestioning obedience from members. It was identified with radical anti-clerical movements in, for example, Italy. Some bishops actively opposed the Fenians (the name, taken from Irish legend, given by the public to IRB members).

The Catholic Church's attitude has to be viewed in the context of the failure of the Young Ireland insurrection (1848) and the abortive Fenian rising (1867). To be morally defensible, a revolution needed a chance of success. The IRB separatist brand of nationalism was seen as likely to plunge an ill-prepared people into yet another armed conflict impossible for them to win. Irish bishops carried opposition to the extent of ensuring that the IRB was officially condemned as a secret society by Pope Pius IX on 12 January 1870. Thereafter, the Catholic Church in Ireland gave its official support *only* to constitutional means of bettering Ireland's condition.

However, there was always a degree of ambivalence, and some clergy who thought constitutional politics unlikely to deliver justice gave tacit support to suspected Fenians. Notable among such sympathizers were "The Lion of the West" John MacHale, Archbishop of Tuam, Father Patrick Lavelle of the same diocese, and Fathers Gerald Barry and John O'Connor of the diocese of Cashel.

A classic example of ambivalent feeling occurs in *Ismay's Children,* where Father Paul Conroy, guardian of three orphans, knows that one of them has joined the IRB, but does nothing about it until warned by a local police inspector that the boy's activities rate a twenty-year prison sentence. We are told in an earlier scene that Father Conroy's grandfather was killed during the Rising of 1798, and that his brother was exiled for involvement in the Young Ireland movement of 1842–1848.[8] The suggestion is that Conroy, given his background, cannot bring himself to be single-minded about condemning the IRB.

The General Election of 1874 returned sixty Home Rule MPs, not all of whom were equally committed to Home Rule.[9] Laffan's satiric novel *Hogan MP* traces the decline and fall of one of these. Among new supporters of Home Rule at this period were upper-class Protestants who had grown wary of London government. They realized the old order was changing and they felt betrayed. Their role as faithful protectors and upholders of the Crown in Ireland was being taken away from them. The sense of this betrayal shows itself in scenes from *Hogan MP, Miss Ferrard* and *Christy Carew* as strongly as in the writings of notable Irish Unionists of the time.[10] But Unionists were not the only ones who found difficulty in managing change. The members of the emerging Catholic middle class did as well, and their trials are described in Laffan's novels in a satiric and detached manner unusual in the fiction of her age. Conventional political novels in English, such as those of Disraeli or Trollope, emphasised the "party" aspect by introducing politicians as major characters. Laffan did not do this, but she described the effects of political decisions on ordinary people, their understanding of events around them and the extent to which they could attempt to take control over their lives. Her continued contact with her Catholic peasant roots no doubt helped to deepen this understanding.

Still, however much we learn about Laffan's ability as a writer we are left with an essential mystery about her. She was a successful writer, not the most prolific of writers, but a writer of quality, one who enjoyed exercising her skills, received favourable reviews, and seemed to have a long and creative life in prospect. Yet that creative life which began with apparent suddenness in 1874, when she was twenty-five, closed equally abruptly eight years later. We do not know for certain why this happened, because no direct evidence appears to have survived. There are a number of possible explanations, which can be deduced from her writings and the limited personal information available to us.

The personal information is limited because during her lifetime (1849–1916) Laffan avoided being well known, so that researching her life and death has been problematic. The biographical information given here was pieced together from varied sources. Though the information available is far from complete, there is enough of it now to present an outline of the life of this unjustly forgotten writer, the settings in which she lived, and the significance of what she wrote. There is enough material as well to provide a base for theories as to why she abruptly stopped writing.

Perhaps the most obvious reason for a writer to cease production is the conviction that she has nothing more left to say. Extreme examples of this are writers who produce one book, and then no more. But there is no indication that Laffan felt herself to be running out of ideas, or was affected by writer's block. Certain common and eternal social and political themes run through her work, the principal ones being uncertainty regarding identity, the effects of the Catholic-Protestant divide on Irish society, and the shortcomings of the Irish Catholic education system, especially in relation to girls. Different permutations of these occur in all the novels and stories, but they are handled in ways that suggest development rather than loss of momentum.

To give one instance, psychological insights are infrequent in *Hogan MP* where, for example, a number of statements about education are made without being explored in any depth. But in Laffan's second novel, *The Honorable Miss Ferrard,* ignorance forms a major theme. Questions as to the true nature and purpose of education are introduced naturally for the reader's attention. The central character, Helena, is shown at first to be driven by her circumstances; as these alter, her understanding of the world develops. But her most effective teacher is the young man who loves her, and helps her to take control of her life. Whether or not she will finally reciprocate his feeling for her is left an open question, but it is plain that from describing mainly the actions of her characters, Laffan has progressed and is able to show what they feel.

To go straight from a witty, satiric first novel to a *bildungsroman* with a neglected girl as central character is a considerable leap, which Laffan was able to make, as at least one anonymous reviewer acknowledged in the *Saturday Review*:

> There was much that was clever in the author's earlier novel of Hogan, MP., but there can be no question that The Honourable Miss Ferrard shows a very distinct advance on its predecessor.... The author, who seems moderate and impartial in his views, is content generally to do his teaching incidentally, casting it into narrative shape. And, far from objecting to information so conveyed, we are ready to be grateful for it when our instructor is so capable as in the present instance.... It is highly creditable to the skill of the author that he should have made his heroine at once attractive and natural. He brings the faults of her neglected education into the boldest relief. He by no means slurs over the unpleasant vices of her nature, such as a tendency to shy sullenness and to the wild outbreaks of a wayward temper.[11]

Note that Laffan was still being identified as a male writer. But she must have been aware that positive growth and change was taking place in her work, and it seems natural that this would encourage her to continue writing.

Theories about the reason for her silence require for their construction some knowledge of Laffan's family life and background. Her early life, as will be seen, was hard, and it seems evident that writing enabled her to bear with it. She appears to have experienced a psychological crisis in her twenties, which briefly interrupted her writing. When she recovered, she resumed her career without obvious difficulty, but perhaps was left vulnerable to future stress.

Information about Laffan's psychological crisis came from two sources. The first was my father, James Laffan Kelleher (1894–1954), who said that Laffan, a first cousin and close friend of his mother, had a "nervous breakdown" in her twenties. He added that it was thought to be due to clerical criticism of her work, a theory which Laffan's own casual reference to the subject in a letter written in December of 1881 to George Macmillan seems to disprove.

The second source was my father's first cousin, Michael Joseph Laffan (1909–2003), who also mentioned the "nervous breakdown" but said Laffan was always a person who was easily upset and tended to take everything to heart. He said the clerical criticism was not serious, and was, in his view, compensated for by the appearance of her translated children's novel *No Relations* in the libraries of Irish Catholic schools. His information came as second-hand from his own father, who knew Laffan well because he had stayed with her family for two years during a crisis in his own life.

An entry by Frances Hays in *Women of the Day* refers to Laffan's third novel *Christy Carew* (1878) as "written during illness."[12] The "illness" could refer to an early stage of the "nervous breakdown." When she stopped writing altogether, changes appeared in Laffan's personality which were not for the better. These changes are evident from study of the following source: "Rough Notes on the Recess Committee etc. by Mrs. Hartley, 36 Waterloo Road, Dublin. nee Mary Laffan authoress of the famous novel 'Hogan MP.'"[13]

This manuscript, which is not in Laffan's handwriting, seems to have been copied for her by Standish Hayes O'Grady, who contributed and initialled footnotes of his own in the course of editing her submission.[14] How did a popular novelist come to be invited to submit a paper to a Parliamentary committee? Before 1898, local government in each county in Ireland was in the hands of a "grand jury" consisting of a number of large landowners selected by a Sheriff appointed by the Lord Lieutenant (Viceroy). A land tax supplied revenue for provision of basic amenities. This outdated system did not meet the needs of the community. Home Rulers saw reform of local government as essential, partly because the existing system was so inefficient, partly because it was hoped that membership of local councils would educate people for self-government. Their demand for a better local administrative system included state-supported technical and vocational education in its program.[15]

One of the main activists for reform of local government was Horace Plunkett (1854–1932), member of a well-known Ascendancy family, a Liberal/Unionist MP and a pioneer of agricultural cooperation in Ireland. He recruited politicians of all parties to his Recess Committee of 1895 which met during the Parliamentary vacation in that year. They successfully put together the case for extensive reform, which passed into legislation three years later. The committee, confined to members of Parliament and leaders of the business community, did not include women, but Plunkett seems nonetheless to have been sympathetic to women's issues. In his own account of the Recess Committee, he mentions collecting ideas and opinions beforehand from many European experts on technical development and education, but he names very few individuals. His submission from May Laffan Hartley, then still well-known as a writer, was probably requested because he thought she had interesting views on education. Plunkett is also likely to have met her husband Walter Noel Hartley, since he singled out for praise the latter's project to run upgrading courses for teachers at the Royal College of Science of Ireland.

Laffan's response is rambling, abusive and obscure—obscure because a number of the names of people she accuses of various offences have been blanked out. Dated 1896, fourteen years after she stopped writing fiction, it shows May Laffan Hartley as an unhappy creature, now completely lacking the objectivity and sense of humour so noticeable in her youth, hitting out at all around her in a fashion both powerless and pathetic. Nothing is right in her world; and Ireland in particular is hopeless. In her midforties, Laffan writes here as if she were much older, and had become extremely paranoid.

This is the only piece of work surviving from what could be described as her silent period, and it is valuable as offering insight into her state of mind during her middle years, providing a strong contrast with the letters Laffan had written to her publishers some years previously. The notable balance once present in her work is gone. Why did she feel like this? What went wrong? As the outline of Laffan's life unfolds we can see possible answers to these questions, relating not only to her state of mind but also to the reasons why after 1882 she wrote no more.

In addition to this source, there is some anecdotal information available about Laffan collected from people whose parents knew her personally. This cannot, of course, be said to be in any sense objective; we all tend to remember what we would like to think happened, or what seems to us to make sense, rather than what actually took place. Judiciously used, however, anecdotes turn some light onto areas of a subject's life that might otherwise remain dark.

If finding the Laffan books had been difficult, getting together personal information about the writer's life was still harder. The actual circumstances of May Laffan's life (1849–1916) obscured even ordinary details, and recollections of older family members proved not to be always accurate. The details given in "family trees" regarding Laffan's date and place of birth were only approximate, and needed to be verified by searches for baptismal records, as Laffan was born before the keeping of birth records became obligatory in Ireland. In fact, some records of the Laffans were discovered by fortunate coincidence. Most were in the Dublin area, but others, such as documents on Laffan's marriage, were found in London.

Additional biographical source information includes a somewhat unusual item: a short history of the Laffan family. This unpublished document, dated 1908, is the work of Dr. Thomas Laffan (1843–1918), a second cousin of May Laffan. Thomas Laffan was a graduate of Catholic University's medical school, where he was at one time Demonstrator in Anatomy. He later combined a medical career with membership of Cashel Urban District Council, and for his work in salvaging and editing Tipperary's Hearth Tax records was elected a Fellow of the Royal Society of Antiquaries of Ireland. Dr. Laffan was a contributor to D. P. Moran's *Leader* and an indefatigable if somewhat acerbic letter writer to local papers.[16] His family record, updated in 1921 by Rev. Thomas Laffan OSA and in 1987 by Michael Joseph Laffan (both cousins), covers the period from 1640 to the late 1900s. The original manuscript is lost, but a copy in my possession gives ample confirmation of the factors which enabled "middlemen" like the Laffans to survive and eventually to prosper over several eventful centuries.[17]

General details of the Laffan extended family and its background were obtained from relatives. Information about the early history of the Fitzgibbon family came from a local historian, a connection of the Fitzgibbons in Limerick.[18] Legal memoirs of the late nineteenth century and some political lives were extensively searched to flesh out the information on the Fitzgibbon legal dynasty already obtained from the King's Inns Library.

Records of May Laffan's schooling went astray on the way to me, and when at length received were simply a confirmation that May and her two sisters each began to attend St. Catherine's, Sion Hill, at the age of thirteen. The details of her brothers' education at Blackrock College were equally slender. It appears that record keeping in nineteenth-century "superior" schools was generally confined to pupils' admission and leaving dates, plus a mention in the programmes of prize-givings and concerts if the children took part in these.

Information relevant to the lives of the Fitzgibbon/Laffan family, and later of the Laffan/Hartley family, was used to build up gradually a picture of both households.

Thom's Directories of Dublin supplied information as to the surprisingly frequent address changes of the Laffan family, who seem to have moved house six or seven times before settling in Blackrock. Census records of 1901 and 1911 supplied details of the Laffan/Hartley household. The Royal Society's obituary of Professor Sir Walter Hartley by an anonymous friend gave an idea of the personality and achievements of May Laffan's husband; the Royal Academy in London was able to inform me about his artist father.[19] The University of Wales at Cardiff and the British Army records of military service in the First World War confirmed details of John Hartley, the Hartleys' son.

The *Irish Times* on microfilm at the Boole Library, University College, Cork, supplied the death-notices of May Laffan Hartley, her husband, her parents and her sister. The Laffan family grave in Glasnevin was located and photographed, as were the last three houses where she lived and the place where she died.

Projects undertaken in relation to the original manuscript included a very necessary and fairly extensive "crash course" in late-nineteenth-century Irish history; a brief study of the notorious Yelverton/Longworth marriage case of 1861 and its wider implications; and, in relation to Laffan's interest in deprived children, a tentative study of the provision of care and help for such children in late-nineteenth-century Ireland. With regard to the social history aspects, it was interesting to note that although Irish work on some aspects of welfare history is increasing it has still some way to go. I refer particularly to an apparent scarcity of Irish works on residential institutions, on child-care theory and practice, and on issues relating directly to mental health.

Not all the research was fruitful and much was simply frustrating. The British Library, undergoing its recent reorganization, took almost two years to supply photocopies of letters to May Laffan from letterbooks in the Macmillan Archive. Photographs which would have included relatives and perhaps a picture of Laffan—for we have none—had been destroyed by one of their owners. The National Photographic Archive was unable to help with any identifiable picture because no one was able to tell them what May Laffan had looked like.

Richard Bentley and Son, publishers to Queen Victoria, were Laffan's first publishers and may well have kept her correspondence, but their archive, now located in the University of Colorado, appears to be as yet uncatalogued and is apparently inaccessible to foreign students and scholars.

Requests to see the records of the Royal College of Science of Ireland were met initially with denials of the existence of any such records. This situation has now been remedied. Medical records relating to Laffan's illness and death were so sketchy as to be of little use—this is often the case with early medical records. Until very recently it was impossible to get accurate information regarding nineteenth-century burials in the principal Dublin cemeteries, a circumstance which hindered initial searches for the Laffan family grave. This situation has also improved.

In 1916 May Laffan, then Lady Hartley, died intestate. Details of her estate and that of her father were found to have been destroyed with other Four Courts records during the Civil War. Attempts to trace descendants of the children of May Laffan's surviving sister Catherine Laffan Morier have so far failed.

Finally, overcrowded conditions in record offices coupled with the weight and size of the heavy Victorian record ledgers in both Dublin and London present genuine physical difficulties to those needing to consult them for purposes of research. It is to be hoped that computerization of records will eventually put this right.

As against obvious difficulties, then, it can be seen that I found help and interest in many quarters, expected and unexpected. Without this encouragement and help, generously given and gratefully acknowledged elsewhere, it would never have been possible to complete this book, which has taken from start to finish about six years. That time will have been well spent if it contributes to the rescue of an interesting writer and her work from oblivion.

꧁ᙏᙏᙏ꧂ **CHAPTER 1**

Origins and Early Years

The questioning and challenging disposition in May Laffan, which
drew her towards controversial themes, had its origin in a divided inheritance. She was the child of a religiously mixed marriage. Her father, Michael Laffan, came from a Catholic family in Tipperary; her
mother, Ellen Sarah Fitzgibbon, came from a newly converted Church of
Ireland family settled in Dublin but originating, a generation back, in rural Limerick. It is important to take into account the influences of these
families because, unalike as they were in some ways, they were characteristic of their country and their time.

Each family was, to begin with, Catholic and Norman-Irish, renting
land of which they had been dispossessed, at the will and convenience of
new owners with whom they had little in common. The Laffans saw their
religion as an essential part of their identity, which they had no desire to alter. Part of the Fitzgibbon family elected to change its religious allegiance
and so to change its identity and fortunes; and this, also, was in keeping
with the times. Following the Act of Union (1800) there seems to have been
an expectation that *all* remaining penal laws against Catholics would be
repealed at once, and then they would and could rapidly achieve parity of
opportunity with Protestants. Frustration at the failure of this to happen
may have contributed to a temporary increase in the number of impatient
and ambitious Irish Catholics converting to the Church of Ireland.[1]
Among these were the members of the branch of the Fitzgibbon family
from which May Laffan's mother came.

The Fitzgibbons had been tenants on the Knight of Glin's estate in
County Limerick since the early eighteenth century at least. They became
freeholders of a farm at Ballyhoulihan, near Tarbert, on the Shannon estuary. The date when this actually happened, as well as the circumstances,
cannot now be ascertained with any degree of accuracy because records
concerning the administration of the Glin estate were destroyed in 1850.
Ballyhoulihan is right out on the edge of the Shannon estuary, facing Co.

Clare, and on the county border between Limerick and Kerry. There would have been few neighbors in the 1700s, and no surfaced roads. The "town-land" was the smallest administrative area recognized for tithe and valuation purposes. The next biggest official area was the parish. Ballyhoulihan town-land was part of the parish of Loughill, but almost cut off from it by the lie of the land.[2] When the Fitzgibbons traveled any distance, they probably went by boat as that would have been easiest. The land is fertile, and landlord/tenant relations there seem to have been good, to the extent that the Rising of 1798 did not affect them.[3] In the early nineteenth century the family was headed by Garrett and Mary Fitzgibbon, née Widenham. They had five sons; John, James, Thomas (May Laffan's grandfather), Gerald, Henry; and two daughters, Mary and Elizabeth. The sons, at least, were educated at a local hedge-school.[4] In 1805 the whole family moved to Limerick city, where the eldest son, John, operated a textile mill with the help of Thomas. A tithe record of the period shows that in 1816 John returned to Ballyhoulihan, and set up another mill at Glin, which made checked cloth and employed local people.[5] John is identified as Seanin Giobun or Jack Gibbon, later steward to the Knight of Glin. In the 1830s Seanin refused to contribute to the salary of a teacher and was named from the altar in a satiric verse composed by the parish priest,[6] who seems to have been talented in this way:

> "Ten pounds and fourpence from the generous Knight
> And two red pennies from innocent Breedeen,
> Five golden guineas from hospitable Donal –
> It is not from the wind or the sun he got his good qualities—
> Two pounds and a crown from Charles Brown,
> But nothing I got from Seanin Giobun!"[7]

There is a tradition that John's failure to contribute to local education was due to his chagrin at being unable to read.[8] If this is true, it would help to explain why he went a different way from the rest of his family. He must have felt he had little in common with them, especially with those who sought higher education. He may also have associated thirst for secular learning with Protestantism. His grand-niece May Laffan was to record the feelings of the unlettered in a way that suggests she knew something about the frustrations involved, though she may not actually have heard John's story.[9]

Communication between John Fitzgibbon and his immediate family seems to have lessened when, in the early 1800s, they decided to go to live in Dublin. If John really was illiterate, he would have been unable to correspond directly with them, and their decision to join the Church of Ireland is likely to have upset him. We do not know exactly when the decision to convert was made, any more than we know the date when Garret and Mary Fitzgibbon and their younger children moved to Dublin.

After his parents and siblings left him, John would not necessarily feel isolated, as most of his big extended family was still nearby. Once the Dublin Fitzgibbons had risen in the world, they were probably not anxious to remember their origins, and accordingly they may have wanted to distance themselves from Limerick relatives, none of whom had followed their example and converted to the Church of Ireland.

In 1944, a descendant and namesake of John Fitzgibbon at Ballyhoulihan wrote to Gibbon Fitzgibbon of Clonskeagh, Co. Dublin. The letter, which has not survived, was evidently written to fill gaps in family history. Gibbon, a great-grandson of the original Gerald Fitzgibbon (I), wrote back that he did not know anything about his Limerick ancestors, but did possess some old papers. He sent John Fitzgibbon a roughly drawn Family Tree.

We have no reply to this letter, but Gibbon wrote again to ask if his correspondent could trace kinship with the celebrated John Fitzgibbon, Lord Clare (1749–1802), who was Lord Chancellor of Ireland at the time of the Act of Union (1800). Evidently no proof to support any kinship could be found, for there the correspondence ends.

Garret and Mary Fitzgibbon went to live at Irishtown, Co. Dublin, and were buried in the graveyard attached to St. Matthew's Church of Ireland—Mary in 1830, Garret in 1837.[10] Of their children, James (1780–1863) had a highly successful career in the British Army in what was later to become Canada, ending as a Colonel and a Military Knight of Windsor, and finally marrying an Englishwoman and making his home in England.[11] Thomas (1785–1836) married Eleanor Mackay Cunningham in 1822[12] and died fourteen years later.[13] On his daughter Ellen Sarah's marriage certificate he is described simply as a "gentleman," but in *Thom's Directory* as a merchant.[14] He was May Laffan's grandfather. Henry (1796–1853), the youngest Fitzgibbon brother, became a barrister.[15] Of the two Fitzgibbon girls, Mary married a Mr. Haley, and Elizabeth married James Dore, of Dublin.[16] No more information about either has yet come to light.

It seems clear that in terms of social status the Fitzgibbons had risen greatly in the Irish world. But the shining success of the family was the fourth son, Gerald (1793–1882), who was at first employed c.1820 as a clerk by Jameson's, the whisky distillers.[17] On one occasion Gerald had to give evidence in court on his employer's behalf. The presiding judge commended him, saying he ought to be a barrister.[18] Gerald, then in his late twenties, took this seriously. He prepared for and passed the entrance examination for Trinity, and there studied law, supporting himself by tutoring others. He was greatly helped in this by the brothers Mortimer and Samuel O'Sullivan, clergymen associated with the University, and like himself converts to the established church.[19]

Gerald was called to the Bar in 1825, became a Q.C. in 1841, and in 1844 unsuccessfully defended Dr. (afterwards Sir) John Grey in the state prosecution against Daniel O'Connell and his associates.[20] Eventually Gerald was made a Judge, and subsequently Master in Chancery.[21] Gerald moved from 29 Upper Gloucester St. to live at No. 10 Merrion Square, and purchased a country estate, Larkfield near Clondalkin, a fashionable address west of Dublin where he died at ninety.[22] He had married late, and the elder of his two sons, also named Gerald (1837–1909), continued the legal tradition. Gerald (II) was to become State Solicitor, Lord Justice of Appeal, a Commissioner for Education, and the personal friend and mentor of Randolph Churchill.[23] Gerald (II)'s younger brother Henry (1841–1912) qualified as a surgeon and eventually became President of the Royal College of Surgeons of Ireland.[24] The Fitzgibbon family, therefore, at the time when May Laffan's father married into it, was a part of the dominant social caste in the country, and was headed by Gerald (I), then a well-known barrister.

Michael Laffan (1815–1895) was a clerk in the Custom House—then an unusual post for a Catholic to achieve. Not until the late 1860s was the British civil service open to competitive examination, and so the use of influence and patronage were still essential for appointment to any government post.[25] Michael had, however, been educated at the Erasmus Smith grammar school—the "Abbey School"—in Tipperary town where he had relatives, and this may well have helped him into the civil service. If not a Protestant, he had at least been to a Protestant school. Also, Michael's family name Laffan was uncommon and Frenchified, hinting at possible Huguenot origins, though like the name Fitzgibbon it is actually of Norman origin.[26]

Michael was the eldest of three brothers whose parents had made the transition from farming in the Templemore area to shopkeeping in the north Tipperary town of Templemore itself. His brother William, a successful miller and publican, was one of the traders who supplied the military barracks in Tipperary. Martin, the third brother, farmed near Borrisoleigh, in the same county.

There had been Laffans in Ireland since the twelfth century. Coming originally from Northern France by way of England and Wales, they settled mainly in counties Wexford and Limerick. The Tipperary branch of the family apparently started in 1640 when one John Laffan married a Miss Doughan, one of seven sisters. Her dowry was a farm in the townland of Kilcurkee, near Loughmore in North Tipperary. Nothing whatever is known about John's antecedents, but he must have had some money to contribute to the marriage, for example to stock the farm. The couple built a farmhouse (still standing, but now a shed) and as the land was poor they raised sheep. Succeeding generations became millers and eventually tillage farmers.

We owe this information to Dr. Thomas Laffan's unpublished family history referred to in the introduction. He goes on to state that the Laffans intermarried with the Purcell family who were the local Catholic gentry. The Purcells occupied a fortified house, or "castle" at Loughmore, and took part in the Williamite war (1689–1691), in which a Major Purcell fought, and was a signatory to the Treaty of Limerick (1691). Following their defeat the Purcells managed for a considerable period to hold on to their land and their social importance. In order to do this, it was usual that one family member made outward conformity to the state religion, for instance by attending local Protestant services. They would then be awarded the confiscated land of the rest of the family, who could be secretly named as official tenants (but in fact would not be expected to pay rent). This Purcell connection would have been very useful for the Laffans and possibly explains how they held on to their land. By the time the local Purcell family died out, in the mid-nineteenth century, the Laffans had prospered enough not to need their protection, and the laws against Catholics holding land had anyway relaxed.

There were now several local priests and even a bishop, Robert Laffan, in the extended family, not to mention missionaries, brothers and nuns.[27] This indicates that the Laffans were doing well, being able to educate their children to the level of acceptability for priesthood and the religious life.

Michael Laffan, though working in the capital, was not cut off from his origins. One of his uncles, solicitor Daniel Laffan, had an office in Dublin as well as an office in Cashel, Co. Tipperary. Michael was successfully appealed to by the extended family for help in such delicate tasks as "buying out" a runaway nephew from the British Army.[28] He had frequent visitors from that rural hinterland of Tipperary and Limerick which contrasted greatly with Victorian Dublin, and which his daughter was to describe so vividly in two of her novels.[29]

The Fitzgibbon and Laffan families were united when, on 11 June 1846, Ellen Sarah Fitzgibbon married Michael Laffan in St. Thomas' Church in Dublin. They were married according to the rites of the Church of Ireland, which was the religion of the bride.[30] As Michael Laffan was a practising Catholic, it is therefore likely that the couple also had a brief and private Catholic ceremony, record of which has not yet been found.

Thomas Fitzgibbon, the father of Ellen Sarah, had died ten years previously, but Gerald (I) witnessed the marriage and signed the register. Gerald, then in his early fifties, was apparently Ellen Sarah's guardian, since she gave her home address as his. We do not know how Michael and Ellen Sarah met, nor do we know what Gerald thought of his niece's marriage to a Catholic in Michael Laffan's modest circumstances, but it is hard to think that he approved. Curiously, some contemporary biographical accounts of May Laffan describe Ellen Sarah as Gerald Fitzgibbon's *daughter,* not his niece.[31] In support of this possibility, one authority credits Gerald (I) with a daughter (unnamed, and mentioned nowhere else) in addition to his two sons.[32] The family tree, supplied by Gibbon Fitzgibbon, his great-grandson, in 1944, even gives Gerald (I) a different wife—one T. Rowe—instead of (or perhaps, earlier than) Sarah Patterson whom he married in his forties. It is always possible that Gerald made a brief early marriage, even an irregular one, that is, a union not recognized by civil law, which produced a child brought up for convenience and discretion as a niece until of marriageable age. For, if there *was* anything about Ellen Sarah's status which made her less of a matrimonial prize, this could account for her being permitted to marry out of her social class, as she certainly seems to have done in marrying this particular Catholic.

Mary (May) Laffan, the future writer, was born on 3 May 1849 and christened in the Catholic Church of St. John the Baptist at Clontarf, Dublin. The only named sponsor for her baptism was her uncle William Laffan's wife, Catherine Mary. The local custom of the day in the case of a mixed marriage was to rear sons in the religion of the father and daughters in that of the mother. The fact that all the Laffans were baptised as Catholics suggests that Michael was either more devout or more forceful than his wife.

May already had a one-year-old brother, William Mackay, and eighteen months later was to have a sister, Ellen Sarah. Three other children followed in succession: Michael Fitzgibbon (1852), James (1854), and Catherine (1859). The family lived until 1852 at Number 41 Phillipsborough Avenue Clontarf, a house that no longer exists. According to *Thom's Directory* for that year, they moved to Rathgar, and Michael Fitzgibbon was on the baptismal register at Rathfarnham. The move south of the Liffey suggests greater prosperity, Rathgar being then an upper-class and therefore largely a Protestant enclave. According to census records of 1901, for example, most Catholics living there at that time were domestic servants.[33] But as if to deny the very idea of prosperity, the Laffans began a series of removals. From 1854–1858 their home address is unknown; but 1859 found them back on the Northside at 10 Mountjoy St. Lower, until 1862 when they moved out to Number 4 St. James's Place, Cross Avenue, Blackrock.[34] This was to be their final family home.

Unlike Clontarf, which is described nostalgically in Laffan's first novel *Hogan MP,* Blackrock is not commemorated in any of her novels. In the early 1860s it was a seaside village with a few shops and two extremes of housing—grand villas with big entrance gates, and thatched cottages in the back lanes where outdoor servants and tradesmen servicing the big houses lived. Like other places along the Dublin coastline it was beginning to develop, as city people became aware of the benefits of living in a clean, fresh environment. A sea-bath had been constructed among the rocks near the harbour, the railway had come out from town, and a new Catholic chapel was going up to supplement the one at Booterstown built for the servants on local estates. Some middle-income housing was available to let, as renting rather than buying was still usual practice. But the great attraction of Blackrock for parents must have been its schools. There were several small private ones, a Church of Ireland parochial day-school which some Catholics attended, the new French College for boys, and the Dominican Convent School for girls right in the village, the latter two taking secondary day pupils in addition to boarders.[35]

The Laffans' new home was only just built in 1862; they were its first occupants.[36] At the village end of Cross Avenue the house still stands, second of four in a stuccoed mid-Victorian terrace alongside the Church of Ireland

Church of St. Philip and St. James. The house is narrow, with three floors above a dark basement, and high by today's standards. The children would have been able then to see the sea from the upper windows, and access to the seashore itself would not have been too difficult. There is a steep flight of steps up to the front door, and behind the house, a little sheltered garden. Laffan's stories often mention gardens; large, romantic gardens, the settings for love scenes which cannot be private elsewhere. She never writes about a restricted garden like this, the real one. A room on the first floor overlooks this garden, a quiet room with one large window. Perhaps it was the room in which on 28 October 1862 Mrs. Laffan died.[37]

Deaths were not registered in Ireland before 1864, so there is no way to know with certainty how or why it happened. As with so much in May Laffan's real life, we have to seek out traces of her personal history from her fiction. Mothers of characters in her novels mostly die before the opening of the story. But in *Hogan MP* the mother of the heroine, Nellie Davoren, dies after an illness during which "another stroke" is perpetually feared. In the last of Laffans's novels, *Ismay's Children*, the mother-figure Aunt Juliet is disabled by one stroke and killed by another. If these fictional occurrences can be taken as clues to what actually happened, they indicate that Mrs. Laffan probably suffered from hypertensive disease, or some similar chronic condition for which, at the time, there would have been no treatment apart from rest and avoidance of stress. Her death was almost certainly not anticipated. The house removal would hardly have been undertaken if she were acutely ill and expected to die very soon.

At this time May, the eldest girl, was thirteen years old. Again, we have nothing to tell us directly about what the death meant to her, apart from her novels. Bereaved Nellie Davoren in *Hogan MP* weeps for days, shut in a darkened room. Some of the mourning is for her recently dead mother; some of it for the conduct of her unfaithful suitor John Hogan. Nellie is delivered from her grief by a new lover who comes out of nowhere to draw her from the darkness. Orphaned Helena, in *The Honourable Miss Ferrard*, mourns her father's death not as the Catholics around her do, with prayers, candles and the sharing of memories at a wake. Helena Ferrard refuses to open the house to the community; her brother Isidore and herself are the only mourners, and no prayers are said for the departed. This practice is in accord with the restrained Calvinistic mode of the Protestant Ascendancy culture from which she comes, and the whole account may reflect the manner in which Mrs. Laffan's funeral rites were conducted. But it is in May

Laffan's third novel, *Christy Carew*, that we are brought closest to the reality of loss: the tough little motherless heroine Christy feels pain every time she sees her friend Esther's mother demonstrate affection for her daughter, and remembers bitterly that there is no one who cares like this about her.

It is very likely that both Fitzgibbons and Laffans helped the family when Mrs. Laffan died. Again in Laffan's *Christy Carew*, we are shown the motherless children being treated kindly by Harriet, an aunt who is overtly critical of "Romanists" but, when the children stay with her, makes certain they say their Catholic prayers and are taken to Mass. In *Hogan MP*, the novel-situation which comes nearest to the real life one, Cousin Dorothy O'Hegarty gives concerned and active assistance. She is a childless elderly woman with a kind heart but an unfortunate habit of making tactless remarks about "R.C.s." Dorothy is well-to-do and generous-minded. During the illness of Nellie's mother she sometimes sits with the invalid to allow Nellie to go out. She introduces Nellie and her brother to the theatre, gives them presents and pocket-money, and brings them to dances and parties that they would normally not attend because, unlike their benefactress, they have no connection with the upper reaches of Dublin society. Harriet/Dorothy would have been modelled on Fitzgibbon relatives, women who were close geographically as well as in family terms to May and to her mother, and who were able to let genuine family concern about Ellen's motherless children override any class feeling about Irish Catholic inferiority. This passage from *Hogan MP* illustrates Fitzgibbon involvement as it is likely to have been. Nellie Davoren, following her first ball, stays overnight with her cousin, who is clearly fulfilling a parental role:

> Miss Davoren's cousin, Dorothy O'Hegarty, sat in a sunny bay-windowed parlour of Fitzgerald Place, waiting breakfast for her young relative. The wintery November sun shone in, lighting up the silver on the breakfast table, and brightening the grim visage of Desmond O'Hegarty, staring with hard grey eyes from his gilt frame over the sideboard. Everything in the room was bright and burnished; the carpet, an old well-worn Brussels was brushed to perfection; the breakfast-cloth was spotless; you might see yourself mirrored in the heavy old plate that decked the table and sideboard, and the fireplace was nothing short of a picture. Seated with her slippers on the edge of the fender, reading with gold spectacles on nose the fashionable intelligence in her favourite Tory paper, Miss Dorothy herself deserves a passing word of description. Tall and thin, not to say angular, with round, hard grey eyes and bushy eyebrows, she had a good nose, in profile—it was rather sharp at the point—strong white teeth, and a weak chin.... a broad forehead and thick grey hair—on the whole a rather handsome and un-

common physiognomy, but stamped with hardness, and unmistakeably cynical
. . . Nellie entered, fresh as a rose . . . Miss Hegarty dropped the paper and specta-
cles into her lap.

"Now, child, good morning. Are you rested? No one would imagine you had been
dancing all night. Perhaps you were not; you were a wallflower, hey?"

"Not altogether, Cousin Dorothy," said Nellie, laughing as she rubbed her hands
at the fire. . . .

Nellie's mother had been ward and niece of Desmond O'Hegarty, Miss Dorothy's
father; and she had lived with him until she fell in love with, and married, Mr.
Davoren. A long enstrangement ensued on this step; but gradually the old
friendship had been renewed, and had lasted since the birth of her first child....[38]

This scene gives a picture of Dublin life, but from those parts of her novels that describe life in rural Ireland it is clear that Laffan's frequently visited relatives in County Tipperary and got to know the way of life there
from the inside. Moreover, although nominally there was no contact between the Dublin and the Limerick Fitzgibbons, this would not have prevented the Laffans, who had Limerick connections, making contact with
Fitzgibbons still at Ballyhoulihan. On the baptismal certificate of May's elder brother William Mackay Laffan, one Anne Fitzgibbon appears as godmother, and on the certificate of May's youngest brother Michael
Fitzgibbon Laffan, the godmother is named as Margaret Fitzgibbon. It is
likely that these two, who would have to be Catholics to be godparents,
were from the Limerick branch of the Fitzgibbon family. Godparents then
were often natural relatives of their godchildren, and were expected to take
a personal interest in them, and particularly in their religious upbringing,
if the natural parents died.

At the time of their mother's death, the three Laffan boys were already
attending the French College (now Blackrock College) as day pupils; in fact
William was preparing there for entrance to the Cecilia Street Medical
School of the Catholic University.[39] He was only fifteen, but it was then not
unusual to matriculate and begin medical studies at about that age. The
mode of education used by the Holy Ghost Fathers at Blackrock was at that
time French rather than English. The boys wore cadet-style uniforms, they
had organized gymnastics instead of team games, and much emphasis
was placed on art classes, debating skills and modern languages—French
being the language of instruction. At Blackrock College no corporal punishment was then used, and the decision to send the boys there suggests a

considered and well-informed choice on the part of the Laffan parents. The records of individual pupils are scanty so that we only know that the Laffans were not remarkable pupils. A biography of Pere Jules Leman, the founder and first headmaster of Blackrock College, has recently been published and is informative about the daily life of the pupils and the ethos of the school.[40]

At about the same time as her brothers began to attend the French College, May began as a day pupil with the Dominican nuns at St. Catherine's, Sion Hill. This was almost literally across the road from No. 4 St. James's Place, the entrance being at the start of Cross Avenue. Part of the school grounds actually backed on to those of Blackrock College. A year later, Ellen Sarah followed May there, but it was 1871 before Catherine became a pupil.[41] Unfortunately, there exists as yet no account of the life of the Sion Hill school at that period. Record keeping then depended on individual school heads, most of whom do not seem to have envisaged people of the future being interested in school matters of the past. However, as Laffan was later to remark, some features were common to all the convent schools, and many of these were later described in novels and autobiographies of the time.[42]

In the 1860s, the usual method of educating middle- and upper-class Irish Catholic children was by home instruction with the help of a governess or tutor, followed by boarding-school. English convent schools were favoured for Irish girls, as a sure means of losing the stigmatised "brogue." For those who could afford them, schools in Belgium or France held the additional advantage of instruction in continental languages, proficiency in which was seen as useful at a time when many Catholics became involved in trading wines and spirits from continental Europe.

Boarding education in the nineteenth century effectively meant that a child lived away from home for almost eleven months out of twelve. They came home only for a summer holiday. Pupils of religious congregations followed a strict regime in which they shared the restrictions associated with the religious life of their teachers. This was generally more the case with girls' schools than with schools for boys. Parental visiting—indeed, any direct parental involvement—was not greatly encouraged either. These circumstances have to be seen in the context of a time when most children of well-to-do families were cared for by servants, and led lives apart from their parents, whom they saw only occasionally.

Originally, the day schools attached to Irish convents were charity schools, intended for children whose parents could pay no fees. Gradually by the 1860s this picture altered. Convents began first to educate a limited number of day pupils together with their boarders, and then to provide separate day schools, sometimes called "academies" or "high schools" for the Catholic middle classes.[43] In doing this, the nuns met a growing demand. Some parents could pay for a child's education, but not as much as the usual boarding fees, while others simply did not want to send daughters away from home. The Dominican convent school at Sion Hill, Blackrock, founded as a boarding school in the 1830s, appears by the 1860s to have begun to take a small number of local day pupils of secondary age.[44]

It was usual at the time for middle-class girls to remain at school until eighteen, or even nineteen or twenty, probably because there was for them no other form of education or occupation available.[45] In fact, the options for girls anywhere were extremely limited, consequently such education as was given to most of them was aimed simply at preparing them for a domestic life. Arranged marriages were still customary, especially in rural Ireland. Women who did not marry were seen as failures in life, although in Catholic and Lutheran countries they had at least the alternative of becoming nuns and working as nurses, welfare workers or teachers without loss of status. The restriction of life choices for girls was reflected in the sort of education convents gave them—to be criticised in the article with which Laffan made her debut in print, as well as in *Hogan MP* and, ten years later, and in her contemporary George Moore's feminist novel *A Drama In Muslin*.

The curriculum for girls' schools varied somewhat according to the pupil's social class. Free schools for poor girls concentrated on teaching skills which would help them to earn a living.[46] But schools for middle-class girls were not so practically orientated, and were often criticised for this. To some extent, they appear to have lacked direction. It was felt inappropriate to teach a charity-school curriculum to girls who would never have to go out to work for a living, yet, given the unqualified state of most teachers, it was not easy to know what more could be taught. There was an emphasis on music, drawing, fancy needlework and modern languages. Classics and mathematics were seen as too abstract for the female mind to comprehend, and the higher education to which these subjects were the key was still closed to women.[47] History was taught from somewhat sketchy books written by members of religious communities, because the standard texts available presented an exclusively English Imperialist and Protestant view of life which was not acceptable.⁴⁸ Geography seems to have been taught solely in terms of learning to find places on the terrestrial globe. At least as important as the educational aspect, though, was the semi-maternal role filled by some of the nuns towards children who otherwise lacked the involvement of caring adults. May Laffan does not seem to have experienced or observed this dimension; at any rate she does not comment on it.

In the opening scene of her satiric novel *Hogan MP*, Laffan describes annual prize-giving at a fashionable convent school near Dublin.⁴⁹ The concert programme of miscellaneous musical items, recitations and drama scenes appears showy and pretentious. Children are drilled to deliver from memory pieces in languages they do not understand, secure in the knowledge that the audience will not understand them either. The "musical offerings" are arrangements learned by rote, without any attempt being made to teach basic musical skills. Tasteless examples of popular arts and crafts finished off by the teacher are exhibited as the pupils' own work. Prizes are even reallocated behind the scenes so that the stupid daughter of a rich publican can receive one. Programmes still in existence of similar events at the same period bear out the accuracy of the description.⁵⁰

May Laffan, through the medium of several characters in the audience, ridicules the whole event. But at a later point in the same novel, when John Hogan asks the local Bishop and the Reverend Mother why girls learn only useless accomplishments instead of "real" subjects like mathematics, they reply promptly that the school teaches what parents want their daughters to learn—and showy accomplishments are all that parents want for girls to enable them to occupy their spare time at home prior to marriage, and also to avoid, at all cost, the appearance of competing with possibly eligible young men.

In Laffan's first published piece of writing, "Convent Boarding-schools for Young Ladies" in *Frazer's Magazine*, she attacks convent schools for the inadequacies of their teaching; not practical and realistic enough in her estimation to prepare pupils for life in the world outside:

> Why should teachers persist in using the books in vogue fifty years ago? Why not give English literature its due place among the school studies, . . . young women ought to know something of the cost of keeping a house, and of cooking a dinner, . . . a knowledge of the rules of spelling is highly desirable? . . . Of housekeeping, cooking, plain sewing or indeed any single thing useful as a resource and occupation, the convent graduates are in a state of complete ignorance. . . .⁵¹

The curriculum, as Laffan acknowledged, would probably not have been much different to that in most girls' schools of the period under lay management. What would have been distinctive was the nature of the ethos. In convent schools, the aim was unashamedly that of "forming youth to the practice of solid piety."[52] As a means to this end social and moral behaviour were taught, and character-training was given importance over academic success. This was particularly the case in the schools of French religious orders, where values different to the current English ones tended to prevail. Indeed, it was to offer acceptable alternatives to the latter that Irish clergy encouraged foreign religious communities to set up schools in Ireland.

Laffan believed that the huge increase in religious vocations in Ireland during the nineteenth century was directly related to the overweening influence of nuns and convent life on the unformed mind:

> Home life after four, six or more years in the refined retirement of a monastic establishment, with its beautiful grounds and gardens, flower-laden oratories and dignified sisterhood, is simply unbearable. Another powerful attraction to young and unreflecting minds is the idealistic, romantic esteem, in which the profession and its members are held. The religious habit confers a certain social standing of immense value in their eyes. . . .[53]

Laffan did not agree with the way religion was taught in convents, either. She quotes from an anonymous friend who had boarded in a convent school: "The piety always seemed to me, with its unvarying routine of religious observances, to be rather of the mechanical, sentimental order, than a real engrained and solid religion. . . ."[54] Laffan preferred, in theory anyway, the secular and practical mode of education on offer at Alexandra College, where domestic science was taught in addition to academic subjects, and she went on to say: "Several Roman Catholics have attended this college for years, and in all this time a single word calculated to hurt their feelings as Catholics has never been heard in any of the class or lecture rooms. . . ."[55]

Alexandra College was established in 1866 by the educationalist Anne Jellicoe, with the support of the Church of Ireland Archbishop of Dublin, Dr. Chenevix-Trench. Like other Irish Protestant schools of its time it was influenced by English socio-economic changes that favoured the academic education of women as a necessary route to female emancipation, and it was actually modelled on an English school, the Queen's College, Harley Street London. The function of Alexandra College was to prepare girls of fifteen and upwards for university. As such, it was clearly in the forefront of attempts to advance the status of women in Ireland by opening the professions to them. Later in the century, in 1873, Anne Jellicoe also founded the Alexandra School taking girls from the age of five. The curriculum included classical languages and mathematics, subjects that were not taught in convent schools of the time.[56]

Obviously Laffan wanted more of a formal education than she got, and she resented the restrictions imposed on her learning. She may have felt that she would have benefited from attending Alexandra when old enough to do so. The fees, however, would have been higher than at the convent she did attend, and this would have been a consideration for a family living on a modest income. It is probably not reasonable to assume either, as she apparently did, that nuns were opponents of academic education for girls, since there is evidence that they readily tapped into further education when the means were made available to them.[57] The often precarious financial situation of some nineteenth century convents, detailed in their annals, must have had some bearing on the rate at which they were able to expand their curricula, and try out new ideas.[58]

But so long as the role of women was seen as narrowly domestic, girls would not receive an education comparable to that of boys. If they belonged to the middle-classes, however, the parents of girls were concerned to provide for them as spinsters a standard of living comparable to the one they had enjoyed in the family home. Usually money was invested for this purpose in gilt-edged securities. During the nineteenth century, developments in technology and transport led to wider investment opportunities but also far greater risk of loss. Novelists of the time, for example Charles Dickens, Anthony Trollope and Mark Twain, depict such characters as the crooked financier—and the gullible speculator fated to lose his money. There were many of the latter, and an increasing number of families gave up the struggle to provide a lifelong income for members who did not earn. The novelists of the period began to write about a new sort of heroine, the lone courageous girl struggling against odds to make a living. In Laffan's novella *A Singer's Story* the situation of such a girl is vividly described. George Moore remarks in *A Drama in Muslin* on the relatively high proportion of unmarried middle-class women in Ireland during the last quarter of the nineteenth century.[59] He implies that they were reluctant to marry men below their own social standing, and another possible factor must have been the numbers of eligible young men killed in the Crimean war, the Afghan war, and the Indian Mutiny.

Poor women had always expected to have to work for a living, but now many middle-class women had to support themselves as well. Their expectations were high, and in order to earn enough to keep up a reasonable standard of comfort and security, a woman needed a sound general education that could form a basis for specialist training. Laffan's article was therefore an assertion of this growing need and a criticism of convent schools for failing to meet it.

More sensationally, there was implicit in her article a suggestion that many women entered the religious life for dubious and unworthy reasons; for example, the inability to cope with life outside the institution in which they had grown up; or the desire—in the case of the lower middle classes—for an enhanced social status. To even hint at this possibility needed considerable courage. Laffan published her novels anonymously, but in this case she signed her writing. Dublin was a small place, and her authorship would soon be widely known. Members of religious orders were not usually referred to in this trenchant manner, or at least not by Catholic laywomen. The Irish Catholic sense of identity was too frail as yet for any attempts at questioning an important part of its support system to be welcomed. All criticism was seen as destructive. And Laffan was nothing if not critical; it seemed part of her nature to be so.

In a letter to her publisher George Macmillan four years later, Laffan commented with pride on the *Frazer's Magazine* article: "Mrs. Mark Pattison wants it preserved, and some time or other it will come in *handy*—the mag. had two editions at this time. It was bought by everybody—and had the good effect of reforming the constitution of ever so many schools of that kind as well as almost procured [*sic*] for me a sort of minor excommunication."[60]

Rather oddly, she seems to have thought it would be a good idea to republish the article in one volume with her collected "sketches," or short stories. Understandably her publishers did not agree with her. (She does not enlarge elsewhere on the form the "excommunication" took, but it is unlikely to have been an official religious reaction.)

Markedly anti-clerical though she was in much of what she wrote, what evidence there is suggests that Laffan remained a Catholic until the end of her life, though a nonpractising one. In the census of 1901 which required household members to declare their religious allegiance, she seems to have had no hesitation in putting herself down as Roman Catholic.[61]

Indeed, the most important factor in Laffan's sense of identity was her religion, and in this she was truly a child of her time. In nineteenth-century Ireland religion and social class were inextricably connected. If you were or had pretensions to be a wealthy person or an intellectual, you were assumed to be also at least an aspiring Protestant. If on the other hand you were a Catholic, no gifts of nature or of grace could make you in most respects other than a second-class citizen of your own country. Catholic Emancipation made nominal changes, but did not alter—could hardly alter at once—either the way Catholics were generally perceived or the system of patronage and social contract that had served members of the Church of Ireland very well over many generations.[62] For instance, as described in Laffan's novels, Irish Catholics might now seek election to the English Parliament, but in practice could not actually do so unless possessed of private means, since members of Parliament then received neither salary nor expenses. Individuals or organizations which gave financial help to candidates were all-too-inclined to attach conditions to this help. The shortage of funds that inhibited Catholic Parliamentary candidates does not seem ever to have been a serious factor with Protestants.

Moreover, discrimination was still openly used against Irish Catholics in employment, so that appointments to banks, hospitals, insurance companies, the Bench and the civil service remained largely closed to them.[63] Local rural government was still, in the 1870s and 1880s, in the control of grand juries composed of local landowners, the majority of whom came from the Ascendancy community. In some towns, the holders of all permanent and pensionable posts, from that of local dispensary doctor to post-office lettercarrier, were as a matter of course members of the Church of Ireland.[64] Attempts to reverse such a long-standing system by practising "positive discrimination" favouring the majority community sometimes only resulted, at least to begin with, in the appointment for political reasons of dishonest or incompetent people. Examples of this are common in fiction of the time, and are described not only in Laffan's *Hogan MP*, but also in Capt. Thomas Lynam's popular comic novel *Mick M'Quaid MP*[65] and Michael J. McCarthy's trenchant satire *Gallowglass*.[66]

If middle-class Catholics were often frustrated by their circumstances, the poor people of whom Laffan also wrote were on the sharp receiving end of the system. The midwife who brought a pauper child into the world, the workhouse master or matron who regulated their care, their employer if they were in domestic service, the staff of the hospital where they went for medical treatment, the judge who sent them to prison for a statutory offence and the governor of that prison—-almost all belonged to what was in effect a ruling caste, differing from the poor in religion and sometimes seeing them as inferior on that account.[67] Popularly supposed to have disappeared with the eighteenth century or at the time of Catholic Emancipation (1829), some penal laws actually remained on the statute book until the 1870s. Apart from the marriage regulations already mentioned, it was against the law to bequeath money to a Catholic convent except under stringent conditions; and bequests to Catholic religious congregations of men under *any* conditions were illegal.[68] These rulings of course had an indirect effect on the resources available for helping the poor.

At another level, well-to-do Catholics might since 1794 attend Trinity College, but they were not eligible for its scholarships and exhibitions, nor could they be employed there.[69] Government aid to Catholic secondary education remained minimal, as throughout the entire nineteenth century an influential body of British public opinion opposed propagation, through aid to denominational schooling, of what were perceived as the dangerous errors of Rome.[70] The message was hammered home that Irish Catholics were inferior people to Irish Protestants, and this message provided justification for discriminatory practices. Laffan demonstrates that intolerant statements were frequently redeemed by gentler actions, but she does not seem to have been aware of the great and lasting harm done by persistently telling people in a variety of ways that they are lesser human beings.

Bigotry being universal, some Catholics did prefer to see Protestants as doomed heretics rather than as fellow creatures. Those who thought like this were influenced less by religious doctrine than by prejudice against alien traditions, and perhaps by their own lack of life experience and sophistication.[71] They may also have been rationalising bigotry by dwelling on the spiritual disadvantages of the rich, as outlined in parts of the New Testament. But there does not seem to be any suggestion that Protestants as a group were ever despised by Irish Catholics; rather, they were envied or feared on account of their socially privileged position.

The situation regarding unfavourable stereotyping of Irish Catholics was otherwise. Prejudice against them was general in the United Kingdom.[72] We can read that even a liberal Protestant like Gerald Fitzgibbon (I) saw Catholics *en masse* not as heretics (that term perhaps implying some degree of equality), but as idolatrous and superstitious members of a lesser race, following through fear and ignorance a primitive and outmoded form of Christianity.[73] In this he was not alone, for influential journalists and thinkers of his time like Thomas Carlyle, J. A. Froude and W. M. Thackeray seem to have genuinely believed that people who were neither Protestant nor Anglo-Saxon *must* be inferior to people who were both.[74] Possible reasons for this view are many. The "catholicity" of their church linked Irish Catholics to France, Italy and Spain, countries with which England had in the past been intermittently at war, and over which she had at some time achieved military dominance. Catholics were thought to form a particular threat to the civil order because their faith was seen as requiring allegiance to a foreign power—the Pope. Prejudice against them was strengthened during the 1840s by the Tractarian controversy, which was thought—erroneously—to be engineered by Vatican agents, and which appeared to threaten the survival of the Anglican Church.[75] Other factors were Protestant anger at the restoration of the Catholic Hierarchy in England in the 1850s,[76] added to misunderstandings about Papal infallibility and Catholic religious practice.[77]

Despite having the civil law and most of what may be called the financial power on their side, Irish Protestants seem not only to have feared Catholics as a group because of their greater numbers, but also to have looked down on them as individuals. The jocular stage-Irish stories and songs of the "Father O'Flynn" type produced so plentifully by Ascendancy writers of the time are full of condescension and stereotyping, but the haunting tales of Sheridan LeFanu and Bram Stoker reveal more: ambivalence accompanied by fear. In LeFanu's *Uncle Silas*, described by Elizabeth Bowen as an Irish novel set in England, the heroine Maude Ruthyn, child of a member of a Calvinist sect, lives in a state of siege menaced by hostile, uneducated underlings. She is unable to venture outside the demesne wall, which confines and restricts her.[78] In Stoker's *Dracula* the magician Van Helsing, who alone can rout the Undead, is described as a Catholic foreigner in direct and constant communication with the Vatican. He is shown imposing his will on the other characters in a grotesquely terrifying manner, and using consecrated Hosts of which he has a special supply to seal the vampires into their coffins.[79] In this and other very popular "sensation" novels of the time a lack of factual knowledge about Catholicism is evident; sometimes this is unintentionally comic but also in ways rather disturbing.

There is an overall impression in accounts of the time that paranoid feeling against Catholics actually increased after Catholic Emancipation, presumably because the threat from them was seen to be greater then. (If they had gained this much, what might they not want next?) It takes the form of accusations of lack of deference, and of respect for their betters. It might be thought that attitudes so narrowly characteristic of colonialism would have diminished somewhat by the time Laffan wrote her novels, but this does not seem to have been her perception in the 1870s and 1880s. The Dublin social scene as portrayed in *Hogan MP* and in *Christy Carew*, Laffan's first and third novels, resounds with insecurity, snobbery and a burning desire on the part of the ruling caste to keep Irish Catholics in their place at all costs.

May Laffan was now a young woman at the beginning of her literary life. She felt herself to be under-educated, but she was an omnivorous reader in several languages. She loved to quote, and enjoyed showing off her learning. (In *Hogan MP* every chapter is prefaced by a quotation in English, French, Italian or German.) She was not by nature philosophical or devout, but she had some strongly held beliefs: such as, in the supreme importance of learning, which she defended with an obsessional pertinacity. Somewhat surprisingly though, she did not, so far as is known, attempt to follow any defined course of study.

When Laffan was nineteen, her mother's uncle Gerald Fitzgibbon (I) produced a book that seems to have exerted some influence over her thinking. It was a collection of essays entitled *Ireland in 1868*, and was published in that year. Fitzgibbon was attracted towards politics, but not at party level. He was a committed member of the Church of Ireland, a Freemason and a Unionist. He seems to have been driven to publish when he was over seventy, to give his opinion on the state of the country, and particularly on the proposed Disestablishment of the Church of Ireland which he viewed with foreboding mixed with a degree of paranoia.[80] He argued that as Protestantism was the only logical faith it was the only possible religion for intelligent people. Catholics could not think independently, being under the sinister rule of priests who exercised psychological control on them through the confessional. There would, he felt, be a full-scale religious persecution of Irish Protestants if Disestablishment were allowed to take place.

Fitzgibbon maintained that Irish Catholics were unfit to exercise power through some form of "Home Government," because they were unable, due to lack of intelligence and education, to understand or acknowledge their troubles were largely of their own making. They simply did not work hard enough at behaving in a loyal and responsible way. Fitzgibbon went on to review in his own individual fashion several important issues of the day. He rejected the idea of a Catholic University, seeing it solely as a bid for Catholic clerical control of academic education. He equally rejected the Queen's Colleges, because none of them, he considered, could compare even remotely with Trinity College. Their entry standards were much too low. It was not really necessary for them to exist, either, because the number of students in further education should, to maintain exclusivity, always be kept small, and Trinity could accommodate these apart from medical students, who were thought to have no need of academic training. The lawyers and the few people who were fit to rule Ireland, on the other hand, did need to be highly educated, but this elite could not in general include Catholics, because they were unqualified; the circular nature of his reasoning seems to have escaped the reasoner.

Fitzgibbon acknowledged the shortcomings of the landlord/tenant laws, but he believed Tenant Right, the current agrarian issue, to be unworkable in practice and likely only to provoke expensive litigation.[81]The term "Tenant Right" referred to compensation of outgoing tenants for improvements they had made to the land and the buildings thereon. The fact that Tenant Right worked in Ulster, Fitzgibbon shrewdly attributed to its being non-statutory, simply a long-standing custom which was widely respected by both communities without needing to have the force of law.

Fitzgibbon seems to have had a working knowledge of Irish (to which he attributed his good relations with his farm labourers), and regretted that more Protestants had not seen fit to acquire the language.[82] Proposals for denominational education he tolerated, seeing no practical alternative. He said it was a pity that Catholics were so adverse to attending Protestant schools where, Protestants unlike Catholics being tolerant by conviction, he assumed there would be no harassment. So tolerant were these schools, he wrote, that within their walls religion was never mentioned at all, and Fitzgibbon evidently thought that this was the way things should be.

He went on to give what he thought and felt to be the main reason why Irish Catholics distrusted Protestants. English insensitivity and ineptitude were responsible, and he gave as main instance of this the history of the

Charter Schools founded in 1733 at the instigation of the Anglican Primate of Armagh Hugh Boulter, an Englishman. These industrial boarding schools were set up mainly to facilitate the conversion of Ireland to Protestantism.[83] They were heavily subsidised by the Crown and the linen industry as well as by fund-raising organizations in England and their managers were empowered to collect vagrant Catholic children, and even to remove summarily the children of poor Catholics from their homes. For a number of reasons the scheme failed, and was brought to a close after ninety years in operation; according to Gerald Fitzgibbon it contributed greatly to sectarian stress because Catholics resented its implication that they were suitable candidates for forcible conversion.

They must have resented even more the ill treatment and neglect of their children for which Charter schools became a byword. Though much smaller as institutions than their successors the industrial schools, Charter schools had similar problems and also exhibited the combined effects of severe dysfunction and almost total lack of supervision.[84] When he wrote on this theme, Fitzgibbon's formal and classically influenced style gradually acquired passion and indignation in a way suggesting personal knowledge of the effects of the brutal, abusive system he described. After quoting from eyewitness accounts he added that those who understandably doubted the truth of what he wrote could find it all confirmed in the published reports of John Howard, the celebrated prison reformer, and he gave chapter and page references. Fitzgibbon blamed English clerics and legislators for setting up a scheme so certain to create ill-feeling against Irish Protestantism in the long term.

His book sold well and quickly went into a second edition. According to R. F. Foster both Marx and Engels read it with interest, regarding it as a distillation of Protestant/Unionist opinion in Ireland at the time.[85] From the standpoint of today, it shows Fitzgibbon as a keenly observant pragmatic individual, holding no brief at all for aristocracy, having likewise no sympathy with radical social change—more tolerant in practice than in theory but assuming rather naively that because he succeeded in fulfilling his ambitions most people can do likewise, only laziness or indifference preventing them. A natural elitist, Gerald Fitzgibbon rarely questioned any aspect of the established order and his place in it. He showed a certain sensitivity to individual human need, particularly to the needs of children (in this his grand-niece May resembled him) and he had a strong nostalgic interest in farming which led him to farm as a hobby even though he admitted he could not make it pay.

Given her interest in current social and political affairs, Laffan must have read this book. Multiple echoes of Gerald Fitzgibbon's thinking can be found in her novels, expressed by characters with whose natures she has sympathy, but with whose opinions she is perhaps not wholly in accord. An example of such a character is the eccentric Mrs. Really, speaking her mind on Irish secondary education in *The Honourable Miss Ferrard*:

> "Schoolboards, properly certificated teachers, and compulsion—they'll thank you for it in the long run. And of this I am certain now, if the school system were placed in the people's hands tomorrow, you would not see the priests at the head of it; and if they were, what harm? They could even succeed if they could modify the present system. . . . if there were intermediate schools you would create and consolidate a bourgeois class educated in fair ratio to their wealth. That is what is wanted here. . . . How can the country improve? It is improving as to wealth if you will, but the people are fearfully illiterate. . . ."[86]

Mrs. Really, with something of an obsession about the need for control and maintenance of class structure, seems to be at times her creator's *alter ego* but is also drawn from Gerald Fitzgibbon. A convert to the Church of Ireland, she is an example of the intelligent and humane Unionist, supporting a measure of reform and devolution in Ireland but equally anxious to uphold the concepts of the unity and integrity of Empire, providing Hibernia might not always, as in Punch cartoons, be cast in the role of the simple maiden given condescending good advice by her big sister Britannia.[87]

In her teens Laffan was to suffer two major losses in addition to the death of her mother. In 1864 her younger sister Ellen Sarah died from consumption, and in 1868 her elder brother, the twenty-year-old William, gave up his medical studies and left for America. From the most simple viewpoint, this meant that she at fifteen experienced another major bereavement, and by the age of nineteen she was taking the responsibility for running a household and caring for three younger children. The siblings next to her in age, with whom she could normally expect to share her load, were no longer there. At a time when life expectancy was shorter than it is now, the death of a young brother or sister was not uncommon. The departure of William, though, was another matter.

Emigration, in the class to which Laffan and her family belonged, was not usually undertaken from dire economic necessity, but could follow the family's rejection of the emigrant, as a result of conduct that they were not prepared to tolerate. There was a social stigma attached to it, as is made clear in novels of the time, in which the troublesome son is banished to the outer vastnesses of the Empire. That Laffan resented her brother's absence we know from the following reference to it in her Recess Committee submission. Characteristically, too, she found scapegoats:

> I well remember my eldest brother, whose wish and hope it was to enter Trinity College, being forced by the interference of priests to enter the unchartered useless Catholic University, as were hundreds of boys. Where are they now? Many an empty chair and solitary hearthstone could tell their fate: sacrificed to the personal ambition of a pair of Satans (Cardinals Newman and Manning, H.K.). Six months or less of it sufficed for my eldest brother; and that now he is a millionaire in New York, is no fault of those pests. Talent and character such as he possessed, are badly needed here; but in this poisoned atmosphere such qualities cannot live and thrive.[88]

Laffan's assertion that her brother spent only six months as a medical student does not tally with information about him from other sources.[89] But we do not know how much stress and disruption had gone before these two events, the death and the departure. In two of the novels we can find some indications, first with regard to Ellen Sarah's death.

Christy Carew in its subplot tells how Esther, the daughter of a parvenu Catholic family, following an unhappy love affair becomes seriously ill. The illness develops into tuberculosis, and despite all her wealthy family can do, she dies after about a year of suffering. Little description is given in the book of the physical changes in Esther; much more about the effect her illness has on her parents, whose opposition to her suitor set off the train of events leading to her death. Of course, the circumstances of Ellen Sarah can hardly be directly compared to those of the unhappy Esther, but the somewhat indirect and reflective method used in the novel to describe a young girl's dying is highly effective as a technique and probably commended itself to Laffan as less painful to employ than other means. She could use the essentials of her experience of her sister's death, without having to recount the details. These must have been distressing, although less shocking than we might think in an era when dying normally took place at home. But the need to process and analyse painful experiences is surely one of the strongest driving motives there can be for a writer, and Laffan was not short of these experiences.

There would have been few families in Ireland at that time without experience of the death of a member from the dreaded "consumption," which was, generally speaking, a disease of young people. The course of that disease, with its insidious onset, remissions awaking false hope, and then almost invariably fatal outcome, was described by many contemporary writers and was of course widely known. The mood swings known to affect sufferers led some observers to make an erroneous connection between emotional instability and tendency to develop the disease; for the organic cause of tuberculosis was not proven until Robert Koch's discovery in 1882, and effective treatment had to wait another sixty years. Possibly for these reasons—dread, allied to uncertainty about both the unknown primary cause, and the method of infection—there existed something of a conspiracy of silence around tuberculosis, as around mental illness, and this is borne out very well by the case of Ellen Sarah Laffan. It is a good instance of the human tendency to try to obliterate tragic events.

Copies of available family trees drawn up at different times by different members of the Laffan family did not include Ellen Sarah. None of the living Laffans had ever heard her name mentioned. There was nothing to indicate her existence, therefore, until a search for baptismal records of May and her siblings turned up details of a hitherto unknown child—Ellen Sarah of the same parents and address. A search for Mrs. Laffan's death certificate, undertaken at about the same time, found instead the certificate of her daughter Ellen, giving the date and cause of death. Sion Hill Convent had a record of her admission to the school in the year 1863, but under the name of Rose, not Ellen Sarah. She died at home on 23 November 1864, at the age of fourteen. There was no death notice or funeral announcement in the Dublin papers, and the child was buried beside her mother in the family grave in Glasnevin, with its weighty recumbent tombstone in the form of a large casket bearing a cross.

For probable events leading up to William's emigration, on the other hand, the main descriptive sources are detectable in *Hogan MP*. A retelling of the Faust legend, it contains a number of episodes in which Dicky Davoren the heroine's student-brother is shown brazenly embezzling money given to him to pay college fees. He tries unsuccessfully to recoup by gambling, then by borrowing money, all of which he loses and at last, terrified of the consequences when his father finds out, he disappears. For some time no one at home knows where he is; but he is in fact working his passage to South America. Once in Rio de Janeiro, Dicky's luck turns and he becomes a clerk in a prestigious firm. He keeps contact with his sister, but not with his father who never forgives him for throwing away the chances in life which he had been given.

From semi-contemporary sources such as obituaries, biographical reference books, and the history of the newspaper he came to own,[90] it seems that William Mackay Laffan was a "chronic medical" student who neglected his studies, preferring to spend time and money investigating the junk shops of Dublin and collecting bric-a-brac, especially pictures. He was already a keen amateur artist, employed occasionally in that capacity by the Pathological Society of Dublin, presumably to illustrate articles on abnormal medical conditions which did not lend themselves to photography.[91] William seems to have been secretive about his activities and to have caused his father a good deal of anxiety and expense. In America he became a journalist, then in succession an art critic, a newspaper owner and finally before his sudden death in 1909 a very wealthy man, a patron of the Metropolitan Museum of Art, and a personal friend of the millionaire J. P. Morgan. William Laffan seems also to have been instrumental in getting his sister's books published in the United States, rather than pirated there as frequently happened at the time.[92] It is clear that his early experiences were transmogrified in a somewhat unflattering way to meet the needs of Laffan's fiction; and one wonders what he thought of that. As a professional journalist, however, he was probably accustomed to the occasional tendency of a writer to make use of some member of their own family as a model for a fictional character.

As she became more practised in writing May Laffan certainly processed her emotional experience more thoroughly, but the detached standpoint from which she viewed the customs of upper-class Dublin, as in *Christy Carew*, did not arise solely from her own attitude but reflected a reality. Some of the scenes she recorded were quite remote from her own daily life. The Laffans were not a wealthy family. Any Fitzgibbon cousins of May's own age—and we do not actually know if there were any—would have led a life far different to hers. To begin with, they would have been rich enough to be insulated from many of the distressing aspects of life in a city as poor as Dublin was then. There was a world of difference between the Laffans' modest rented house in Blackrock, a fishing village become a suburb, and the luxuriously appointed Georgian mansion with a staff of six or eight servants occupied by Gerald Fitzgibbon and his family in Merrion Square. The Laffans would not have kept a carriage or owned a country house. They would scarcely have been in the set that gave dinner-parties to dignitaries or attended the Lord Lieutenant's Levee at Dublin Castle. Nor would they have been able to afford holidays abroad, fashionable clothes or new books. The girls would not have been presented at Court; the boys would not have been commissioned in famous regiments. They would have had little to do with the celebrities and celebrations of late nineteenth-century Dublin, or with the land-owning county gentry slyly mocked in *Christy Carew* and *Hogan MP.*

But they must have encountered some of these people. Dublin was a small and intimate place. They would probably have been invited to family gatherings at Merrion Square, and perhaps asked to an occasional dinner where the number of guests would otherwise be unlucky thirteen. They would have been invited to wedding, christening and funeral receptions—being family, after all. They would have gone to fringe events of the Dublin Season of the kind caustically described by George Moore in the 1880s.[93] They would have made, through school, friends from the emerging and wealthy Catholic middle-class whose amusements they were occasionally invited to share. They would have encountered, though not on equal terms, the Dublin aldermen and the county gentry.

Social experiences of this kind are related in *Hogan MP* and in *Christy Carew*, with enough circumstantial detail for us to believe them genuine. That material must have come from somewhere actual—it is too rich to be altogether imaginary. But it also shows limitations. For example, it is interesting to note the marked difference between a vivid, amusing account in *Christy Carew* of a family's muddled preparations for attending the Lord Lieutenant's Drawingroom—followed by a rather perfunctory account of the actual presentation ceremony there.[94] It reads as if the writer had witnessed the first scene but for the second had to fall back on descriptive information gleaned at second-hand from others, who were present but unable to make their experience live.

The day-to-day life of the Laffans would have been comparable to that of the family to which James Joyce belonged, in its stable early phase. (Incidentally, it is likely that Michael Laffan knew James Joyce's father John, because the latter then personally collected the domestic rates from Number 4 St. James's Place in the 1880s.)[95] The Laffan income would have been about the same as that of the Joyce family, and they most likely lived up to every penny of it, "pulling the devil by the tail." There would have been domestic help, probably in the form of a living-in general servant and a charwoman who came in every week to scrub floors. But May as the actual housewife would still have had to do a considerable amount of housework, budgeting, washing, mending and cooking. It is significant that it was not until she was twenty-six and the younger children were old enough to help themselves that she emerged into print.

It is not known exactly when Laffan left school, but at a time when girls did not mark school's conclusion by taking public examinations this process could have been gradual. Laffan describes in *Hogan MP* and in *Christy Carew* the life of a middle-class young Catholic woman living at home in Dublin. She still goes to have foreign-language lessons at the convent where she was educated. She attends lectures and charity sermons, one of which, given by the famous Dominican preacher Father Thomas Bourke, is minutely described in *Hogan MP*.[96] She meets her friends when they all go—unchaperoned—to daily Mass and weekly confession in a fashionable city church. Sometimes they go—always chaperoned—to select entertainments such as concerts, events at the Royal Dublin Society, college football matches, and the theatres, where second-rate English touring companies present second-rate London plays. There are musical evenings at home, a feature of Victorian Dublin life. One of these is described in detail in *Christy Carew*.[97] The evenings sometimes concluded with dancing, though usually quadrilles rather than the "fast dances" which had been condemned officially by the Irish Bishops at the Synod of Maynooth (1870), although the edict does not seem to have been taken equally seriously by everyone.[98] (The adjective "fast" had nothing to do with actual pace, but with the alleged moral danger incurred in dances, such as waltzes, in which the couples embraced.)

Music, in the form of muted piano accompaniment, was also a feature of the "At Homes" or afternoon tea parties, the resource of hostesses unable or unwilling to entertain more grandly. For those with a social conscience there was always charity work. References to this are frequent in Laffan's stories. Literacy then as now was a matter for concern, and classes were organized in some city parishes where volunteers taught reading and writing to specific groups, such as servant girls or street children. But unless one had a vocation to the religious life, marriage was the real and unmistakable aim in life of every girl. Married women had normally more security and freedom than spinsters, added to a social status based on the income and profession of the husband. Although she describes first love in a touching and realistic way,[99] it is noteworthy that Laffan does not say much about marriage in her books. In *Hogan MP* the only marriage described in depth—that of Eric and Adelaide Poignard—is an abusive one. In *Christy Carew* the heroine's stepmother and her husband appear to lead separate lives. A wry description of the course of an aunt's marriage to an alcoholic is also given. In the other Laffan stories, the adult principal characters are almost all either widowed or unmarried.

Social life was more leisurely and structured than now, although it was hedged in by rules which to ignore could lead to ostracism. Women over the age of twenty-one could marry without parental consent, and some did so, hoping to be reconciled with their families at a later date. But married or not, many intelligent middle-class women felt bored and frustrated. In Dublin, it was difficult for them to train for a career or to support themselves while they did so.[100] Most single women did not earn enough to live independently, which convention forbade anyway. If they lived at home they could be restricted in petty ways, for example questioned as to their comings and goings or have their letters and reading censored. There is no indication that May Laffan personally suffered in these particular ways, though she describes the sensations of those who did.[101] Yet on the whole Irish society was perceived as less rigid and class-conscious than that of England, and it was differently organized, for, as has been said, class division tended to be on religious lines.

The Protestant Ascendancy itself was divided between landed gentry on the one hand and urban professional people (lawyers, doctors, civil servants and Trinity College academics), all mainly Dublin based, on the other. The latter group looked down somewhat on the former, which it saw as uncultured. Both groups, to the outsider, appeared very sure of themselves and their social position, but in fact they were, like Gerald Fitzgibbon, feeling under threat when the Church of Ireland was disestablished. Too many changes were taking place, and too quickly.

In theory, many Unionists now felt themselves to be Irish, and thought they should support some kind of "Home Government."[102] It might be preferable to English rule, which they had come gradually to realise was centred mainly on English welfare. But all these new-rich "Romanists" at Viceregal parties; those whiskey sellers and grocers, their overweight women vulgarly and expensively dressed, dripping with jewelry and furs! It went against the grain, thought Laffan's Protestant characters, to accept such creatures into their society, to "share power" with them even when there were clear material advantages in doing so. Moreover, the increased military presence (because of the recurrent threat to civil order) had brought in more Army people, equally socially undesirable, hard-drinking officers and their "barracky" wives, loud voiced and coarsened by military life. The Ascendancy world, as its inhabitants were frequently heard to complain, had become more complex than it formerly was, and the common people were beginning to lack deference.[103]

Meanwhile, May Laffan in her early twenties was taking in the complexity of the life around her, and finding in it material for realist fiction. It is significant that her first successful literary attempt was made, not with a poem or a story, but with a critical article on a controversial social theme—the education of girls. Awareness of the perceptions at different levels of the society around her seeped into her consciousness, aided by the measure of detachment she gained from being part of each side of the class divide. From her vantage point on the fence, she felt she could see both aspects of most problems, and that there were advantages in this.

CHAPTER 2

Adult Life and Works

The world presented to us by the novels and stories of May Laffan is almost unique to her, that world of the Irish middle class in the second half of the nineteenth century. Other storytellers had written of peasant life or the trials of the gentry; but she chose to write about the alcoholic ex-student, the impecunious solicitor, the farmer or merchant turned politician, and their often resentful wives and children. On the whole her world view was pessimistic. Rural Ireland was a beautiful intellectual desert. Dublin was a place to leave, not to live in. Unlike most writers who were her contemporaries, Laffan did not give downright approval to one side or the other of the social and religious divide, but weighed both and often found both wanting, as the following passage indicates. It is spoken by Nellie Davoren, child of a mixed marriage: "This country is so cut off from the other nations of Europe,—for it is a nation, in spite of geography, ethnology and all the rest of it. Thanks to our rulers, we have no manufactures to employ our time; and then, worst of all, these wretched castes of Protestant and Catholic hinder so."[1]

It has been said that Laffan was a critical person. Her first novel, unusual for first works, was a satire. She set high standards and castigated those who failed to achieve them, being one of those anti-clerical Irish writers who, according to Dr. James H. Murphy, rejected not so much the ideals of their faith, as the priests and the people who consistently failed to live up to those ideals.[2]

People in both cultures, Anglo-Irish and Irish, read novels; it was the main recreation of the literate and, despite Laffan's criticisms of the education system, the number of literate people was on the increase everywhere. Ireland then as now produced new writers in plenty. It has been calculated that during the nineteenth century alone there were upwards of five hundred women writing and publishing in Ireland.[3] This number does not include the expatriate women writers, for example Hanna Lynch, who lived in France and published in America. Once the number of male Irish writers is taken into account, the total doubles. However popular they were at home, Irish writers did not expect to gain much from Irish publication, as the native book-buying population was far too small for that. England and her colonies, with America, formed the main market for Irish fiction, and it was the London publishers and the London reviewers whose opinions mattered most. Irrespective of the viewpoint from which they were written, most Irish novels of the time were somewhat didactic, attempting to instruct the foreign reader about Ireland and perpetually interpreting the country and its situation to them. Inevitably, too, there was political discourse, which most English readers found incomprehensible and some indigestible as well. It has been suggested that the novel was not in any case a really appropriate art form for Irish writers, although they used it extensively.[4]

The fashion for ethnic novels which Walter Scott and Lady Morgan helped to inaugurate in the early nineteenth century had diminished after the Famine, and novels with Irish settings were less popular than they had once been.[5] In keeping with the Celtic Revival there began to be, towards the end of the nineteenth century, some renewal of interest in short stories, poems and plays set in Ireland. Novels however were not highly regarded by leaders of public taste like W. B. Yeats, as they seemed unfitted for the propagation of national spirit which he considered essential. Yeats did, though, include Laffan's short story "Flitters, Tatters and the Counsellor" (which was published as a book) in his list of best Irish fiction for 1895.[6]

The first of her novels to be published was *Hogan MP*, in 1876 when she was twenty-seven. We do not know how long it took to write; as in the *Recess Committee Notes* she refers simply to correcting the proofs in the year of publication with the help of Barbara Corlett, then head of the Queen's Institute in Dublin. Miss Corlett was a member of the executive committee of the Dublin Women's Suffrage Society, and Laffan accompanied her to its inaugural meeting on 3 March 1876, but it is not known if she actually became a member.[7]

Laffan's first publisher was Henry S. King, of London. King was brother-in-law to George Smith, of the well-known Smith, Elder & Co., publishers to the Brontës and Mrs. Gaskell. We do not know either how much May was paid for her novel. Publishers at that time were arbitrary in the amounts they paid new writers, but the fact that she retained her copyright, and did not place any other books with them, suggests that she was not pleased with them. They should have been pleased with *Hogan MP*, which received favourable reviews and sold well, to judge by the fact that it is easier to find a copy of it today than of any of the other Laffan novels.

The following extract comes from a lengthy anonymous review of *Hogan MP*, in the *Dublin University Magazine* of August 1876. It is interesting for three reasons. It assumes the writer of a realistic book to be male, it confirms the topicality of the subject of the story, and it presents a typical Irish Unionist viewpoint:

> There is a considerable amount of cleverness in this novel, though we cannot say that the ability of the writer has proved quite equal to the ambition of his design. He had evidently two leading objects in view—to exhibit a ridiculous picture of the pretension and vulgarity of a certain class of parvenu society in Dublin, and to expose the demoralizing tactics of priests and agitators who trade on party in Ireland. These aims are kept consistently in view throughout, and in many respects are realised with much rough force and striking effect. Hogan is a model of the unprincipled patriot of our day. He represents fairly the class of unscrupulous adventurers who obtain seats in Parliament by pandering to the revolutionary incendiarism that is a curse to the country. He is a Roman Catholic, the nephew of a Bishop. . . .[8]

Then follow several quotations describing Hogan and his actions (chapter three) and the review is concluded thus:

> Such, briefly, is the outline of Hogan, MP, and if, instead of refined, delicate and pungent satire, there is too much of rather broad and coarse caricature in the filling up, still we must admit that the descriptions generally have truth and point, more especially in the sketches of society, in which the Raffertys, the Brannigans, the Muldoons and the Cogarties (sic) so conspicuously figure.[9]

The reviewer clearly missed Laffan's acidic side comments on Ascendancy snobbery and instead dwelt mainly on the passages ridiculing the pretensions of the Catholic middle class. Appreciative of the writer's skills the reviewer may have been; objective he was not.

Laffan's second novel, *The Honourable Miss Ferrard*, was published in 1877 by George Bentley. It seems to have impressed reviewers as a more satisfactory work, that is, more conventional. Bentley specialised in publishing romantic novels by authors such as Rhoda Broughton and Mrs. Henry Wood. *Miss Ferrard* follows the Cinderella tradition of stories in which a beautiful Irish girl is rescued from poverty and neglect. The twist in this tale is that the rescuer is not a wealthy foreigner, but an Irishman. Political discussion, as before, tends to focus on the shortcomings of Irish education, although the statements made about it in this novel sound on the whole fairly positive and hopeful. Reviewers found the principal characters attractive, but the portrayal of the chaotic domestic life of the careless, unconventional Irish shocking. Laffan in all her books describes the homes of the provincial middle-class Irish as comfortless, ugly and dirty.

It is tempting to take the novel's principal character, Helena Ferrard, as to some extent drawn from reality. She is shown as a displaced person because her lack of education and means do not "fit" with her beauty, her title and her Protestant Ascendancy ancestry. Her disadvantages would have been more acceptable, it is inferred, had she been a Catholic. Did Laffan know someone like this, and extrapolate from what she was able to observe about them, and if she did, could that person be a relative of her mother—or that mother herself? The name given to this heroine leads one to associate her with a first cousin of May's—Helena Laffan—who was born circa 1861 and so would have been about the same age, when the book was written, as the fictional Helena. Like the latter, she was orphaned and brought up in unusual circumstances, though not as a Protestant. Laffan and she were friends, so it is possible that part of Helena Laffan's character and experience went to make up the tomboyish heroine so disadvantaged by her lack of education. It is interesting to learn that during 1877 May Laffan was seeking further education for herself. She is on record as attending Alexandra College for one term, to study Italian. She was obviously taking the opportunity afforded by royalties from *Miss Ferrard* to pay for a further education course—practising what she preached, in fact. Her experience was evidently favourable, since she seems to have arranged for her younger sister Catherine (Casy) to attend Alexandra College full-time for a period of over two years.[10]

Christy Carew, the third of Laffan's novels, was published in 1878, again by Bentley in London but simultaneously by Holt of New York to avoid pirating. This was arranged presumably by William Laffan, as he later made a similar arrangement for the novels re-issued by Macmillan. *Christy Carew* appears to be based most closely on May Laffan's own life experiences, and as such it is particularly interesting. The story, set in Dublin and its environs, concerns two middle-class Catholic families with differing value systems. The main character, Christy, is an adolescent girl at odds with her father and stepmother who want her to marry a rich suitor. Her character is shown in greater depth than those of the heroines of Laffan's two earlier novels. Her appearance is described also in some detail:

She was something below the middle height, and had a handsome face. The fore-head was perhaps a little too low, but her thick brown hair curled so prettily round it, that the fault was hardly perceptible. Her eyes were brown too, al-mond-shaped. To most people they had a good-humoured, lazy look, but there was a satirical expression sometimes in them, and they could light up with a firey sparkle.[11]

Little definite information is available about Laffan's physical appearance. No photographs known to be of her or her parents seem to have survived. As a family, the Laffans tended to be large and fair, with a curl to the upper lip which was characteristic of the Laffan men; but Michael J. Laffan, a cousin whose father knew May, reports her as resembling her brother William. From a photograph and description of William, appearing in a history of the newspaper he came to own, we can see that he was of medium height and build, with broad forehead, straight dark hair, and rather small, shortsighted dark eyes.[12] There is also the hint of a cleft chin—but no curled lip. His mother is most likely to have been his dark-haired parent, as portraits of her uncle and cousin show both men with dark hair and eyes. It is therefore possible that Laffan truly was small and dark, and did look something like Christy Carew. Is the latter character modelled on what May thought to be herself?

People with a critical perspective on the world may set unreasonably high standards for themselves as much as for others, and experience depression and anxiety when inevitably they fail. To go by family anecdote, something like this happened to May Laffan.[13] At some time during the writing of her third novel *Christy Carew* (1878), she became ill. We do not know the circumstances, but we know that illness was apparently given to the publishers as a reason for delay in completing the novel. The source of this information is twofold: the British Biographical Index,[14] and family tradition which described the illness as a "nervous breakdown." This vague and useful term can cover almost anything, but the most likely thing for it to be covering in this case is some form of depression. According to the legend, this was caused by clerical hostility towards Laffan on account of her scathing portrayal of Fr. Jim Corkran, the bullying parish priest in *Hogan MP.* No details are recorded of the form the hostile reaction took, only that it was serious enough to cause emotional upset, and to cause Laffan to give up writing for a time. It may have been at a local level, for example, a reaction by an individual; or it may have been more public, such as an attack from the altar or the pulpit. Her casual reference to negative reactions to her article in *Fraser's Magazine* in 1874 does not suggest an over-sensitive nature so there may well have been other depressing factors which she or those around her chose to deny.[15] About her emotional life at this time we know nothing, and she seems to have made a complete recovery. But we can infer from this incident that Laffan was more vulnerable to the disapproval of others than she would have been ready to admit, and this seems to have had implication for later events in her life.

Christy Carew is of a restless nature, manipulative, mischievous and impatient, recalling Becky Sharpe in Thackeray's *Vanity Fair*. She can be charming, but only for short spells at a time, and her darker moods conceal a certain aggression, an intolerance of people less quick-witted than herself. Her idle and enervating existence without point or challenge exasperates her at times, and then she dreams of running away, of leaving home to become an actress. She plays with the affections of her honest if not very bright English suitor, pleased at the sense of power it gives her to do this. Then, as she has from the beginning intended, she marries an Irish Protestant barrister of Huguenot descent, an ambitious and socially upwardly mobile workaholic. He is taken into partnership by an Anglo-Irish Q.C. resident in London who has just disinherited his only son for becoming a Catholic and is clearly looking for a "replacement" who will not disappoint him in this way.

May Laffan's decided gift for characterization is prominent here. We may not like Christy, her worldly family, her unsuccessful suitor and her too-successful fiancé, but we cannot help believing in their existence.

The boredom, tension and barely concealed aggression behind the scenes in this picture of middle-class urban life as lived in nineteenth-century Ireland is at times startlingly realistic, leading the reader to wonder how far it describes the realities of the writer's own youth. Indeed, it is this impression, rather than any separate incident, that takes us nearer to experiencing something of May Laffan's early life and times.

Christy Carew is in atmosphere a sad, almost tragic novel. The following short contemporary review which agrees with this opinion is part of an assessment of Laffan, which appeared in *The Cabinet of Irish Literature* together with some extracts from her published work:

> Miss Laffan is to some extent the precursor of a new school in Irish fiction. The Irishman always witty, goodhumoured and blundering was almost annihilated by the stern realism of Carleton, who painted him as he too often is—sad, brooding and among unhappy surroundings. But Carleton wrote only of the very poor,

and his realism, though sometimes unsparing enough, was usually sympathetic. Miss Laffan draws most of her pictures from the middle classes, and she cannot as a rule be accused of too much sympathy with the people she describes. Even her admirers cannot acquit her of overdrawing occasionally; for she is a satirist, and satire can rarely keep within the modesty of nature; but on the other hand she deserves the highest praise for the courage and the remarkable skill with which she has exposed some of the shams and narrownesses that deface the society of Ireland as of every other country. Her writings in this respect mark unquestionably a new era in Irish literature. . . . In *Christy Carew*, which is the last book the authoress has produced, she is back again among the middle classes of Dublin, and her biting satire of some of the meannesses of metropolitan life cannot be read without a certain degree of sadness.[16]

In *Catholic Fiction and Social Reality* (Dublin, 1997) Murphy attributes this evaluation to Katherine Tynan (1861–1931); but it is questionable if the latter, just over twenty in 1883 and at the start of her literary career, wrote for *The Cabinet of Irish Literature* until she became editor of the later edition in 1900. This review seems more likely to be the work of T. P. O'Connor or of Charles A. Reade who were joint editors of the 1883 edition. The comparison with Carleton probably refers at least partly to his striking portrayal of an obsessive character in *Fardorougha the Miser* (1839), comparable to and not unlike the character of Hugh O'Neill in *Christy Carew*.

The story "Flitters, Tatters and the Counsellor" was published next, in 1879, in the form of a little book. It had four separate and apparently simultaneous publishers: Simkin & Marshall, London; Hodges, Foster & Figgis, Dublin; John Menzies, Edinburgh & Glasgow; and L. Smith, Aberdeen. Finally, later in the same year Bentley also published *Flitters*. The story, a funny and unsentimental account of two days in the life of a group of vagrant children, went into a number of editions. Sensitively written, it indicates that the writer has had actual experience of such children. In view of Laffan's later involvement with the Dublin branch of the Society for the Prevention of Cruelty to Children (SPCC), it seems that she must have had a special interest even then in the lives of vagrant children. Though "street arab" stories formed a *genre* attempted by many women writers of the time, their productions varied widely and some were over-sentimental and unconvincing. "Flitters, Tatters and the Counsellor" was certainly one of the more successful ones, and Laffan was proud of it. She also seems to have retained the copyright, at least until she tried to get Macmillan to accept it in 1881.

In 1880, Laffan followed "Flitters" with the stories "Baubie Clarke" and "The Game Hen." The former story, about a Scottish street child, is set in Edinburgh; the latter is a story about a woman who fights other women. "Baubie Clarke" and "Flitters" both attracted favourable attention from John Ruskin, and were reviewed by him at some length. All these stories are noticeably different to run-of-the-mill Victorian fiction about poor people, being more compassionate and less overtly moralistic. In addition to these stories, Laffan produced in 1880 an English translation of Hector Malot's popular children's novel *Sans Famille,* under the title *No Relations.* This was first published in New York in 1880; its European debut did not take place until 1886 when Bentley published it in London. Laffan's translation is sympathetic and lively and does justice to the book, which again is realistic in its depiction of hardships and the manner in which children adapt to them; but its second volume develops into a more conventional and coincidence-laden tale about a conspiracy and a missing heir. Laffan's version seems to have run into two editions, the second of which was illustrated by Emile Bayard. She never refers to this work in any of the texts we have, but both *No Relations* and the last Laffan novel, *Ismay's Children,* are mentioned in the popular American novels of Sara Jeanette Duncan.[17]

It seems clear that Laffan had an excellent working knowledge of French. The account in her last-published work, *A Singer's Story,* of a young girl living cheaply in Paris is so factual and real that it suggests personal experience. She must have spent time in France to acquire the French she had, and it is probable that, like the student she describes, she worked at teaching English there. The ability to read French easily would have opened to her the riches of French literature and to some extent Russian literature as well, when we remember that in the late nineteenth century the works of most contemporary foreign writers had not yet been translated into English, but were available in French.

In the following year—1881—Laffan established contact with Macmillan & Co, who were to become her English publishers in succession to Richard Bentley. Most of the scanty background information available to us about Laffan as a young woman comes from the ensuing correspondence. This consists of an incomplete series of thirty-six letters, dated from 7 January 1881 to 17 April 1882. One section—those written by Laffan—comprises eleven letters from an archive now at Reading University.[18] Seven of them are addressed to George Macmillan, and four to George Grove, editor of *Macmillan's Magazine.* The other section, extracted from

Macmillan letterbooks in the British Library,[19] consists of twenty-five letters to Laffan from George and Frederick Macmillan. Frederick was then head of the firm; George was his cousin and assistant. Macmillan & Co., in the words of one authority, "Even in fiction . . . contrived always to retain two features of their early character: highmindedness and intimate friendly relations with authors."[20]

They were one of the most successful English publishing firms, and they published, in addition to famous English authors such as Charles Kingsley, Lewis Carroll and Thomas Hughes, Irish authors like Thomas Moore and writers, like William Black[21] and Annie Keary,[22] for instance, of books set in Ireland. At first, the (unrecorded) approaches made to Macmillan by Laffan met with a muted response. A formal letter from the firm acknowledged hers, and explained: "With regard to the republication of your Gutter Stories we should be very glad to consider the matter but should like to know first your views as to terms, whether you expect a payment down or some share in the profits. As the stories have all been published already we cannot of course afford to pay for them as for new work."[23] May replied in her usual letter style. She used dashes for punctuation, which gave a somewhat breathless impression:

> The stories are new enough as regards the English readers—The Game Hen has never been seen in London save by a dozen people to whom I sent copies—the enclosed reviews reached me yesterday—the Scotsman came out only last week.
>
> 600 Flitters were sold and no more and I know nothing of Baubie Clarke save that everyone likes it and I dare say you have seen the revs in the *Athenaeum* etc I enclose you an *Aberdeen Journal* notice of it.
>
> What I want to do is to sell it out and out and I can give you shares of Flitters.[24]

Gradually the Macmillans thawed towards their correspondent. Over the next few weeks, George Macmillan at any rate read *Hogan MP* and the "sketches," and accepted them, but asked for another story to make up a publishable set: "We must of course await your convenience for the new story. I can easily understand that such fresh and natural work is not produced offhand, or written to order. But I hope you will let us have it in the course of the year, if the spirit moves you. I shall be glad, if chance brings us together again before you leave town."[25]

Laffan was staying with friends in London and evidently had visited her prospective publisher. We learn from occasional asides in her following Macmillan letters that she came to know several people of importance in the English literary world. Indeed, we have a tantalising glimpse of the range of her acquaintance which, given her background, seems remarkable. One of her friends was Rhoda Broughton, a prolific and very popular novelist specialising in stories about exploited young women.[26] Broughton was a cousin of Sheridan Le Fanu, who published her first stories in the *Dublin University Magazine*; but she had settled in Oxford where she was part of a coterie led by Laffan's friends the Pattisons.[27]

Mark and Emilia Pattison were popularly supposed to be the originals of the characters Edward and Dorothea Casaubon in George Eliot's novel *Middlemarch* (1860). In 1879 Laffan's name was mentioned to Mrs. Pattison, apparently for the first time, in a letter from her friend Sir Charles Dilke,[28] who had met May at the home of Lady Russell, widow of the Prime Minister, Sir John Russell. Dilke thought Laffan was "great fun" but also that she "looked immodest."[29] Mrs. Pattison held a literary salon, in opposition to that of Mrs. Liddell, mother of "Alice in Wonderland."[30] A writer on eighteenth-century art, Emilia Pattison knew the novelist George Eliot well, and had herself a considerable reputation as an *avant-garde* intellectual. She was also, like Laffan, an advocate of better education for women.

Mark Pattison, Rector of Lincoln College, was a former follower of Newman. Influenced by J. A. Froude, he became agnostic but remained a clergyman. By 1881 the Pattison marriage was in difficulties. Emilia having left him, Mark Pattison had fallen in love with Meta Bradley, the niece of a colleague, causing scandal in Oxford. He enlisted the help of May Laffan to detect the sender of a particularly insulting anonymous letter, but her forthright attempts to do this made the whole situation much worse, causing him to complain to a friend about the tactlessness of Irish women.[31]

Another friend was Thomas Arnold, brother of Matthew Arnold, the Poet Laureate. Thomas was from 1856–1865 a Catholic University lecturer. During his time in Dublin, he was robbed by a servant girl recommended to him by Laffan, who would herself have been no more than sixteen at the time. She relates the story in sardonic detail in the *Recess Committee Notes*, but she does not take any responsibility for the occurrence.[32]

R. E. Francillon, a lawyer turned journalist and a writer of highly complicated stories, was another of Laffan's circle.[33] He was harassed by a begging-letter writer who got his address (and Laffan's) from Macmillan, and she expressed great indignation to her publishers about that: "being made a target for such missives as the enclosed. This letter to my mind bears every impress of duplicity. . . . It is clearly a case for the Charity Organization Society. I never felt so angry as when I read Mr. Francillon's letter one of the kindest and best of men and all very heavily weighted too. This fellow has clearly imposed upon him."[33] Once accepted as a Macmillan author, she made several attempts to recommend friends who were also trying to get work published. The first of these was a Professor Baldwin of the Richmond Commission.[34] May Laffan suggested that he should be invited to write the preface to what she considered to be a long overdue popular edition of Arthur Young's *Travels in Ireland and France*.[35] She also recommended a book by a Mr. Beljames, who has not proved traceable, and one by J. J. Tylor, an Egyptologist.[36] These attempts were not successful; George Macmillan showed considerable skill and patience in fending them off.

Macmillan decided eventually to bring out a new edition of all of Laffan's works to date, apart from *No Relations*. They did not do this without persuasion—their reluctance seems to have been natural enough as the books had originally been launched by other publishers who reaped the first benefits. At length they offered Laffan profit-sharing terms with which she agreed. They refused to make her an offer for the copyrights, and, as Frederick Macmillan explained:

> I think it would be a pity to print your books in a cheap edition. If they are worth reprinting at all they are worth decent paper and binding.
>
> More useful to bring out six-shilling editions of "Hogan" and "Miss Ferrard" on half-profit which means that we take the risks and divide the profits with you when they come. . . . How would that suit you?[37]

It seems to have suited Laffan very well. There were still, however, some difficulties. She had arranged with American printers to print her works for publication in the United States simultaneously with London publication. William Laffan was arranging this, and she had to persuade Macmillan to agree. Eventually they did. Next, their printers objected to the spelling in the dialect passages. It differed from conventional English spelling. In the same page, they confusingly encountered "owld" and "old," and "wan" and "one." This problem was sorted out, and the printer told to follow copy, however spelt. But a more serious matter then arose.

The story which Laffan had newly written was to be published in the September issue of *Macmillan's Magazine*, their house journal, as a sort of appetiser before the republication of her novels in the autumn. Unlike the other sketches, it did not feature children or the urban poor. *Weeds* was a study of rural Irish deprivation and degradation, and its consequences, that is, murder in this instance. George Grove, editor of *Macmillan's Magazine*, was evidently shocked by what he perceived as clear support for physical violence. We do not have copies of any of his letters to Laffan, but their content can be deduced from her replies. He seems to have remonstrated with her and insisted on changes to the text before he could publish *Weeds*. Reluctantly, she agreed to the changes. Then, probably inadvertently, Grove published *Weeds* under Laffan's own name, despite her previous express stipulation that all her writings should be published anonymously. Her reaction was prompt:

> I suppose it was to pay me out for not putting a moral to "Weeds" that you went and laid my name to it. I shall in all probability be shot by my erst friends of the Land League. . . . I thought I had clearly made it understood to the Messieurs MacMillan that I did not want my name to appear—it is such a bore. My father & sister arrived yesterday from Buxton & say that their friends there from the day of Macmillan's appearance worried their lives out. My sister Casy says they took to quoting poetry to her, & asked her opinion on all sorts of literary matters—I will not have my name to my books or stories. The plague is too much altogether. Rhoda Broughton told me that if she were to begin again she never would put her name to her books. Really, out of London it is not pleasant to be noticed & worst of all people are either on the defensive or get on their hind legs—all pleasure in life is destroyed —if the famous Caliph had not gone about incognito, where would the Arabian Nights have been. It is a detestable thing to be ticketed Novelist. . . .[38]

At this period, May Laffan's father Michael Laffan was sixty-six years old, and probably had just retired from the Custom House, where he had attained the level of Chief Clerk. Had he been still employed in the civil service when the offending story appeared under his daughter's name there might have been repercussions for him—as, according to W. E. Houghton, anonymity was really necessary in Victorian times to permit free expression of opinion by civil servants as well as by serving officers in the Army and Navy.[39]

What is also evident is that May Laffan disliked personal publicity anyway, feeling that it inhibited her in the collection of material. It seems clear that at this stage of her life she had no intention to give up writing fiction. In October of that eventful year, George Macmillan wrote again to her:

Mr. O'Brien's copy of Miss Ferrard went to him before his misadventure. We will send Hogan MP to his present address, where I hope it will help to cheer his hours of loneliness!

How would you like me to show your letter to Mr. G? I fear that you would then share the fate of your best friends. . . . [40]

This letter refers to the imprisonment of William O'Brien (1852–1928), editor of *United Ireland*. The paper had been suppressed and O'Brien was in prison. It seems likely that Laffan's request to send the books to O'Brien was a simple gesture of sympathy and friendship; for she had had similar copies sent to a number of her friends. The reference to "Mr. G" (Gladstone) is not altogether facetious. Letters from Laffan to George Macmillan, to which he referred and in which she clearly criticised British political leaders and their policy in Ireland, are all missing from the archive. It must have been felt prudent to destroy them. In a letter dated 24 October 1881 from George Macmillan offering £20 for the copyright of *Christy Carew*, he mentions casually that Laffan's recent letters to him (which are among the missing) are "rather dangerous."

Some of Laffan's letters during this period are addressed from Blackrock, some from different London addresses. One from McKeown's Hotel, Leenane, Connemara reveals a vibrant social life:

Thanks for your note. The proofs came yesterday and the friends with whom I am yachting here have one and all pronounced me a murderer & worse.

The alterations you suggest shall be made though it is against my principles to put my own sentiments into anything I write. The Athenaeum spoke of the "characteristic cynicism" of the author of "Hogan MP."[41]

I am not a bit cynical and I should like to hang with my own hands anyone who tortures a cow or horse—but I try to let people speak for themselves without any showman comments. . . .

You ought to be here, if you like roughing it. I have been wet to the skin twice a day since Monday out fishing. It is a splendid place for sport—almost a solitude—with scenery, unsophisticated natives, and unmistakeably good salmon and trout fishing—I took two of the last with one throw yesterday. You are in easy reach of sea, lough and river fishing. 3 good rivers, and such appetites as a horse— It rains every other ten minutes but the rain is warm and makes one rather comfortable than otherwise.[42]

The overall impression is of happiness. Life seems to be going well for her. In December Laffan is back in London, and preoccupied with illustrations for "Flitters". She knows exactly what she wants—a frontispiece only, and it must be a reproduction of a painting by "Dolly Tennant." This could be name-dropping, a fault from which Laffan was not free. Dorothy Tennant (Lady Stanley) was a well-known *genre* painter of children.[43] But perhaps she really knew the artist. However, the picture of a little girl nursing a baby which was the frontispiece to the Macmillan edition of "Flitters" and looks remarkably like that child's description, is signed "Paterson" and could be the work of Helen Allingham, née Paterson, also a painter of children and wife of the poet William Allingham.[44] Laffan goes on to explain that she actually possesses a portrait of "Tatters," one of the characters in the story. It is an original by Sir George Reid, President of the Scottish Royal Academy; and Laffan says she intends to exhibit the picture. She says it is even better than Miss Tennant's—but the engraving from it is "odious" and not in any way acceptable for a book. Laffan seems to have developed a genuine interest in pictures, as if she were starting to collect them.

In the same letter she compares the Liberal Government to the Gadarene swine, apparently because of their Irish policies.[45] George Macmillan, replying, commiserates with her on the "awful state" of Ireland, but is glad to see that if she disapproves of the Government she at least approves of J. M. (John Morley). He mentions the booksellers to whom he has sent copies—he thinks the Dublin and London ones have been influenced by events in Ireland to take fewer copies than he had hoped. However, he is sending a copy to the editor (Gallaher) in the hope of a *Freeman's Journal* review. George Macmillan then adds:

> I am rather sorry you are at a one-volume story. It is a poor speculation compared with the regular 3 volume novel. You had better try to get what you can out of its serial publication. . . . When "At the Back Gates" has run its serial course we shall be very happy to treat for its publication in book form.[46]

This is the last "personal" letter to Laffan from her publishers, the few later letters being notes to do with business only. These were generally written by Frederick Macmillan, the senior partner in the firm.

The one-volume story referred to in the letter above was the novella *A Singer's Story*, eventually published by Chapman and Hall (London) in 1885, and by Munro (New York) in 1887. So far as known, it was the only venture by Laffan into the area of the Moral Tale, so popular at that time, and so widely promoted by the Society for the Promotion of Christian

Knowledge (SPCK) and similar evangelical organizations. These stories, written mainly for adolescents, were intended to demonstrate Divine intervention in ordinary life, usually through the use of Bible study to affect a change of heart. The action of *A Singer's Story* takes place wholly in London and Paris, and describes the reaction of a middle-class English girl, a devout evangelical Protestant, to a catastrophic change in her life circumstances. Inspired by finding a scrap of paper with a biblical text on it, Hester eventually succeeds in having her voice trained, embarking on a professional career as a singer of sacred music, and marrying a clergyman.

A Singer's Story differs from most Moral Tales in the liveliness of the characterization and the flashes of humour when Laffan describes professional singers and musicians, their in-fighting and posturing and the stresses and uncertainties of their lives. This aspect of the story carries immediate conviction; you feel Laffan knows these people and writes from her experience. In fact, there are frequent references to music and musicians in all her books, and Hester is the fourth of her characters to make a living from music. The religious aspect does not appear so genuine, somehow it does not convince. A certain amount of pandering to English taste, also, is shown by portraying all the English characters as sincere, kind and noble. The non-English, including Irish, are stereotyped as deficient in most of these good qualities, and in fact are shown as inferior people. The novella seems to have been a one-off attempt, perhaps just to see if Laffan could work as successfully in this *genre* as she had in others.

It has not proved possible so far to trace the magazine in which *At the Back Gates* was serialised. Nor is any novel of that name listed with Laffan's other works in the British Library catalogue. But this is almost certainly the same story as that which was finally published by Macmillan in 1887, under the name of *Ismay's Children*, for the children of the title do in fact live by the back gate of the demesne inhabited by their wealthy cousin. The novel, obviously written before 1882, impressed reviewers by its analysis of the reasons that led men to join the Irish Republican Brotherhood (IRB), and they looked forward to the future Laffan novels.[47] This hope never came to anything. *A Singer's Story* was, so far as is known, the last piece of writing Laffan ever published. Her life as a writer seems to have come to an end with the Macmillan letters, in or about April 1882.

About a year later a curious incident took place involving Fannie Gallaher, a writer on similar social and political themes and a contemporary of Laffan. Fannie Gallaher attended Alexandra College over a period of several years, and was a student, possibly also an assistant teacher there in the year 1877, when Laffan was also a student, so they might have come to know each other then. Fannie's father John Blake Gallaher edited the *Freeman's Journal,* one of the reputable papers which Laffan relied upon to publicise her books. Fannie Gallaher had written and published in 1880 a short story called "Katty the Flash: A Mould of Dublin Mud." It is a powerful and dramatic tale of a destitute mother and daughter, and the attempts to help them. In 1883 the story reappeared in *Temple Bar* and also in the *New York Sun,* in a version amended, indeed almost rewritten, by Laffan. A note informed the reader that the story appeared by permission of Miss Gallaher.

The *Temple Bar* publication was anonymous, but was later attributed to Laffan by the *Wellesley Index of Victorian Publications,* and it still is so attributed. William Laffan was then publisher of the *New York Sun,* and no doubt open to consider the submissions of his sister's friends, but apparently not prepared to question the way his sister chose to edit them. The alterations made to this story were quite radical, the form being altered and its savage, satirical character modified, except in one instance. Laffan allowed her personal anti-clerical prejudice to take over when describing a nun prison visitor, about whom Fannie Gallaher had been far more positive. Understandably, Fannie was very angry about the alterations made to her story and complained in a letter to the editor of the *Morning and Evening Mail* that she had given no one permission to tamper with her work in this way.[48]

It is difficult to know why Laffan should have done this. Did she really hope to take credit for the work of another writer? At the very least it seems as though considerable misunderstanding arose between the two women as the result of an ill-judged impulse on Laffan's part.

May Laffan during her single years seems, from the evidence of her letters, to have been an impulsive and generous person; outspoken, assertive and ready to help others whether they asked for it or not. She enjoyed her own literary success and the good things it brought her—money, travel, opportunities for new experiences, and above all, contact with other writers. There is no hint or suggestion whatsoever that she was tired of writing, or that her publishers and her public were tired of her. It is true that fashions in fiction alter and certain themes and techniques become dated, but what is known of Laffan and her ability to write different kinds of books suggests that she was versatile enough to cope with such obstacles to her progress. Nevertheless, she did give up all her creative life, the life which must have become in the course of a productive eight years part of her identity as a human being. Why did this happen? She was young, and had received much encouragement to go on with her work. We can only speculate from what is known. In July 1882 May Laffan married Walter Noel Hartley, recently (1880) appointed Professor of Chemistry at the newly founded Royal College of Science in Dublin.

Walter Hartley (1846–1913) was an Englishman and came originally from Lichfield in Staffordshire; his father and his maternal grandfather were both artists. His scientific training had been in Germany, and when appointed to Dublin he was Senior Demonstrator in Chemistry at King's College, London—a distinguished chemist working mainly in the field of spectroscopy. Later he was to become a Fellow of the Royal Society and the recipient of a knighthood and several international awards.[49] He seems to have been an only and a delicate child; for he was educated at home and there is no mention of siblings. In temperament he was, according to his obituary

> . . . very reserved. This was perhaps due to a slight deafness, which troubled him all his life. Though reserved, he was full of human sympathy, and never forgot any act of kindness in others.

> Although hampered all his life by frail health and none too easy circumstances, he turned out an amount of first-rate work that the most robust might have been proud of. . . . [50]

From a surviving copy letterbook of Hartley's we learn that he suffered from severe asthma which he treated by changes of scene and climate.[51] Asthma is one of the conditions affected by emotional stress. His health apparently grew progressively worse over time, and it does not seem that he found married life helped.

At the time when the marriage of May and Walter took place, the Catholic Church in Ireland had developed strict regulations about religiously mixed marriages. These rules may have originated in a belief on the part of bishops that "mixed marriages" disadvantaged Catholics, and were to be strongly discouraged on that account. A Catholic living in Ireland who wanted to marry a member of another Christian church had to formally request their Bishop to apply to Rome for leave (dispensation) to do so, although in other countries the application was made routinely through the local parish priest.[52] In the Dublin diocese "the dispensation" was taken very seriously and official permission to marry a Protestant was rarely granted to a Catholic Dubliner. The well-to-do found a way around this, by fulfilling the residence qualification in London or Paris, applying for a dispensation there, and marrying there. Laffan does not seem to have considered this as a possible option. She and Walter were married on 4 July 1882, at St. Marylebone Parish Church, London, under the auspices of the Church of England to which Walter belonged. By her action, Laffan at that time was seen as declaring herself to be no longer prepared to follow Catholic practice.

In many ways, it was a curious thing to do. Laffan was, as has been said, bitterly critical of the Irish Catholic Church, but she was hardly less critical of the Protestant Churches. Irish law since 1871 had acknowledged Catholic marriage ceremonies as valid for Protestants also,[53] and it is hard to imagine Walter Hartley insisting on a Church of England ceremony—if he had been so insistent, would he have wanted to marry a Catholic girl in the first place? According to family tradition, he was himself an agnostic.[54] However, the Church of England was nearer the Catholic tradition than the Church of Ireland, notoriously Calvinistic at that time; and perhaps Laffan saw herself as bridging a gap between the two communions. Another possibility is that the elder Hartleys, Walter's parents, may not have been prepared to attend a Catholic wedding.

The marriage was witnessed by Catherine Laffan, May's sister, and by a "Michael Laffan" who could have been either her brother or her father. Walter Hartley's parents at that time lived in London and so could also have been present. As Walter's father Thomas Hartley was a portrait painter one might ask whether he ever painted his daughter-in-law, but it seems that his career as an artist ended for health reasons in 1860, long before May and Walter met.[55]

The Hartleys went to live at 36 Waterloo Road, near Ballsbridge. Now the office of a merchant bank, it is a large, plain red brick terrace house with gardens front and back and it certainly represents a step up from the modest Blackrock house. An advantage was its relative nearness to 51 St. Stephen's Green, the Royal College of Science where Hartley worked. The neighbourhood was redbrick, middle-class and residential, with long tree-lined roads and few shops. The visible churches were those of Protestant denominations. It was peaceful, conventional and respectable and in many ways resembled a suburb of an English city. But if their living quarters were peaceful and secure, Walter's work environment was not always so.

The Royal College of Science of Ireland (RCSI) had come into being in 1865, gradually evolving from origins in the Museum of Irish Industry and the Government School of Science Applied to Mining and the Arts. The RCSI, part of the Royal University which was an examining body only, was affiliated to Dublin University (Trinity College) and to Queen's University, Belfast, and was modelled on the future Imperial College, London. Though funded, unlike them, from central government, its purpose was to offer: ". . . as far as practicable, a complete course of instruction in Science applicable to the Industrial Arts, especially those of Mining, Engineering and Manufactures, and in Physics and Natural Science, and [was] intended also to aid in the instruction of Teachers."[56] As was the case with many similar institutes of the time, the RCSI suffered from chronic lack of funds and general resources such as laboratory equipment and space. Staff salaries were paid greatly in arrear and expenses were paid likewise but with even greater reluctance.[57] Walter Hartley, Professor of Chemistry from 1880 to 1911, seems from his surviving letterbook to have been engaged in an ongoing struggle with the Treasury. At one point, unable to continue working in the teaching laboratory due to inadequate ventilation there, he sent in a doctor's certificate for four months sick leave—the time needed to get the extraction system replaced. He seems to have been a successful teacher and, as Dean of the Faculty (1902–1911), considerate and supportive to his students but not combative by nature. The RCSI's economic difficulties improved somewhat from 1900 onwards, but Hartley's health problems did not improve, and led him to take early retirement in 1911.

On May Laffan Hartley's married life in its early years there is little information, but there is one known fact. The Hartleys were childless for the first seven years of their marriage. We can only speculate on the reason for this, but, assuming that they wanted a child, the situation must have made them both anxious. Laffan married in her thirties, and time was going by. And if she had to endure a series of miscarriages or stillbirths as many women had, it would certainly contribute to the depressive and negative side of her personality. It is likely, also, that she was uneasy about the gesture she had originally made in marrying outside the Catholic Church. In Catholic terms, her marriage would be seen as valid, but unlawful. She may even have believed that her infertility was connected to her gesture—that it was some kind of punishment. Yet, so far as is known, she made no attempt to use her suffering as she had done in the past, by transforming it into fiction.

She did, however, keep up her burning interest in the educational needs of Irish women. At a dinner party in 1884 Laffan met William J. Walsh, soon to be appointed Catholic Archbishop of Dublin in succession to the formidable Paul Cullen, and in the following year she wrote a series of letters to him about the need for an academic school for Catholic girls.[58] She began the proceedings by sending him a seven-page manifesto, allegedly representing the collected views of Dublin middle-class Catholics, with a short introductory letter from herself. The manifesto described Ireland as "in a state of ignorance and vice, the second growing direct out of the first," from which condition, it was said, only a radical change in the way girls were taught could deliver the whole of Irish society. Laffan mentioned her personal experience of Alexandra College, and suggested that Dr. Walsh should found its Catholic counterpart. But she recommended that it should be governed by a lay committee and staffed by lay women, because nuns, she thought, were not practical enough or well enough educated to be effective, although they might be allowed to run the boarding side of the establishment. She diverged abruptly to complain about the "scandalous farce" of the Catholic University, which, according to her, permitted its college library to be misappropriated, was only allowed to confer medical degrees, and employed Catholic converts of pension age who were useless as lecturers. In three following letters Laffan added to the details of her original scheme, but it also began to be clear that middle-class Dublin Catholics were not quite so enthusiastic about her ideas as she had hoped they would be. Finally, she requested an appointment to see Archbishop Walsh, who seems to have been answering her letters politely but without committing himself to any of her views. The four letters and the accompanying manifesto are preserved in the diocesan archives, but the outcome of Laffan's interview is not recorded. Dr. Walsh finally did act to promote the further education of women, but along academic lines suggested to him by the Loreto and Dominican nuns.[59]

On 25 April 1889 the Hartley's only child, Walter John, was born. The birth took place at home, as then only the very poor, unable to afford private attendance, made use of hospitals. That birth is likely to have been difficult, considering that Laffan was forty and it was her first confinement. At some time shortly afterwards, probably during the summer months when it would have been safest to take a newborn infant out, she took her son to a Catholic church and asked the priest to baptise him. The priest refused to do so.[60]

The evidence for this incident is anecdotal only. We do not know why baptism was refused. On the face of it, the only obvious reason would rest on the doubt of whether any undertaking could be given that John (as he was to be called) could be brought up a Catholic. What is significant, though, is the apparent absence of Walter Hartley from the scene. If Laffan did not discuss her action with him, and get his consent to it, then the priest may have been wise to refuse. On the other hand, it was a not unusual practice at the time for nurses and female relatives, concerned about a delayed baptism, to take the law into their own hands by bringing the baby into a church and asking a priest to officiate secretly. No other accounts of a priest refusing to do this are known.

The result of this incident was, again according to anecdote, that Laffan never again entered a Catholic church. This suggests that she had been attending Mass up to that time. That she still saw herself as a Catholic much later appears from the Census of 1901 in which the religion of participants was recorded. Laffan, like the three servants, was entered as "Roman Catholic"; Walter was entered as Church of England and the twelve-year-old John as Church of Ireland.[61]

Information about Laffan's life at this time comes mainly from the *Recess Committee Notes*, mentioned in the introduction. This extract gives some idea of her state of mind, seven years after the events referred to above:

> In Ireland the law is not administered. . . . compulsory education is suffered to become a dead letter because Boards of Guardians, controlled by the priests (whose pawns they are), refuse to enforce it until the Christian Brothers' claims are allowed. . . .You complain of the silence, the cowardice, of the Roman Catholic laity. Just now, my Protestant friends taunt me with the ignoble timidity of the Roman Catholic body, all afraid to speak out. . . . What example does the Government show them?. . .continuous knuckling down to the unwashed rustics who in this country masquerade as bishops and by their perfect organization hold the others in thraldom. No wonder that, via the confessional, it is the Roman law that is administered . . . the priests, while openly disavowing Fenianism, worked it up secretly, aided by their allies in the Privy Council ... to impoverish and drag down Protestants is their avowed intention. . . . idle and dissolute men and women have the burden of supporting their children shifted to the ratepayers' shoulders. . . Jesuits . . . the "Black International". . . .[62]

And so it goes on in a fairly continuous stream. In one sense the document is interesting, for the amount of contemporary gossip and rumour it contains; but in another way it is sad and gives cause to wonder that such an intelligent and perceptive woman could have changed so much; her worldview whittled down to the point where everyone lies and cheats, and no good is to be found anywhere in life. The first impression made by the twenty-two foolscap pages of derogation is one of suppressed rage needing an outlet. The second impression is of insecurity and fear of the future. Laffan seems to have believed that Walter Hartley and his colleagues were likely to be downgraded to teach in "a training school for artisans."[63]

She seems to have believed this to be the main aim of the Recess Committee's deliberations, and O'Grady, from his comments, appeared to agree with what she wrote. In fact, there is no evidence that anything of the kind was contemplated. Years after Professor Hartley's retirement, the RCSI was subsumed into the National University on terms disadvantageous to the development of science in Ireland, but this policy seems to have arisen from other factors than the ones known to the Hartleys.[64]

There are interesting passages in the *Recess Committee Notes*, from some of which it appears that Laffan was a friend of Michael Davitt, and sympathetic to his socialist ideas, though not to the extent of supporting land nationalisation. Her accounts of Davitt's prison experiences are somewhat confused. She was well informed, though, about the use of explosives by republican activists, because Walter Hartley was sometimes involved in analysing captured explosive devices and materials. Laffan also relates, somewhat surprisingly in view of their confidential nature, details of four cases brought before her when she served on the Executive Committee of the Dublin branch of the Society for the Prevention of Cruelty to Children (SPCC) from October 1889.[65]

This branch of the famous organization was set up in Dublin, in May 1889, and affiliated to that in London. It was well supported by the Ascendancy and for that reason did not receive much initial help from wary Catholics, though Count and Countess Plunkett were founder members.[66] The main practical function of the Society was the prosecution of people who neglected or abused children. Laffan was one of the first Irish members. To begin with she was involved in fundraising, but was later on the committee which reviewed cases and decided on strategy. Her name appears as "present" in the notes taken at meetings, but nothing she said has been recorded. The fact of her involvement suggests a real interest in and commitment to the welfare of children. She remarked in the *Recess Committee Notes* that the nature of the legal system made the collection of enough evidence to take a case to court very difficult—a situation which persists to-day. Evidence from young children was not acceptable by itself, because it was assumed that they could not distinguish truth from fantasy. Laffan commented scathingly on this assumption.

She blamed lack of action in serious cases on the armed services, the political establishment, and the Catholic Church respectively. When, as in two cases of child rape, the accused were members of Her Majesty's Armed Services, no investigation could be pursued. It seemed that soldiers were rarely convicted of breaking civil laws. Another case involved a man charged with giving his two stepdaughters poisoned sweets. The children died but no *post mortems* were carried out—the stepfather had politically powerful friends. Laffan then described how a child was apparently strangled by her mother, a recent Catholic convert; and that a priest prevented the servants from giving evidence against the mother, who only received a one-year prison sentence as a result. Laffan felt she should have been given a much longer sentence, although from the details given one might deduce extenuating circumstances, i.e. mental illness. Laffan seemed to take the view that the SPCC's main function was to punish, rather than to prevent situations which lead to violence against children. This simplistic approach would, however, have been a usual and acceptable attitude at the time.

Records of the SPCC do not say for how long Laffan was a member of the Committee, but in 1895 she was still active in the organization. A continuing interest in the welfare of poor people seems also to have caused her to become involved with some practical projects to help them. Her name is recorded on 18 October 1898 in the *Irish Daily Independent* as one of the speakers at a conference held to support schemes for low-cost housing. In other ways, though, her ideals appear somewhat unfocused and inconsistent. She is at one moment lambasting Catholic institutions:

> Helpless children starved and brutalised in the Industrial Schools; farmers' and shopkeepers' daughters humbugged into entering "the religious life" at 14 or15 years of age, to die of consumption at 35. . . . boys taken at ten years or twelve and put through a discipline which (if medical psychology is to be trusted) makes them for life no more than disciplined lunatics.[67]

At the next moment she is castigating the same institutions for spoiling inadequate parents, by removing the responsibility of child care from them, and educating their children so efficiently that the civil service is able to employ them and pay them well—and all at the ratepayer's expense!

There is no information at all about how Laffan coped with their own son. John seems to have had his early education at home (a nursery governess is mentioned); he eventually studied at Cambridge and trained as a bacteriologist, a career Walter Hartley once told a friend he would have liked to follow himself but could not for lack of money. Money does not seem to have been a great problem just then with the Hartleys, for some time between 1904 and 1907 they moved to No. 10 Elgin Road—a grander house, but still in the Dublin suburb of Ballsbridge. May's father Michael Laffan and Walter's father Thomas Hartley both died during the 1890s; the former left little, but the latter left Walter a house at Norwood, in South East London. Trips to London, Austria and the south of France are mentioned; and the family kept three resident servants.

Two personal letters written by Laffan have survived from this period. They were both written to her first cousin Michael Dwyer Laffan, who after a somewhat adventurous early career had joined the Hibernian Bank. The following extract from the first letter is suggestive of trouble: ". . . I fancy it was Helena who sent me a paper with the very pleasant account of your promotion to Mullingar—with all the family worry and *desolation* I have endured it is agreeable to know that *some* are different and not evilly disposed."[68] It is not easy to guess what desolation and evil Laffan is referring to here. There is no rumour of any particular difficulty at home. There seems not to have been anything going particularly wrong with the rest of her scattered family. William Laffan had married the daughter of a Baltimore judge and was now a wealthy newspaper proprietor in New York.[69] He was followed into American journalism by his younger brother Michael, who joined a news agency in San Francisco.[70] James Laffan, the youngest of the brothers, qualified as a doctor in 1881.[71] He seems to have joined the Army Medical Corps, as in 1887 he was registered as working in Larnaca, Cyprus, where there was a British garrison. But since 1890 he had been living in Australia,[72] where Casy (Catherine), Laffan's surviving sister, had emigrated in the 1880s. She married Dr. Charles Drummond Morier there on 13 June 1885, and they had two children.[73] So, although separated from her brothers and sisters, Laffan had no obvious reason to be anxious about them. It is therefore possible that the anxiety came from within herself; that her depressive state of many years before threatened to recur, and the dark was closing round her. Colour is given to this theory by the close of the second of her two letters to Michael:

I'm more pleased than surprised at your pleasant news today. Mr Hartley also joins me in congratulating you. I suppose you saw in the paper that the Germans have put him first chemist in his branch, it is not any money but great glory which I'm afraid runs in this family. . . . I will write soon again when better able.[74]

Laffan was close to her cousins, and appears to have seen them regularly, including her cousin Helena who lived in Cork city with an ailing husband and a large family. Laffan was remembered by these children as an eccentric and somewhat temperamental woman, who drank whiskey—something women did not usually do openly at that time.[75] This circumstance gives rise to the suspicion that alcohol may have played a part in her problems. These problems, whatever they were, moved rapidly towards a crisis. In November 1909 William Laffan died suddenly following an appendicectomy. Whether the shock of his death contributed to what followed is not known, but ten months later, on 5 September 1910, May Laffan Hartley was committed to a psychiatric institution at the request of her husband. The admission was supported by two doctors, as the law then required, but the diagnosis was not recorded.[76]

This compulsory admission was an unusual occurrence in Ireland at the time, given the comfortable circumstances of the family. As Joseph Robbins states in his account of the treatment of psychiatric illness in nineteenth- and early-twentieth-century Ireland, well-to-do families kept their insane or disturbed members at home for as long as they could, there being a great reluctance to "put them away."[77] Indeed, to do this was seen as shameful and wrong. Only when it became absolutely impossible to cope was institutional care considered. Taking this into consideration, Laffan must have been a very difficult patient—so difficult that not even with continual nurse attendance, which the Hartleys were able to afford, could they continue to keep her at home.

The Bloomfield Institution, to which Laffan was committed, was probably the best place of its kind in Dublin. Founded in 1812 by the Society of Friends, originally for members of that Society needing psychiatric treatment, it occupied an elegant eighteenth-century house near Morehampton Road, with a modern extension (circa 1900) housing patients. These patients—all paying— had rooms opening on to a wide corridor, or lounge, overlooking a large garden which supplied their vegetables as well as flowers. The daily regime seems to have followed that of the Society's famous Retreat at York, a psychiatric hospital which avoided harsh and restrictive treatment and aimed at what would now be called holistic medicine.[78]

Laffan was never to leave Bloomfield. A year later, Walter Hartley was knighted for his services to science, and Laffan, probably without knowing it, became Lady Hartley. Walter Hartley then retired; but his health was no better and he died in his sleep on 11 September 1913 at Braemar, Scotland, while visiting friends. He is buried there.[79]

The start of the First World War in 1914 found John Hartley, son of May and Walter, lecturing at University College, Cardiff. He joined up, and was commissioned in the Irish Fusiliers. A year later, he was killed at Gallipoli.[80] In the same year, 1915, May's brothers Michael and James also died, but she may not even have known about it.[81] News of the Easter Rising in 1916 could have penetrated to Bloomfield, but probably more real to Laffan would have been visits from her sister and brother-in-law from Australia. They had returned to live in London, but came to Dublin to see her and, when she died, organised her private funeral and inherited her few belongings.[82] According to the death certificate, Laffan died on 23 June 1916, from the effects of a cerebral haemorrhage occurring two months earlier. She was buried at Glasnevin, in the Laffan grave.

Writers on nineteenth-century Irish literature speculated as to what had happened to the promising May Laffan. Some thought she must have died young—perhaps in childbirth. Her long silence puzzled those who had hoped she would be the herald of a new literary dawn.[83] These speculations continued after her death, which went unnoticed. The *Irish Times* death notice was as brief as possible, referring to her as Lady Hartley and giving no details, that is, nothing about Bloomfield, or about the funeral. To date, no obituary has come to light. May Laffan the writer had completely disappeared, vanished from the earth.

There are several possible explanations for Laffan's thirty-four year silence, if we assume that it was not just a case of running out of ideas. First, there is the possibility that she wrote because she needed to exorcise a demon. This demon could have taken the form of recurrent bouts of depression, a state commoner than we like to think in talented young people. Her marriage relieved the depression, and so removed the compulsive need to write. A problem with this hypothesis is that the *Recess Committee* submission is anything but happy and positive; on the contrary, it seethes with anger and anxiety, emotions which are very much a part of depression in many individuals. It is hard to credit that Laffan was happy in her marriage when one compares the almost paranoid writer of the *Recess* papers with the confident, up-beat writer of the Macmillan letters. Fourteen years separated those two literary sources. It does not seem as if those years brought contentment.

The reverse hypothesis is that Laffan was inhibited from exercising her talent by her husband. For some reason, Walter may have felt that her literary career was not important enough to continue. He may even have seen the measure of independence it would have given his wife as a possible threat to his status as the family's sole provider, and her role as home maker. Laffan herself may not have felt able to oppose such a view. The objection to this theory is that there is no evidence, either way.

The marriage may well have been stressful, however. It is not easy to live with a satirist; for there must always be the knowledge that they can, and probably will, turn their wit against you at some time. As has been said, Hartley was a delicate, reclusive man who had, apparently, no rivals for his parents' full attention. How did he adjust to Laffan's exacting nature, and the "mood swings" with which she is credited?

Laffan's ideas on marriage are not expressed openly in any of her books except the novel *Ismay's Children*, but are implied in the three other novels. It is interesting that all the marriages she writes about are "mixed." In *Hogan MP* the hero of the title, John O'Rooney Hogan, is trapped into a loveless marriage by a designing Ascendancy belle, and his own foolishness. The heroine, Nellie Davoren, child of a "mixed" marriage herself, is swept off her feet by a returned colonial. He takes her to his ancestral home in Kerry, where they live happily ever after. Both of these marriages are "mixed"— the first is a failure, the second a success.

In *Miss Ferrard* the story ends with the departure of the aristocratic Protestant Helena to Canada with her Catholic fiancé. They are going because his parents opposed the marriage on grounds of the religious difference. Helena has accepted him in preference to her English Protestant suitor—or has she? What the outcome will finally be, is left uncertain.

In *Christy Carew* we are told about three couples and what becomes of them. Christy's father and his young second wife Caroline were originally of different faiths, but she converted to Catholicism before the wedding. Because the implication is that she "turned" for unworthy reasons, her step-children cruelly make fun of Caroline's attempts to live her new faith. Christy, the heroine, herself says that she is "not religious" and she has no scruples about marrying a Protestant; but consciously or not, she weighs up the advantages of such a marriage—and one of these is that they will live in London and need never return to Dublin. Esther, Christy's friend, falls deeply in love with a young officer from the Anglo-Irish nobility. At first infatuated with her, he loses interest when her parents resolutely forbid the match, and Esther refuses to elope to Paris on his vague promise of a Catholic marriage there. When Esther pines away and dies of T.B., the Irish Catholic Church's rulings on "mixed marriage" are ostensibly held responsible, but the story is in reality highly ambivalent. One's impression is that Laffan began by trying to attach blame to the Church for making mixed marriage difficult, but then to some degree the novel began to take its own course in a direction she did not originally intend. Perhaps she realised that the whole story was not as simple and clear-cut as it had seemed at first.

Laffan's last known novel, *Ismay's Children*, has a plot centred on the validity or otherwise of a marriage between a Catholic girl and a Protestant Ascendancy officer—the long-dead parents of the children of the title. The novel ends with the betrothal of Marion, eldest of the children, to a young English aristocrat whom she loved, in the best romantic tradition, before she knew who he really was. Shocked at the violent and tragic events he witnessed in Ireland, her lover wants to take her back to England and civilization. Marion, not convinced by her friends' cynical comments about selfish men, seems happy to agree to go—indeed, to go anywhere so long as it is with him.

The conclusion one can draw from the above can only be tentative: Laffan seems to say that marriages between people of differing faiths depend for their success on mutual respect and the ability to tolerate difference. That difference, as Laffan perceives it, is less ideological than social. It is easier to cope with "difference" in an unfamiliar setting, such as Kerry, London, Canada—above all, not Dublin. Laffan does not feel happy in Dublin and would ideally like to live elsewhere. Her idea of the wife's role in a marriage is apparently very traditional—the only working women she portrays are the singers in *A Singer's Story*, and they give up singing in public on marriage, unless they are so poor that they must continue to earn. Husbands are normally the wage earners; it is their privilege, and so it is vital for a woman to marry someone who can give her a measure of financial security.

There is in Laffan's novels little real sense of marriage as a relationship of mutual concern and support. Perhaps she did not feel that this was important, if she had had to lead her single life without much emotional help from anyone. This leads one to speculate again on the quality of her life with Walter Hartley, and the degree to which their expectations of marriage were met.

The most probable of the theories, then, regarding the reason why Laffan ceased to write when she did, seems to be that which sees her thinking that marriage would solve her difficulties without further need for self-expression in fiction writing as a safety device. By the time she discovered herself to be mistaken in this, she had lost her balance (rather like a tightrope walker), and she never regained it either in terms of having the confidence to start again, or in terms of regaining the impartial and even-handed outlook which she had formerly. She may have relapsed into a state of chronic depression which was hard for Hartley to tolerate and which led to her admission to a private mental hospital. Her life was therefore in its later aspects tragic. Her husband and son both predeceased her, as did most of her siblings. She had no descendants, and her death went unremarked. The Laffan side of the family knew what happened, mourned her and remembered her, but we do not know if the younger generation of the Fitzgibbons knew of her at all.

Her work, apart from its literary merit, may be considered as a unique concealed link between romantic, partisan writers like Charles Kickham and William O'Brien, and later realists such as George Moore and James Joyce. The latter especially is often perceived as inhabiting a sort of mountain fastness of his own, but were he and Moore as unique and isolated from contemporaries as we like to think them? Laffan was a highly gifted writer from a slightly earlier age but almost identical social background to that of Joyce. Like Moore, she was very conscious of being uneasily poised between two cultures. She seemed to veer between giving approbation to one or the other, and blaming both. She was successful in her art without any of the resources of money and patronage which Moore early in life and Joyce later both achieved. Her work shares with theirs the brooding, occasionally hopeless perspective of *fin-de-siècle* Ireland, and allowing for her more limited range of experience, it approaches and sometimes overtakes theirs in its unsentimental compassion, its wry humour and the quality of its observation. Some of these attributes will, it is hoped, become evident in the chapters which follow, in which analysis, comparison and description of May Laffan Hartley's work is attempted.

Class and Politics in *Hogan MP*

"A seat in Parliament must be obtained—by any means."

M ay Laffan's first and most successful novel, *Hogan MP*, was published by Richard Bentley in London in the spring of 1876, when
its author was twenty-seven. A satirical novel, it may be fairly
compared with two other much better known novels also dating from the
last quarter of the nineteenth century: Anthony Trollope's *The Way We Live
Now* (1875) and George Moore's *A Drama in Muslin* (1887). Comparison between *Hogan MP* and the work of other contemporary female writers has
not proved possible, since the main theme in *Hogan MP*—social and political dishonesty—apparently lacked appeal to women writers of the time.
Possibly for that reason, *Hogan MP*'s anonymous author was at first assumed, as in this *Spectator* review, to be a man:

> We have seldom read through a modern novel which left a worse taste behind it
> than this. At the same time, we cannot but admit that the author shows consider-
> able power in handling his materials. His canvas, indeed, is crowded to such an
> extent that the sketches are of the slightest; but each character stands on its own
> feet, and is not merely a lay figure, and the story, such as it is, never flags. Our ob-
> jection is not to the handling of them, but to the materials themselves.[1]

Hogan MP is a complex novel with several overlapping themes—the "materials" referred to above. Here we will concentrate mainly on two of these,
class and politics—on which the perspective offered by Laffan is valuable
because unique. Few Irish Victorians wrote satirical novels, and so far as
can be ascertained no other woman from an urban middle-class background did so in the 1870s. Moreover, the working knowledge of French
and German which Laffan apparently possessed, and her consequent fa-
miliarity with European literature, give a realistic and unsentimental

quality to her writing not generally found in the novels of her contemporaries.

Because copies of *Hogan MP* are difficult to find it seems useful to give an outline of the story here. The action takes place between the summer of 1872 and the winter of 1874 in Dublin, London, Paris and "Peatstown" (probably Tipperary town). The plot is based on Goethe's *Dr. Faustus*, a work with which Laffan was familiar as her use of chapter-heading quotations in the original German would indicate. Like Dr. Faustus, the barrister John O'Rooney Hogan is a poor and ambitious man on his own in the world. He wants wealth, power and eighteen-year-old Nellie Davoren. She is the child of a mixed marriage, and for Hogan, who believes Protestants to be his superiors, this is an added attraction. Nellie's Catholic father, a civil servant, is selfish and remote; her Protestant mother is an invalid. Nellie lovingly cares for her with help from her mother's cousin Dorothy O'Hegarty, who although bigoted is genuinely fond of Nellie and of her brother Dicky, a Trinity College student. Through Dorothy's generosity, they experience what Dublin society of the time has to offer.

Cosmo Saltasche, a neighbour of the Davorens, appears in the story as the Mephistopheles to Hogan's Faust, offering him wish fulfilment—at a price. (Saltasche, a mysterious figure, has features of Trollope's villainous character Melmotte.) Like the latter, he seems to be personally wealthy, but has a craving over the lives of others. Claiming to be the grandson of a French émigré, Saltasche is widely travelled, speaks several languages and has, unlike Melmotte, a large circle of friends and acquaintances.

Hogan is not very discerning and accepts readily when Saltasche offers to help him to a seat in Parliament. We can date the time of the event closely. The by-election which gives Hogan his chance takes place in either North Cork or South Tipperary, after the Secret Ballot Act of 1872 and before dissolution of Parliament in 1873, prior to the General Election of 1874. There are only two candidates—John Hogan, Liberal Home Ruler, and Theodore Wyldeoates, Conservative. Neither comes from the district, though Wyldeoates's uncle Lord Kilboggan is the local absentee landlord, and Hogan makes full use of Nellie Davoren's local connections.

Once elected, Hogan finds himself under pressure to promote fraudulent investment schemes. Saltasche, who loves to control other people's lives, introduces him to Diana Bursford, a fading beauty from the Protestant Ascendancy who is looking for a husband. Separated from Nellie and his familiar Dublin surroundings, Hogan soon begins to feel lonely and out of

his element. Diana knows how to flatter his personal vanity and social aspirations. Saltasche meanwhile falls passionately in love with Adelaide
Poignarde, the South American wife of one of his debtor clients, who does
not love him but uses him to get away from her abusive husband. Inspired
by passion, Saltasche executes a series of swindles robbing half of Dublin,
his London brokers and incidentally John Hogan. The only way in which
Hogan can avoid financial and professional ruin is to borrow from Diana,
who exacts engagement to marry as the price of her help.

Saltasche and Adelaide flee to the Continent, one jump ahead of the
law. They live luxuriously on ill-gotten gains until Adelaide, following an
episode in which she unwittingly attracted police attention to them both,
admits to her lover that she has never really cared for him. On his way back
to England in custody, Saltasche, realising that prison life would be insup-
portable without the hope of rejoining his love, gives his guards the slip
and drowns himself in the Channel. Conscience-stricken, Adelaide returns
the stolen money to Saltasche's victims.

With a general election in prospect, the English Prime Minister Gladstone resigns over his failure to carry through a University Bill for Ireland.
Hogan has been neglecting his duties as an MP, all his time being taken up
by the tasks exacted by Saltasche. Now the Peatstown electors make plain
they will not have him again as their Parliamentary representative, preferring Dinny "The Hare" Houlihan, a reputed informer but a more forceful
character. The financial journal Hogan was editing changes hands, and he
loses his job. Hogan then tries— unsuccessfully—to break off his engagement to Diana. On a flying visit to Dublin he sees Nellie, assures her of his
love, and tells her to disregard rumours about him. But they are interrupted
and so she is unable to ask him any questions.

Nellie had agreed to keep their engagement secret, but grows uneasy at
hearing too seldom from Hogan, and too often from Anglo-Irish friends
about Hogan's involvement with Diana. Nellie's mother becomes acutely
ill following the sudden disappearance of Dicky, who has run away to escape creditors. Mr. Davoren reacts to the news with a temper outburst
which terrifies his wife, hastening her death.

Shortly after Hogan's visit Nellie reads in the paper an account of his
wedding to Diana Bursford. Dermot Blake, a Protestant cousin returned
from the colonies, observes Nellie's reaction, guesses the reason and tries to
comfort her. Some time later, he succeeds in persuading her to marry him.

Dermot is an unconvincing character who seems introduced solely to provide the obligatory happy ending.

Diana, through her contacts, quickly finds a colonial job for Hogan and the pair departs for Honolulu. But already Hogan is showing signs of depression, and taking to drink as a comforter. There is no salvation in sight for this Irish Faust.

Such are the bones of the novel. It may be inferred that John O'Rooney Hogan, the nominal hero, is attractive and talented but also weak and insincere, whereas Cosmo Saltasche, the villain, is unscrupulous and devious but has a humour and passion about him which make him likeable. Characterization was one of Laffan's gifts, and the empathy she seems to have had with people at the margins of society is demonstrated here.

We see John Hogan to begin with mainly through Nellie's uncritical eyes. When with her, he appears most sincere and at his best. When away from her, as on his political campaign in Munster or during his brief London career, he lies, he pretends, he prevaricates and temporizes. The rural voters are not fooled, but they prefer him to the landlord's nominee, and accordingly vote for him. En route to Westminster, Hogan does have one moment of insight when he is tempted to give up politics, try to make a career in the law, and ask Mr. Davoren for Nellie's hand. But the world and the devil, represented by Saltasche, alternately threaten and tempt him, so that finally Hogan goes off to Westminster with the addresses of Saltasche's friends in his pocket. We are left with the suspicion that he has taken on too much.

Laffan analyses John Hogan in one of her rare asides:

> Hardship of any kind was antipathetic to Hogan's nature. That which was soft and easy in life he clung to. He could work hard; but if he did, it was not as men do who work for the love of working and for the love of their calling. He worked hard that he might the sooner play. There was a strong tinge of the peasant nature underlying all his polish: the ingrained hatred of work, the fatalistic indifference engendered by a social and religious system of long and complicated standing, the curious reverence and love of power and authority peculiar to those who have been oppressed. All this old leaven worked under the super-imposed layer of training and culture. . . . He had his cleverness from his mother; and as often happens when such is the case, his mind ran in rather a feminine mould. There were some parts of his character, at all events, which were not what the world calls manly.[2]

Laffan here shows awareness of the over-respectful attitudes to authority often found in people living under colonial rule, and this awareness is unusual for the time. She reveals the high value set by Anglo-Irish society on the "manly" image and Protestant work ethic by suggesting how poorly her hero can measure up to them.[3] Consciously or not, she gives him a history which suggests some reasons why he fails. John O'Rooney Hogan was the only child of shopkeepers in a midland town. Educated at a junior seminary, he proved not to be suitable for the priesthood and so reluctantly joined his father in the shop. Both his parents died early, and by the age of nineteen Hogan was his own master, with a legacy in prospect from the sale of the shop. After consultation with his maternal uncle, Bishop O'Rooney, the latter agreed to help educate Hogan for a legal career. Hogan, a Trinity graduate, has now the manners and appearance of a gentleman, but lacks the self-assurance which marks the genuine member of the ruling caste. He is out of touch with his origins, and he survives by imitating his social superiors, almost to the extent of playing a part. His mistakes show failure of confidence and social skill; these shortcomings are assumed by Laffan to be due to his Catholic upbringing but could equally be due to his keen sense of his own inferiority as member of a subject race. The reference above to Hogan's "peasant nature" is not meant to be complimentary either to him or to peasants. It implies that Hogan shows traits of laziness, ignorance, passivity and subservience to authority, altogether an Ascendancy stereotype of Irish Catholic characteristics, linked to class and religious prejudice.

Nineteenth-century scientific discoveries regarding evolution and genetics unfortunately were used in some instances to support an electionist view of human society.[4] Not only were certain races thought to be intrinsically superior to others in terms of reasoning power and devotion to the work ethic, the Anglo-Saxon race in particular was believed to be naturally selected for the task of governing other races. The "others," in order to justify their suppression, were told that they were incapable of self-government. John Hogan, though an intelligent and presentable young man, is therefore seen by the ruling caste as an inferior, and he inwardly believes this to be true. Perhaps the greater part of the attraction Nellie Davoren has for him is her connection to the Protestant Ascendancy from which the ruling caste in Ireland of the time was drawn. She, at any rate, is not an inferior, and marriage to her would mean social advancement.

John Hogan's great disadvantage, as he sees it, is the fact that he is not a
Protestant. This circumstance alone, in the Ireland of that time, places him
in an inferior social caste, as the *Hogan MP* characters strolling on
Kingstown Pier are well aware:

> "The Pier is really crowded with very common people this summer. Every year it
> gets worse," said Miss Braginton, "now, just look at these costumes. R.C.'s, my
> dear, of course."

> "These costumes" were the Raffertys' and the Malowneys', who looked like a
> walking flower-garden as they passed.

> "R.C.'s—what's that for, eh?" asked Mr. Blake.

> "Roman Catholic," explained Dorothy; "common people—trade, you know."[5]

Discrimination and lack of formal education having kept Catholics from
the professions, they were over-represented in occupations involving buying and selling, and thus became identified with "trade," that is, became
inferior in Irish Victorian terms.

A society with but two main social groups—a small Protestant upper
class consisting of landowners, civil servants and professional men, and a
much bigger inferior class consisting overwhelmingly of Catholics in less
skilled occupations—is the Ireland depicted in the works of most nineteenth-century novelists.[6] The eighteenth-century term "Ascendancy"
originally referred to the political and material advantages of being a
member of the Established Church of Ireland. In fiction Protestants are
shown in a relatively good light as reasonable, industrious and intellectually honest people; Catholic characters are depicted as volatile and amusing, but also intellectually dishonest, easily dominated and unreliable.
Clearly the latter do not function in an "Ascendancy mode," and this pre-
vents them aspiring to Ascendancy heights.

Religion more than nationality is the indicator of social class in Irish fiction as well as in fact, although some romantics in the Walter Scott tradition bring in characters drawn from the remnants of Catholic Gaelic
nobility,[7] and some later Victorian writers conscientiously try to endow upper-class Catholic characters with middle-class Victorian values.[8] This
practice, intended to counteract negative stereotyping that "Catholics are
not respectable and civilised" by nature, accurately reflected changes in
the urban society of Ireland; for there was by the 1870s a Catholic middle
class, and even a Catholic upper or professional class, although relative to

the whole of Irish society the latter group was small.⁹ Laffan, as can be seen from her writing, took the view that Irish Catholics, however able, however prosperous, were rough diamonds needing the social polish to be gained by contact with Irish Protestants.

To the English, Irish Protestants did not differ greatly from the Irish Catholics they despised, which possibly explains a tendency, noted by Laffan, for Irish Protestants, who were already critical of the English, to emphasise their own separate status and identity. The Church of Ireland, as from 1870 the Irish Anglican church came to be called, was naturally based in Dublin, as the centre of population. Within the Protestant community, there were various subdivisions, some of which are mentioned in *Hogan MP*. People "of good blood," that is, belonging to a family with a traceable history, took social precedence followed by members of the learned professions, seen as more altruistic than those who made their living by trade. Landowners, unless titled, were regarded by the educated middle classes as somewhat boorish and unsophisticated; and Dissenters, apart perhaps from Presbyterians, were seen as socially inferior to members of the Church of Ireland. It is clear from contemporary accounts that in spite of legislation (the Church Act of 1869) aimed at altering the special position conferred by its Establishment on the Irish Anglican Church, Irish Protestants continued for some time afterwards to be a privileged and powerful minority, although at the period in which *Hogan MP* is set they were increasingly if indirectly aware that their days of unshared power were coming to an end.¹⁰

It has to be remembered that the public which Laffan hoped would buy her books was not Irish, but in the main evangelical Protestant, English and middle class, for it was this prosperous social group above others which bought and read novels.¹¹ Stories involving political and religious questions were very fashionable, as they helped people to explore in a gradual manner new ideas of the day.¹² Fiction with an Irish setting had a certain exotic charm for those who knew little of countries other than their own. Expectations as to the form and content of Irish novels, however, were likely to be founded on the works of Maria Edgeworth, or the humorous stories of Charles Lever and Samuel Lover. These did not generally contain much of history, overt politics or nationalist propaganda, being written from a broadly Unionist standpoint and therefore on the whole uncritical of English relations with Ireland.

But to please the readers, certain fixed ethical values must always be maintained; and these were derived from evangelical Protestant not Roman Catholic tradition.[13] For instance, the civil law was viewed as virtually identical to the moral law—therefore the possibility of some laws being unjust was not acceptable. Authority, however exercised and set up, in every case must be respected and obeyed without question. Racial prejudice was endemic and was not seen as wrong; indeed, its existence was taken for granted as justified—it being a "known fact" that some races were superior to others.[14] Cleanliness, orderliness and thrift were regarded as virtues almost on a level with faith, hope and charity. Sinners must meet with visible punishment and virtue must be materially rewarded, even to the extent of going against the genuine beliefs of the writer or their perception of psychological truth. Sin itself was rather narrowly defined in terms of sexual misconduct, overtly violent behaviour, and theft.

Not only *avant-garde* writers like George Moore had difficulty with negotiating this moral code; the devout and high-minded Irish writer Rosa Mulholland (Lady Gilbert) collided with it as well in one of her novels.[15] The chief offence of both writers was to suggest that a woman who gave birth to a child outside wedlock was not beyond redemption on that account, and so there was no real reason to kill her off in the course of a novel as punishment. This seems to have been seen as a shockingly over-lenient approach, acceptable to Catholics, perhaps, but not at all to strict evangelical Protestants. There is no doubt that London publishers were aware of this difficulty, and it dictated the terms on which they accepted an author's work.

In the 1870s when Laffan's writing career began, deliberate realism in the manner of Balzac or of Zola had scarcely yet appeared in novels written in English, where characters and situations still tended to the stereotypical and conventional. George Moore, as a critic of the English literary scene, declared that too many nineteenth-century English novels appeared to be written solely for young girls to read.[16] Moore himself, writing *A Drama in Muslin* a decade later than *Hogan MP*, found it necessary to devise a traditional love affair for his heroine in order to make the story end in a way acceptable to readers. Another convention of the Victorian novel in English was that most leading characters should resemble the readers, that is, should be Anglo-Saxon, white and Protestant; but preferably not too High Church, or they might be suspected of leaning towards Rome.[17] There were of course some departures from this rule, but they seem to have been very few.[18]

It is a measure of the originality of *Hogan MP* that it scarcely follows the conventions referred to above. Within the limits set by any satirical treatment it is a surprisingly realistic novel, and in general a witty one (this cannot be said to have been usual either). The deviant behaviour of a group of college students is gleefully as well as accurately described in alternating chapters of *Hogan MP*, probably to provide the story with lighter contrast. An example of this is the following passage which shows at an early stage the progress of Dicky Davoren and his friends down the slope of insolvency. Here the group is meeting in "Botany Bay," a part of the residential student quarter of Trinity College:

> Mahony Quain stooped his great back over the table, and in company with his friends perused the enticing bill of fare set forth in the columns of one of the most largely circulated and influential papers in Dublin.
>
> "Ten pounds realise four hundred. Augh!" grunted he derisively, "the lowest thing they notice is five pounds."
>
> "Five hundred it might as well be!" cried Dicky scornfully.
>
> "What do you think of a joint stock concern?" asked Mr. Orpen, "Quain, you're in cash; Davoren, couldn't you manage twenty-five shillings, —hey? . . . "
>
> "I shan't," said Mr. Gagan; "I'm cleaned out. You did it, Billy Orpen, so put down for me, else I won't."
>
> "Have you your Ulster coat?" suggested Mr. Quain, who was credited with a perfect genius for raising money.
>
> "No, I haven't my Ulster coat," returned Mr. Gagan savagely, "it's pawned two days ago."
>
> A silence fell on the quartette. It seemed as if their scheme was to fall through, but Orpen, inspired by a sudden thought, cried, —
>
> "Day after tomorrow we give in our fees, don't we? Suppose you—ah—just postpone paying yours for a week, Gagan. I have done that: it works beautifully. They never mind a few days delay; and something's always sure to turn up in a week."
>
> Mr. Gagan looked a little frightened; he had not tried this expedient yet; embezzling the fees was looked on in college as a rather go-ahead practice.

"And what if your new financial dodge turns out to be a bilk?" asked Mahony Quain, stretching himself lazily against the opposite wall of the little grimy room.

Orpen shook his head. "Perfectly safe, my boy; take thirty, forty, whatever is given against their selection or your own, I bet you we'll win."[19]

By the end of the story, Gagan has pawned his mother's cashmere shawl and his father's law books, Quain has eloped to Australia with the housemaid, and Dicky has run away to sea. Laffan seems to have possessed a thorough knowledge of different forms of gambling and the practices of Dublin moneylenders, as well as of adolescent male attitudes towards life—and towards girls not of their own social class. Nellie and her brother Dicky, going out for the day, have the following encounter:

They came upon a tawdrily dressed nurse carrying a baby, and followed by a number of little children. These belonged to an acquaintance of the Davorens, and Nellie stopped to enquire for their mother from the nurse.

Dicky, who was a little in advance, turned round with such an angry face that she hastily quickened her steps to overtake him. He stood quite still until she came up, and then said in an angry and serious tone, "Did I possibly see you speak to that girl of the Wildings?"

"Yes; I asked for her mistress."

"Don't you ever dare to speak to her again: never notice her on any account. You hear me, Nellie?"

"I do. Why not speak to her. What can you mean?"

"I mean this, then, since you must have meanings and reasons,—she's not a person fit for you to speak to. I know what she is very well."

So he did, for the "person" in question was a companion and associate of several of his college friends.

Nellie made him no rejoinder. She felt shocked and mortified.[20]

Nellie has been made suddenly aware of another social convention concealed from the world with which she is familiar—a convention which treats servant girls as destined for sexual exploitation by middle-class young men like Dicky. These girls incurred social blame for their situation as if they had a choice in the matter—which often they had not. This incident can be seen as a foretaste of James Joyce's short story "Two Gallants," written on the same "double standard" theme nearly thirty years later.[21]

The pervasive low-life element is more subtly and convincingly dealt with in *Hogan MP* than in *The Way We Live Now*, where Trollope's Felix Carbury, the dissolute young socialite who "tries it on" with various girls and is finally badly beaten up by the sweetheart of one of them, is difficult to credit. Trollope seems to have intended him as comic relief to set off the darker chapters of the novel, but somehow he is not funny enough, and even rather pathetic.

A sharper and closer comparison with Dicky and his friends is the "broken down swell" Fred Scully in Moore's *A Drama in Muslin*. Fred, in fact, represents a further stage in the rake's progress—he is what the students in Laffan's story are likely to become:

> After having been in London, where he spent some years in certain vague employments, and having contracted as much debt as his creditors would permit, and more than his father would pay, he had gone through the Bankruptcy Court and returned home to wearily drag through life. . . . Fred was about thirty years of age. His legs were long, his hands were bony, and stable yard was written in capital letters on his face. . . . Such was the physiology of this being, from it the psychology is easy to surmise: a complete powerlessness to understand that there was anything in life worth seeking except pleasure—and pleasure to Fred meant horses, women, eating—beyond these three gratifications he neither thought, felt nor saw.[22]

Fred Scully is indeed motivated only by desire for instant pleasure, and a wish to escape consequences. In this he strongly resembles Dicky Davoren and his friends; their desire is consistent with what they do—and say, in the case of Laffan's characters only, as Moore gives almost no dialogue to Fred. With Trollope's Felix Carbury, even the motivation is not gone into. All that we are shown are his actions, which are comical but not consistent with each other—a state which has the effect of depriving the character of depth.

The points in common between characters in the two Irish novels mentioned above underline the differences between nineteenth-century Irish society and that of Middle England as portrayed by Trollope. Tension appears in Trollope's novel *The Way We Live Now* between the comfortable, predictable English world and the deviant people who upset it. Like Jane Austen, Trollope chose to start from the baseline of a peaceful and ordered society, disrupted by unexpected happenings which he would then proceed to describe. Irish writers could not use this approach, as they were unable to count on peace or stability as a norm, living as they did in a *milieu* where life was far less predictable. However, the solution found by all three writers to dispose of their troublesome characters was the same: emigration to foreign parts, ranging from Germany to South America, and guaranteed to produce eventual reformation.

The progress of Cosmo Saltasche's infatuation with a South American and the gradual fading of his dream once attained are realistic enough to make one consider a possible origin in real life. Certainly *louche* international power brokers like Saltasche made regular appearances in the daily news as well as in American,[23] English and French novels of the period. Expansion in the transport and mining industries, particularly during the second half of the nineteenth century, led to a general increase in speculation which opened possibilities for financiers prepared to venture beyond the limits of the law. As fictional characters, these could be menacing, like Vautrin in Balzac's *Pere Goriot* and Melmotte in *The Way We Live Now*; or they could appear benign, like Sidonia in Disraeli's *Coningsby*, and occasionally just furtive, like Merdle in Dickens's *Little Dorrit*. But there is no doubt that they were modelled upon real people, usually self-made men on the margins of society, men who had narrowly escaped from poverty and obscurity.

In contrast to Augustus Melmotte, Trollope's impressive confidence trickster, Cosmo Saltasche is a genuine mixture of good and evil. He is shown to be charming, generous to the poor, sympathetic to women and a good listener. But he is also inquisitive, unscrupulous and controlling. When, at one point in the novel, Saltasche becomes aware that Hogan regrets their bargain, he turns on the latter with such ferocity that Hogan, shocked and frightened, gives way at once. This incident shows Hogan as the weaker man and, possibly to emphasize this, Laffan makes him less convincing and even less positive than Saltasche. The shady financiers of the time, on whom this character was modelled, probably really were deceivers of the public who began by deceiving themselves, got carried away by greed or ambition, and eventually destroyed the fantasy they had created, and along with it, the legitimate hopes of many other people.[24]

In fact, Cosmo Saltasche, self-styled intimate of international statesmen Metternich and Gortshakov, has been called the first known representative in Irish fiction of the cultivated international scoundrel.[25] A likely Irish model for him would be the lawyer, banker and MP John Sadlier

(1814–1856).²⁶ Saltasche resembled him in appearance—both men were dark-haired, brown-eyed, olive-skinned and short—and he resembled him also in being able to inspire confidence and liking in many people, including those he afterwards ruined financially. Sadlier, too, made a personal fortune as a speculator, and dramatically took his own life when faced with the loss of all he had striven for. Just before he took poison, he apparently visited the dancer Clara Morton, thought to be his mistress. The fact that she did not perceive his state of mind suggests that her attachment to Sadlier may have been like that of Adelaide to Saltasche—a matter of expediency rather than affection.²⁷

Details of the career of John Sadlier would have been well known to Laffan. Her father's people came from the original scene of Sadlier's operations, and at least one—Archdeacon Michael Laffan—was among those whom Sadlier deceived both into giving him political support, and later investing church money in his ill-fated Tipperary Joint Stock Bank, destined to crash resoundingly in 1856.²⁸

In class terms, Cosmo Saltasche and his predecessors both real and fictional are outsiders, not true participants in the official scheme of things upheld by the powerful English social system. Outsiders in English novels of this time are frequently foreigners, often Jews or Catholics originally, but anyway prone to conceal their true origins. Typically, Augustus Melmotte in Trollope's *The Way We Live Now* says he is English, is assumed by all to be a Middle-European Jew, and is finally discovered to be an Irish American. To a conservative and xenophobic readership, financial speculation was a foreign invention and reinforced the bad name foreigners already had. Their "different," presumably shady backgrounds were held to account for any lack of openness; their persuasive charm and social skills were seen as vanities deployed solely to deceive investors.

In the Ascendancy enclave of South Dublin, Saltasche ingratiates himself with poor people, and manifests sympathy with Irish Nationalism and Catholicism, the creeds of the underdog. The poor people like him; but he is less successful with people of his own station in life. Though he contributes lavishly to charities and organizes money-raising events, he is never ever invited to events at the Viceregal Court:

> It was in his own immediate neighbourhood, precisely where he expended his best efforts and a vast income to attain the goodwill of everyone, that his enemies were keenest. There was a class of Protestants—not the best set, nor the second set, but still a very respectable and old-established faction—who stoutly

denied Saltasche's supremacy and would have none of him, "a half-foreigner," "a fellow come from God knows where," "a mongrel,": they even declared him to be a freethinker. And one gentleman, who, on the strength of an avowed atheism, had acquired a sort of reputation for general information, if not erudition, imparted under the seal of secrecy to his most particular friends his opinion that Saltasche was a Comtist.[29]

Cosmo Saltasche, unlike John Hogan, is able genuinely to fall in love. Adelaide Poignarde, an aloof girl apparently contemptuous of her surroundings, inspires in Saltasche an obsessive devotion from the first time he sees her:

> She was looking, as it happened, straight in his direction, and he caught the very glance of her splendid liquid brown eyes in his. The pure oval of her face was well relieved against the braids of brown hair hanging low on her neck. White and scarlet camellia buds were set, in defiance of the mode of the day, right behind her left ear,—just where the Spanish beauties put them; the white above the scarlet, so that the one set off the ivory-white skin it caressed, and the other glowed in the setting of her luxuriant hair. Not a jewel did she wear, save a gold and diamond star, fixed in a black velvet ribbon on her neck; and her wrists, slender, round and supple, bore not a single bracelet.[30]

Saltasche, we are told, "revelled in the picture that she made"—evidently a picture after Ingres, as the description recalls the latter's cold and voluptuous style.[31] Saltasche is shown as a knowledgeable patron of art and music. Adelaide Poignarde is a gifted musician. Her skill, her style and her exotic appearance set her apart from the upper-class Dubliners who enjoy her playing but feel uneasy in her presence. Conscious of this unease, and unwilling to provoke it, she resists attempts made to get to know her. An alienation similar to hers is experienced by the wife and daughter of Melmotte in *The Way We Live Now*. They do not feel comfortable in the English upper-class world any more than Adelaide does in the world of the Ascendancy. Saltasche and Adelaide, the two aliens, should have enough in common to make a success of their relationship. The fact that they fail at this could have to do with the natural disposition of both of them to exploit others. Adelaide feigns a love for Saltasche which she does not feel; he conceals his dishonest financial transactions from her. Like most of the other characters in *Hogan MP*, they practice deception and are caught in their own trap.

It is noteworthy that Laffan, writing about two deviant characters (Adelaide the tough-minded woman who cares only to pursue her musical career and readily agrees to jettison an alcoholic husband, and Saltasche the trickster of uncertain origins who becomes her accomplice and lover) describes their individual thought processes and motivation in an impressively realistic manner but without expressing judgment on them. She hardly even judges their actions. Such moral detachment is far commoner in French novels, such as those of Balzac, Zola and Flaubert, than in English fiction, to the detriment of the latter, as Henry James was later to argue.[32] They acknowledge the complexity of human nature and the need for fiction to take into account that the truth about any individual's behaviour is seldom simple or straightforward.

This does not mean that Laffan herself was not a moral novelist—on the contrary, standards of morality concerned her. She was, however, a compassionate writer, avoiding the tendency to see characters as perfectly good or totally evil, and accepting the reality that good people sometimes cause bad actions. She was quick to demonstrate that social class is not a measure of probity. John Hogan is dishonest in trying to use his status as an MP without doing anything to earn his position. Cosmo Saltasche uses written lies to exploit the financial greed of others. Their social superiors behave differently but no better. Lord Brayhead, for example, is uninterested in anything but proselytism and financial gain. As a leader of the evangelical community in Dublin, he attends a charity concert at which Adelaide makes her successful *début*:

> His Lordship . . . had serious doubts as to the becomingness of ladies excelling in anything. . . . He had a dim idea that these sort of things were marketable commodities, bought and paid for, and that it was infra dig.[33] for a lady or gentleman to meddle with professional pursuits. . . . Then he was not sure who the musician was. She might have been a governess, or some "person" obliged to support herself. So he deemed it right to qualify his approval.

> "Do you consider that music in itself repays or justifies the expenditure of so large a portion of our allotted time?"—and the long sheep's face inclined sideways towards her. "Is it not open to question whether we are justified in encouraging trivialities that pass with time itself?"[34]

Brayhead considers that it is legitimate for him to question the value of Adelaide's performance, which he is unable to appreciate. He puts a puritanical gloss on his remarks by drawing a distinction between "valuable" and "worthless" activities and suggesting music to be worthless because there is no tangible end product. His reason for backing Hogan, a man from the class he despises, is typical—he needs an MP to introduce a private

Railway Bill which will open access to mineral deposits on his estate. And he cannot support the obvious candidate, Kilboggan's nephew:

> "With Lord Kilboggan I have nothing to say or to do in common, I thank the Lord. I trust I remember him in my prayers, but he is a godless man, who would not scruple to injure me in any way he could; and if he were aware that I had any interest in the election for Peatstown he would oppose me."[35]

Intolerant as he is towards "Romanists," in his zeal to overcome an enemy and make a profit Brayhead lowers himself sufficiently to invite Hogan to dinner, which is delayed by an hour to accommodate the Lord Lieutenant, Lord Spencer. The latter is held up, according to Lord Brayhead, by the need to censor Meyerbeer's opera *Les Huguenots*. Saltasche is highly amused, but pretends otherwise, except to Hogan:

> "Did ever mortal man hear such foolery? His Excellency, I suppose, is holding a Privy Council to decide whether the Rataplan chorus is to be excised or not. He'll send alarming dispatches to Downing Street over it, to show them what he is doing. Pooh! he must give a little value for his money, you know, or seem to do so."[36]

Laffan does not spare her ridicule of Brayhead, yet, social status being all-important, she makes it clear that he and his family are highly influential in the little Dublin world. They are integral parts of its Protestant upper-class, as also are Diana Bursford and her mother, Dorothy O'Hegarty, and her gossip-circle, Theodore Wyldeoates and his vacuous friends, Nellie's mother Everilda Davoren and Dicky Davoren's mentor the hypocritical Divinity student William Orpen. These all perceive themselves (and are perceived by others) to be superior people solely because they are upper-class Protestants. Others are expected to aspire to their heights, although never to actually reach them; and English society is seen as inferior to that of Dublin, because it is less narrow and socially exclusive.

John Hogan himself, Bishop O'Rooney, Rev. Mother Assumption and the nuns at St. Swithin's Convent, Nellie's father Mr. Davoren and his Tipperary cousins, the Lord Mayor and his entourage of aldermen with "overdressed and underbred" wives and daughters—all these are Catholics, and therefore lesser people. But Adelaide and Saltasche cannot be placed within this system; and Nellie and Dicky Davoren, children of both traditions like their creator, have a more complex and ambivalent relation to it.

Ambivalence is in fact one of the features of this book, and more so than in either *The Way We Live Now* or *A Drama in Muslin*. Laffan uniquely shows us both Irish communities in their natural colours, even if usually for the purpose of castigating both. In her books, Irish Protestants are depicted as far better educated than Catholics, more sophisticated and more cultured. The accuracy of this can be inferred from the relatively greater numbers of Protestants who in the Ireland of the period received higher education, joined the professions, or made successful business careers.[37] But they are also depicted as complacent, arrogant, narrow-minded and insensitive. Irish Catholics by comparison are generous, imaginative and lively. Their responsiveness to religion, the arts, and the needs of others is consistent with this description. But they are also shown to be ignorant, careless, dishonest, and too deficient in self-esteem not to take offence at any suggestion of criticism. Some recognition is given to the idea that Catholics in other European countries do not seem to have the faults attributed to those in Ireland, but the implications of this are not discussed.

There is little scope for ambivalence in *The Way We Live Now*. Trollope wrote from the viewpoint of the middle-class nineteenth-century Englishman, but unlike most of them he had been educated at famous public schools.[38] Little as he seems to have drawn from this experience at the time, he found in adult life that his school background had effectively ensured him a livelihood—made it possible for him to have a rewarding career in the civil service, with the time and opportunity to become a writer. Perhaps because the rest of his early life was lonely and hard, Trollope valued greatly the part of his history and identity connected with his famous schools, and their reputed standards of honesty, responsibility and "decent" behaviour became, for him, the level to which all good men should aspire.

The Way We Live Now, the longest of Trollope's works and the only one in a sustained satirical mode, was intended as an attack on changes in the value system of society, changes which he felt were hostile to his creed and denigrated it. In middle life he did not welcome social change, adopting the general if sub-acute distrust of the foreign and unfamiliar common to English writers of the time, and illustrated in *The Way We Live Now* by Trollope's intense and obvious dislike of the Conservative Prime Minister Benjamin Disraeli, although he was at the same time a sincere supporter of the party Disraeli led. Trollope was no friend to ambivalence or ambiguity; he liked things to be straightforward, and often interpolated his own personal views in his novels to make clear to the reader what these were and why he held them. Trollope liked Ireland, where his first career as a civil servant had flourished and his second career as a successful novelist had begun, but his view of Irish politics was little different to that of any other English Conservative.

Most novels set in the Ireland of the last quarter of the nineteenth century were written either from the standpoint of the Anglo-Irish Protestant or from that of the Irish Catholic. *Hogan MP* is written from the two standpoints alternating, because its writer stands between both sides. She is therefore in an ideal position to shift the mocking light of ridicule from the pretence and snobbery of the Ascendancy ladies at Dorothy's tea-party to the pretence and vulgarity on display at St. Swithin's Convent prize-giving. And as is usual with satire, there is a general impression of underlying pain and a sense of disconnection, of half-hidden uncertainty as to what is right, or who is in the right, and a deep dissatisfaction with the way things are.

George Moore shared some of the views of May Laffan, but expressed them with a more conscious art. *A Drama In Muslin*, his first novel to be set in Ireland, was like *Hogan MP* successful in critical and financial terms. Like *Hogan MP* also it was written in a satirical vein; and it had in common with the earlier novel an opening scene in a convent school, and a conventionally happy ending in which we cannot quite believe. The aims of both writers differed though. Unlike Laffan, Moore wanted to shock the public into awareness of the "slave market" aspect of marriage in upper-class Irish circles, first commenting on this in the meditation of his clever heroine Alice Barton:

> For this, and only this, the whole system of their education had been devised. They had been dressed out in a little French, a little music, a little water-colour painting—for this, and only this: to snigger, to cajole, to chatter to any man who would condescend to listen to them, and to gladly marry any man who would undertake to keep them.[39]

Like Laffan, Moore considered the convent education of girls to be inferior; but though he was fascinated by girls, it is not certain that he ever valued their intellectual abilities. He intended *A Drama in Muslin* as an exposure of the humiliating lives of unmarried women in upper-class Irish society, where they apparently outnumbered men. He wrote about what he knew, drawing on his extensive personal experience and that of women friends. The Moore family had converted to Catholicism in the eighteenth century and to Home Rule in the nineteenth. Fulfilling as they did the unlikely role of Catholic landlords, they nevertheless supported social change intended ultimately to eliminate their class.[40] Moore, whose father had been a founder member of the Irish Party led by Isaac Butt, rejected both conversions, preferring ultimately for many reasons a nominal Protestantism and a British identity.[41]

Moore saw little difference between Catholics and Protestants in regard to their attitudes to women and to marriage. The supply of marriageable men of their own class being limited, for many upper-class Irish girls the real choices lay between spinsterhood, the celibate religious life, and marriage to a man beneath one's own social class. This third option—the one chosen by Diana in *Hogan MP*—is chosen also by Alice Barton, Moore's heroine, when the dispensary doctor (regarded by her family as a sort of upper servant) wants to marry her. Alice, by her marriage, is enabled to escape from a society which, during the Land War,[42] was under constant threat of violence to a scene which holds no painful memories and enables her to use her experience creatively as a writer of fiction.

Diana Bursford, on the other hand, by her marriage to Hogan the ex-MP apparently achieves nothing but married status. She, too, is assumed by everyone to have married beneath her; and because Hogan is a Catholic, his shortcomings are no surprise to anybody. But it seems as if the actual status of being a wife is all Diana needs—to liberate her:

> The girl was in truth sick of her life; fourteen years was a long apprenticeship, and she wearied for the day when she might lay aside, literally as well as metaphorically, the war paint and feathers; when she might be natural and unaffected, and above all, independent of the mother bird, whose control, prolonged far beyond the natural limits, was now become distasteful and wearisome to her.[43]

Moore castigated what he perceived as hypocrisy regarding sexual conduct; but Laffan wanted to ridicule pretension and its associated dishonesty in public and private life. She saw these faults as endemic in Ireland, and holds them up to ridicule. In *Hogan MP* she exhibits and characterises them. John Hogan pretends to culture when trying to impress Nellie Davoren, and not really understanding what she is talking about, he mispronounces the name of a famous German poet.[44] Later, he deceives Nellie as to his relations with Diana. In his election campaign he feigns idealism and motivation which he knows are not really his own. Likewise Dicky Davoren and his friends cheat and deceive their families in order to mimic the lifestyle of their social superiors, the hard-living British Army officers stationed in Dublin. Mother Assumption and her nuns at St. Swithin's Convent deceive as well, offering a false and expensive travesty of education to their pupils, who in their turn slavishly copy the attitudes and fashions of the Viceregal Court. Life in Dublin has therefore a meretricious and derivative quality, based as it is on insecure identity and lack of self-esteem. Even the gentle Nellie Davoren expresses this to Hogan:

> "What would become of us all—of our energies and intellects—if we were not given to politics and patriotism? There isn't any outlet for either, as things are."
>
> "How 'as things are' now?" asked he . . .
>
> "Do I need to tell you that? . . . This country is so cut off from the other nations of Europe,—for it is a nation, in spite of geography, ethnology and all the rest of it. Thanks to our rulers, we have no manufactures to employ our time; and then, worst of all, these wretched castes of Protestant and Catholic hinder so—"
>
> A look on her listener's face warned the speaker to stop. She bit her lip, frightened lest she had said too much.[45]

It is significant, perhaps, that the harsh term "caste," with its derivation from Hindu society, and not the gentler term "class" is used. Nellie has her own opinions, even if the convention of the time discouraged young women from expressing these, about issues of class and identity which also were uppermost in the mind of May Laffan.

Laffan seems to have felt very uncertain indeed as to where she really belonged, and she expressed this in the somewhat nebulous character of Nellie Davoren. It has been recently suggested that Laffan, mainly on the evidence presented in *Hogan MP*, chose like Moore to identify herself as Protestant, but taking into account her consistent strictures on Irish Protestant attitudes this seems rather unlikely.[46] There were already a number of contemporary novels which touched on the "mixed marriage" theme, but the touch was very light and no difficulties were explored. Perhaps May Laffan felt that any attempt to look below the surface would take her novel in a direction she did not want. This could account for her failure to develop Nellie as a complex character; exploration would have gone altogether too near the bone for her.

How accurate were the descriptions given in these novels of life in Dublin for the middle and upper classes? In detail, they correspond closely to accounts both in memoirs of the period and in contemporary novels.[47] Certainly, Moore's scathing picture of the Viceregal Court in full swing is more accomplished and detailed than the parallel descriptions of "Castle" events in *Hogan MP* and *Christy Carew*, the two "Dublin" Laffan novels—but Moore deliberately attended the Dublin "Season" for two successive years in order to describe it convincingly from within. It was possible for him to do this as a man, a landowner, and a comparatively wealthy person. Without such opportunities as he had, Laffan managed in her evocations of activities on the fringe of the Court to convey the self-same uneasy, frustrating and inhibiting atmosphere of colonial society in a state of decline.

This decline is shown in *Hogan MP* in a number of different ways, for instance, in descriptions of how Dublin social life at the middle- and upper-class level is obsessed with the doings of "their Excellencies," the Viceregal pair Lord and Lady Spencer and their entourage. At the theatre, they attract more attention than whatever is happening on the stage. At the Royal Dublin Society's Flower Show, no one looks at the exhibits once "their Excies" have arrived—and then everyone follows them about. Their horses, clothes, and banal sayings are reported on and copied to a disconcerting extent. As private individuals, Lord and Lady Spencer are not popular with the Ascendancy, which considers them too free in their encouragement of upwardly mobile Catholics; but they are important nevertheless as representing the Queen and English nobility, a focus of loyalty in fact. Beyond the "echoes and shadows" of Moore's famous phrase describing Dublin[48] lies genuine substance—the real seat of power existing in London, capital of the world's richest and most powerful country.

In *Hogan MP* also, Dubliners with social pretensions fix their eyes firmly on London. During a lengthy tea-party given by Dorothy O'Hegarty to her women friends, all the conversation concerns not events in Ireland, or even Dublin, but the latest London scandals. Not a single one of the people so avidly discussed is known to Dorothy or her friends, but they pretend otherwise. They read London magazines, too—but only in order to copy the fashions displayed in the illustrations. Education is mentioned—but in terms of wealthy Irish people educating their children in England, so that they may be able to pass for English later.

The chief social events Laffan writes about in *Hogan MP* are private parties and dances, held with great ostentation in the large houses of Mountjoy Square and Gardiner Street, the territory of the upwardly mobile Catholic. Her set-pieces depict the social scene much as George Moore found it, but she adds another dimension. All of the girls present are Catholics, and this is because women from the Protestant Ascendancy do not accept invitations to these social occasions. They are therefore perceived as setting the social boundaries. Army officers and gentlemen of the Ascendancy readily accept invitations to Catholic houses to devour the over-lavish suppers where expensive wines (in which their hosts trade) are pressed on them. They come to see the girls, whom they usually perceive as inferiors, as they do most Irish Catholics including their hosts:

> "I didn't know a creature in the place, give you my word. What the deuce did the people mean by askin' us to such a shop? Did you notice the Lord Mayor, old whiskey barrels, with his chain of office round his neck? Law!" continued the young gentleman, after an explosion of laughter, "why hadn't the aldermen got on their gowns?"[49]

But when a drunken guardsman gatecrashes one such party, Mr. Rafferty the ex-publican Lord Mayor comes into his own, removing the offender quickly and unobtrusively with an ease born of long practice. And the guests at these noisy, lively parties certainly enjoy themselves more than at the dismal entertainment to which Lord and Lady Brayhead invite Saltasche and Hogan. Thus do *nouveaux riches* Catholics imitate the customs of the socially dominant class, but their own different nature, barely restrained by deference, is shown as occasionally breaking through. This habit of deference towards social superiors was losing hold in the 1870s, and new ideas on the subject of identity beginning to appear. Bishop O'Rooney, advising his nephew John Hogan, had one way of putting it:

> "Now, John my boy, don't let anyone hear you sneer at trade. You're in a fair way enough, but a rash speech like that would be enough to tumble you over.
>
> . . . Depend upon it, John, the only way to get on—and I know the world—the only chance of consideration or respect you can have from the Protestants, is to let them see—you being a Catholic—that you have the confidence and respect of the Catholics. The Government can't do without the priests; and what use would you be without their back? And to make little of Catholics, and Catholic society, is not the way to go about getting that, I can tell you, sir."[50]

Associated with this robust consciousness-raising is the gradual appearance of a change of attitude towards the Celtic past. Although antiquaries and historians had always shown some interest in the Irish language and Gaelic society, it was certainly a minority interest. No one actually speaks Irish in *Hogan MP*, though in rural Munster episodes of the occasional Irish derivative is used. But the comment is made—and made fun of—that upwardly mobile people who tried very hard in the recent past to anglicize their surnames by changing the spelling and dropping the Gaelic prefixes are now trying equally hard to reverse that process:

> The Raffertys had got home a genealogical tree from Sir Bernard Burke; the Ryans wrote themselves O'Ryan; and O'Donnell, the retired wine-merchant, who bought Lord Ramines' patrimony, insisted on the prefix Mac. There was great talk of the septs and tribes; and sundry extinct peerages seemed to be only waiting for moneyed claimants to come forward. Hitherto Hogan had over- looked the fact that his ancestry might be of service . . . he determined that the chieftain Rhuadne, and that the ruined Castle Rhuadne, near Tara, should both be skillfully introduced as a background, so to say, to the representation of the family O'Rooney.[51]

This popular aspect of the Celtic revival is shown as part of a range of fash- ionable trends, current in late-nineteenth-century Dublin, which fell in with national aspirations in that time of transition from relative accep- tance of English rule to its rejection. Other such manifestations were the re- vival of interest in Thomas Moore's *Irish Melodies* in the 1870s and the popularity of patriotic songs such as *The Wearing of the Green*, which Diana Bursford sings incongruously at the Brayhead's reception. However uncon- sciously, these minor gestures towards cultural separatism went along with the need to develop a more comfortable identity than that of an imper- fectly assimilated, subject people.

Moore's novel *A Drama in Muslin* is almost free from mention of such con- temporary trends, apart from his indirect references to women's rights and their need for education. It is probable that he had read *Hogan MP* before starting on his own more celebrated story. So far as education and mar- riage are concerned, Laffan and Moore seem to have thought on similar lines. The convent-school opening scenes apart, Laffan's characters, Mrs. Rafferty the ebullient Lady Mayoress or Diana the fading belle, for in- stance, could be fitted very neatly into Moore's evocation of the Dublin Sea- son and its sacrificial victims—one can imagine Mrs. Rafferty as a typical chaperone, and Diana Bursford as one of the Muslin Martyrs:

> Poor Miss Bursford! her opportunities were not to be wasted now. Who would think that under the cold, well-bred smiling manner there lay such a torrent of disgust, contempt and fierce self-upbraidings? She looked round and round the room, noted with a sneer that ancient manhunter, Blanche Braginton, playing off all the well-worn tricks in her repertory on the tough hide of Cosmo Saltasche; then noted the sofa, where a couple of women, well-dressed and dull, were keep- ing up a feeble trickle of small-talk with some dining-out professional; Lord

Brayhead, wooden as usual, on the hearthrug, and the place of honour vacant as yet. . . .[52]

The inhabitants of the ladies' sitting room at the Shelbourne Hotel in Moore's story are all Irish Catholics, which would scarcely have been the case in Laffan's time ten years earlier. Social change has evidently taken place; and awareness of it is shown to have hardened some Ascendancy attitudes. Reference is made in *Hogan MP* to a more tolerant climate existing before Catholic Emancipation. It is implied that Catholics did not then present a threat, because they knew their place and were respectful. Not one of the Anglo-Irish characters in *Hogan MP* explicitly states the native Irish to be *racially* inferior; however, their low status is firmly and ostensibly attached to their religion.

Catholicism was perceived from the outside as a primitive, permissive and anti-intellectual form of belief, hardly Christian, but vaguely related to Christianity. Devotion to the Virgin Mary and the saints was understood as idolatry, and emphasis on tradition was interpreted as a deliberate attempt to prevent the faithful from using their intellects. The Catholic Church was considered to be condoning evil by saying *all* sin could be forgiven. Even the use of visual imagery, of music and drama in Catholic worship was suspect as a form of deception.[53]

Both religion and philosophy were taken very seriously by the Victorians, and the writings of Thomas Malthus[54] and Harriet Martineau,[55] together with the research-based theories of Darwin and Huxley, reached a wide audience in one form or another and fed into a general vague perception of threats to civilization posed by racial and cultural inferiors.[56] Mingled with the fear of such threats was distrust of any belief system apparently not logic-based, or any good not measurable in material terms. For some, in fact, religion altogether lacked any transcendental dimension; it was seen merely as a useful emotional prop for political and social systems.

Hogan MP was published in 1876, but one of the most searching reviews it received was to come years later in *The Cabinet of Irish Literature*.[57] This review, quoted in full in chapter two, is unsigned and its authorship therefore uncertain, but the writer compared Laffan to William Carleton, and hailed her as the precursor of "a new era in Irish literature."[58] One of the criticisms it made about *Hogan MP* was

the manner in which political debates are introduced . . . and do not, as in the case of Miss Keary's Castle Daly, arise naturally out of the incidents of the story ...

but they also . . . reveal a penetrating sense of the real issues and the genuine opinions of people that is especially remarkable in an authoress.⁵⁹

The "political debate" criticism refers to a long scene between Saltasche and Hogan in chapter six. Saltasche asks Hogan out to dinner with a view to finding whether he might do as a prospective tame MP for the powerful Lord Brayhead. The two men certainly talk politics at length, but as Robert Lee Wolff remarked, it is reasonable that any political "fixer" at any time in history would sound out a candidate in this manner.⁶⁰ Hogan and Saltasche begin by discussing Catholic-Protestant relations and social interaction, Hogan leading on the subject of bigotry:

> ". . . the root of it lies far back. You have to go back a century or more into the history of the country to see how deeply rooted is the class distinction between the two rival creeds. I assure you even Protestant tradesmen think they have the pull over any R.C. And that is a thing that always gathers force as it gets older. So long as the Protestants were the recognised superiors of the others, they were not nearly so stuck-up and exclusive. . . ."⁶¹

The pair goes on to discuss current politics. Saltasche is clearly drawing his protégé out, testing his powers of quick thinking, verbal expression and communication; and Hogan knows quite well what he is up to though not why the test is taking place. Accordingly he gives, not so much the stock answers associated with politicians, but opinions and ideas which appear to be his own and he gives the reasons he has for holding them.

The topic of Home Rule, ostensibly the major political issue at the time, is not touched on at all at this stage, but the issue of undue clerical influence is:

> "[Priests] abused their influence? . . . I don't know that the Government can charge them with that. They certainly have an enormous personal influence over the people, but in political matters, why, look at this Fenian business: in all Ireland, it is a fact there was but one Fenian priest.⁶² Their lives were actually threatened—you know that. . . . Fenianism was low, too—" said Hogan thoughtfully, "essentially low: it had not a single supporter of the social position of those who were concerned with the Young Irelanders;⁶³ and I may tell you that priests are intensely aristocratic."⁶⁴

Then Saltasche gives his opinion of the fundamental reason for Irish unrest:

"The monstrous insolence of the English is at the bottom of all the troubles here. Talk of Infallibility and the Pope's assumptions,—God bless me, what is it compared to the Anglo-Hibernian Protestantism? A trifle light as air. Their religion is themselves; and everywhere John Bull goes with his egotism and his Bible,—on the Continent, India, Africa—the story is identical; hatred and rebellion spring up at once."[65]

Hogan agrees with his friend, instancing the Indian Mutiny as an unnecessary war brought about by tactless behaviour on the part of English officials and army officers. He and Saltasche are especially critical of the manner in which the English treat their servants as a lesser species. (The few servants depicted in *Hogan MP* are strong characters, shown dominating their employers.) The sensitivity of Hogan and Saltasche to this aspect of life under English rule suggests a shared consciousness of their own perceived social inferiority—as marginal people they too have both been at the receiving end of denigration.

Now Hogan believes the tenant-at-will situation may be ruining rural Ireland, but he cannot envisage a way to change it yet, because it would be asking too much to expect landowners to dismantle their own system. He does not think the electorate well-informed enough yet to help themselves:

". . . What can you expect of the people? What can they do for themselves? Take into account their wretchedness and degradation, and their ignorance . . . how, then, can you expect them to have just or equitable ideas? They really are not one whit more civilised than the peasants whom Arthur Young[66] describes in France a century ago."[67]

Hogan thinks he understands that the issue of the land ownership in Ireland is fundamentally important. What he cannot imagine is how it could be made to alter in any permanent and satisfactory way.

The next topic raised is the proposed reformation of the existing National School system,[68] necessary because, according to Hogan, the present system was destined from the start to be unacceptable to those for whom it was designed:

"They always wanted to force Scripture, in some shape or sort, down the throats of the children, and insisted on their right to do it. Bah! The priests were quite right to resist such aggression. And let the parsons promise what they like, from the very first time they ever established a school in Ireland, proselytism was their business. There is not a brat as high as your knee but knows that, and hates them accordingly. . . . This proselytism was not for the sake of merely winning over their souls to the rival Church, but also, mark you, as a means of obtaining their allegiance, and thereby strengthening and securing the proselytiser's own position as conquerors in a subjugated country. So at all times here a pervert, or, as the Saturday Review says, a 'vert', was looked upon in the double light of a deserter and an apostate."[69]

Saltasche hints that the Catholic clergy expect that the fruits of the Church Act, which disestablished the Church of Ireland, should be used to finance the Catholic University. Hogan disagrees, seeing another University as unnecessary:

> "Trinity is absorbing such Catholic youngsters as want college education and degrees. I think the Stephen's Green University merely draws medical students. After all, they have a very good excuse for patronising Trinity. Few people can afford to lose time and money taking out a degree that has no market value—a mere certificate. . . . Moreover, who are their professors? Mere nobodies,—or men trained in, or belonging to, the Queen's Universities [*sic*] or Trinity."

> "It's a pity, Mr. Hogan," said Saltasche, "that you are not in St. Stephen's[70]; if you were to talk that way, you'd soon make your mark."[71]

Without knowing it, Hogan has passed the test, and without delay Saltasche recommends him to Brayhead.

The views quoted above, leaving out only the strictures on Protestantism and "perverts," repeat almost word for word the views of Gerald Fitzgibbon, Laffan's granduncle, as given in his book *Ireland in 1868* (see chapter one). Fitzgibbon was a Unionist, but his views coincided with those of many socially aspiring middle-class Catholics at the time. These were business people whose profits depended, or so they thought, on the persistence of British Rule in Ireland. They could see no sense in destroying their hopes of personal prosperity and the futures of their children for what seemed the illusory dream of a self-governing country where a more equitable and just society might possibly arise. The system as it presently was suited them and met their needs. Perhaps their children were to take a wider view, but Laffan does not speculate on the future. She seems to have seen her novelist's role at this point as simply recording the ideas of her present time, with some bias towards subjects of special interest to her. In that connection it is notable that, following on the political discussion summarised above, Saltasche and Hogan go on to have a lengthy and slightly irrelevant session on the pros and cons of religiously mixed marriages, an important subject certainly, but not at that time a political one. This topic, like women's education, was a recurrent preoccupation of Laffan.

But caring as much as she did about education she should have been aware that Gladstone's attempt to design a plan for an Irish University which might be acceptable to all parties was being restricted by the insistence of English Liberals, his supporters, that denominational education must never be subsidised.[72] Some at least of the younger Irish MPs supporting Home Rule foresaw this possibility and refrained from placing much faith in the Liberal Party for that reason.[73] Isaac Butt's emphasis on Home Rule as the main political aim was beginning to lose impetus, as other issues rose in importance.[74] One of these issues was the need to fund both a University system and a system of post-primary education acceptable to Catholics, on which the formation of a middle class could depend. It was at the time a matter more urgent than Home Rule to some of the townspeople in the Catholic community, and especially to those who, like Laffan's father, were making regular financial contributions at the church door to keep their Catholic University going.[75]

The Irish town and city dwellers seem to have been most aware of the need for state support to third level education. However, when John Hogan, having received assurance of financial support from Lord Brayhead, goes down with Dicky Davoren as his sub-agent to canvass in Peatstown, he enters an altogether different world: "It was Hogan's first exploration of the country parts of his native land; and he was astonished beyond measure by the Irishness of everything. The dirt, the carelessness, the merriment; the overflowing genuine hospitality,—all were present. . . ."[76] Hogan begins to experience rural Munster, which as regards life-style, weather and living conditions is a world away from suburban Dublin. He is taken to canvass a distant cousin of Nellie, living off the beaten track:

> It seemed almost a desert. Here and there, at long intervals, a cabin sunk below the road-level raised its brown indented roof in a sheltered corner. . . . They turned up a narrow, muddy lane. . . . In front of the hall door was a huge pool of water; stepping-stones laid down in this showed that it was a permanent institution. Barney . . . welcomed the travellers to his mansion and led the way in. Pointing to the holes in the floor of the entry, he . . . related with glee how M'Scutch, the agent, had twisted his ankle the day he came up to inspect the place. [Barney] led the way into the one sitting-room of the house—which indeed looked a great deal more like the robbers' caves to be read of in romance than a sitting room in the ordinary sense of the word. There was no grate; and a perfect stack of turf was

blazing on the hearthstone. A rickety painted table and a half-dozen old chairs, in a fearful state of dilapidation, composed the whole furniture, save for a broken sofa, one end of which was supported in a hole which had been made in the wall of the room apparently for that especial purpose.[77]

Barney is a tenant of Lord Kilboggan, and has no incentive to repair the house or outbuildings or drain the yard because if he does so his rent will be raised; and when his lease expires, he will not be compensated for any improvements. Were he the tenant of an Ulster landlord, he would be compensated—operating the practice then known as Ulster Custom and associated with Tenant Right,[78] which Hogan quickly learns to be a major political issue. In provincial Ireland, Home Rule means separatism; and the most immediate issue in Peatstown is not even so much Home Rule, as Tenant Right. The names Laffan gives to the local absentee and his agent—"Lord Kilboggan" and "M'Scutch"—appear to be mischievous references to more famous literary characters—Lever's Lord Kilgobbin,[79] and Carleton's Valentine McClutchy[80]—illustrating the undeniable influence of both writers on the rural chapters of Laffan's first novel.

In Peatstown there is a unity of purpose apparent between the very different members of Tenant Associations. Some of them, like Hogan's host Ned Shea, are wealthy graziers wanting a share in the running of the country; others are able men frustrated by lack of opportunity, like Pat Daly, a Fenian returned from America,[81] whose only source of income seems to be poteen-making, and the giant horse-breaker Barney Shane, mentioned above, whose sole recreation is politics, and whom no matchmaker will consider because his lease has less than two years to run. In forceful language Barney describes before the parish priest and assembled guests the insecurity of his existence—as a tenant unprotected by legislation designed only to uphold the rights of landowners:

> "You and the likes of you . . . that have nothing to lose, may prate of your peace and quietness, and every man look after his own. We'll look after our own—and trust you to look after yours." Here an assenting shout almost rent the ceiling. "Look at me," he went on, smiting the table with a fist like Thor's; "my lease will be out in two year's time, and what will that gambling blackguard Kilboggan give me? The key of the street! and I born and reared in the place, and my father and grandfathers before me;" and the big man's voice almost faltered as he spoke.[82]

Minor characters in the novel, the three tenant farmers Ned, Pat and Barney, are presented in a sympathetic light, contradicting in a positive way what Hogan has said about "the people" earlier. It may be asked why a tenant farmer did not stand for election to Parliament himself—why bring in an outsider such as Hogan? The reality was that only a man with independent means could afford to be an Irish MP. Of the fifty-odd members of the Home Rule party led by Isaac Butt, only two or three were described as farmers.[83] These would be also among the few who were freeholders and did not have to depend on the goodwill of a landlord. This situation was to alter gradually over the years, and dramatically once MPs became salaried and had their expenses paid.

At a meeting held in Peatstown to introduce Hogan to the electorate and recruit support for him, all three tenant farmers play active roles. Ned Shea opens the proceedings:

> "The Land Tenure we'll never get without Home Rule. . . . We want Fixity of Tenure and Home Rule; and it's to Mr. Hogan and men like him that we must look, and not an absentee like Kilboggan, that's draining every penny out of this country to spend it in London and France and all them foreign parts."[84]

Pat Daly, a reluctant orator, explains in detail the workings of the Secret Ballot, now to be used in Ireland for the first time. Lastly, Barney Shane has the chance to make his feelings known, and he gives these full dramatic emphasis in his account of the parish priest taking bribes from the Conservative candidate. Already Hogan's beliefs regarding lack of clerical interference are shifting, and they are to undergo radical alteration when he encounters the diocesan administrator and parish priest of Peatstown, Father Jim Corkran:

> A lubberly, coarse figure, bulletheaded, and with the prominent round forehead that tells of obstinacy and impetuosity, wiry black hair and brows which contrasted strangely with round light blue eyes, hard and ruthless, and with a fixed staring look most unpleasant to encounter; while the lips were scornful, and pursed out with pride and self sufficiency. And with all this he was utterly devoid of dignity, either of manner or bearing. Those who feared him—and they were many—were servile and cringing before the bully; but those who like Shea and the richer class of farmers, were independent of his good graces, spoke of him, irrespective of course of his saintly office, with a freedom which showed that the reverend Father Jim was valued at his proper rate by them.[85]

This unpleasant individual, a far crueller caricature than Moore's portrait of the peasant priest in *A Drama in Muslin*, is made the target of continual witty remarks by Dicky Davoren, encouraged by his cousin Ned Shea. Fa-

ther Jim supports Hogan's rival Wyldeoates, because the latter has promised him land for a new chapel and given him money. But the priest
launches an attack at Hogan and his supporters, beginning with the unfortunate school teacher Finlay who has dared to attend Hogan's meeting:

> "If ever you presume to attend any such gathering, or to busy yourself with any-
> thing of the sort again, without first consulting me, I'll turn you away on the
> spot, mark my words!" and he shook his forefinger threateningly. "Begone now!"
> and pointing to the door with the gesture he might have used to an ill-behaved
> dog, he dismissed the terrified schoolmaster. . . .[86]

Father Jim succeeds in frightening Ned Shea's pious wife Margaret also, by
ignoring her greeting and cutting her dead whenever they meet in the
town:

> She began to conjure up in her own mind all the dismal stories she had ever
> heard; Hara's haggard burned down not six months after he quarreled with the
> clergy; Mr. Magrath, of High Park, who married the Protestant lady, and drank
> himself to death within the year; Biddy Flannery, that would marry the Presbyte-
> rian sergeant, and had a deaf-and-dumb baby, and never held up her head after.
> It was tempting Providence clearly, with "foot and mouth" raging in the very
> next county; and she determined to send a pound to her sister the nun, Mary
> Columbkille of the Poor Clares, for such "intentions" and prayers as could be had
> for the money.[87]

Father Jim's opposition to Hogan and his supporters reaches its climax
on the Sunday before the election, when after Mass he makes a speech from
the foot of the altar, saying that a good parishioner will vote as the priest
tells him, and going on to threaten horrible but unspecified consequences
to disobedient members of his flock. Threats of this sort from the altar had
actually been banned within the diocese of Cashel and Emly by Archbishop Leahy since 1867, but this does not seem to bother Father Jim, a law
unto himself.[88]

In the chapel yard afterwards, Laffan describes the reactions of the con-
gregation: the men "laughing, indifferent, a few frightened," and the
women "in consternation . . . one or two of them defiant and reckless,
maybe revengeful, cackling shrill sedition from beneath their blue hoods,
the cynosure the while of their more impressionable sisterhood."[89] When
the election finally takes place under secret ballot conditions, Hogan is
brought in with a large majority.

There is a deliberately dramatic quality to the whole incident, and it is hard to take Father Jim's behaviour, outrageous as it is, very seriously, especially as the effect of his speech is shown to be greatest on the women who were in any case ineligible to vote. In the later chapters of the story, he is shown as reconciled to the Shea family—because he is unwilling to lose his fees for conducting the marriages of their many daughters. It is probable that there was more than one "Father Jim" known to Laffan. One possible model for the character is her cousin, Archdeacon Michael Laffan (1791–1861). He had a formidable reputation for using strong language, but an observer records him, unlike Father Jim, as a strikingly handsome man with an impressive presence.[90] He may not have given unqualified support to Home Rule, but, again unlike Father Jim Corkran, he was one who held it was impossible for any sincere Irish Catholic ever to vote Tory (Conservative).

Official political opposition to Hogan begins when Theodore Wyldeoates, Lord Kilboggan's nephew, arrives in Peatstown as Conservative candidate. He represents an absentee whose agent M'Scutch oppresses tenants to raise money for his master to gamble, and pulls down the cabins of the labouring poor, leaving them nowhere to go but the workhouse. It is clear that he, too, will be an absentee if elected. But Wyldeoates says he is sympathetic to Home Rule, which is thus shown to be a kind of general catch-cry; little more in Laffan's estimation: "It was the new shibboleth which was to succeed Fenianism, and to do all that Fenianism had left undone; just as Fenianism was to wipe up the tears of the Young Irelanders or the Phoenix party,—the fatal legacy of unrest and discontent that seems entailed on the Celt."[91] Laffan, who was politically a Whig (Liberal), attacked conservatives in general, and perhaps especially conservative priests. She was equally ready to attack priests who might be thought to sympathise with members of the Irish Republican Brotherhood (IRB).

With a few exceptions the Catholic clergy did not give strong support to the Home Government Association (HGA), which was set up in 1869 to promote what came to be called Home Rule. There were other reasons for this in addition to those suggested by Laffan. From correspondence now available it would seem that initially members joined the H.G.A. for widely different reasons. Some former Unionists who joined it were felt to be over-reacting to Disestablishment of their church and expressing their feelings at being, as they perceived, left in the lurch by England. Their conversions to nationalism were very new and the question was how genuine they were and how long they would last. Concern was also expressed at the time about the Association's urban bias. Most of its members were Dubliners (it has been described as a Dublin pressure group)—and its consequent tendency was to shelve issues relating to the land. In fact, there seems not to have been any inclination on the part of the H.G.A. to encourage provincial branches, probably because the funds were lacking to develop these.[92]

Few knowledgeable people believed that Home Rule would be achieved very rapidly, so the question often arose as to how domestic matters relating to Ireland could be dealt with in the meantime. One of these urgent but neglected issues was Tenant Right, lack of which was thought to encourage emigration.[93] In fact, no detailed and effective plan to call attention to the country's domestic legislation needs was put together until Parnell succeeded in doing this, at a date some years later than the Hogan era.

Laffan's knowledge of the provincial scene derived at least in part from strong family and political connections with Tipperary. A cousin, known as "Honest" John Lanigan, had been Liberal MP for Cashel in Tipperary from 1859–1865. His nickname arose from his refusal to give or receive bribes. Laffan had four other cousins who, during the period 1855–1891, were politically active priests in the Cashel diocese, supporting Home Rule but not separatism or republicanism.[94] From her Macmillan correspondence and the *Recess Committee Notes* it appears also that Laffan knew personally diverse nationalists such as William O'Brien, John Dillon, and the Davitt family.[95] On the opposite side of her family, the Fitzgibbons were strongly Unionist and conservative. She was well placed, therefore, to know how opposites really thought and spoke about burning political issues of the day. She does not appear to condemn either nationalism or unionism, seeming more concerned to investigate, acknowledge and understand something of the roots from which they spring.

It is notable how convincing Laffan is when it comes to describing the political scene at a local level. Moore's picture of similar scenes is coloured by a sense of the landowner regarding tenants with a mixture of apprehension and distaste. The distaste is mainly shown in an incident where landowners and peasants come together at Mass on Sunday: "The peasants came, coughing and grunting with monotonous, animal-like voices, and the sour odour of cabin-smoked frieze arose. . . . Olive and May, exchanging looks of disgust, drew forth cambric pocket-handkerchiefs, and in unison the perfumes of white rose and *eau d'opoponax*[96] evaporated softly...."[97]

Later in the story, Mrs. Barton, watching from a window as the tenant farmers negotiate with her husband, feels only apprehension and anger towards them: "she saw the pretty furniture, the luxurious idleness, the very silk dress on her back, being torn from them, and distributed among a crowd of Irish-speaking, pig keeping peasants. . . ."[98]

Tenants were often perceived by landowners as ungrateful and menacing and their power to perpetrate violence was acknowledged and feared. The idea that they could ever have real political power was evidently unimaginable to Moore at that time; but not, it seems, to Laffan writing a decade earlier. She does not underrate, though she may satirise, the hard-drinking "big farmers" in their frieze coats, the wife who dreads being "told off from the altar," and the bullied school master trying to remain anonymous at a political meeting. She is near enough to these people to understand them and, almost despite herself, to express how they feel. She is unable to condemn or, albeit critical of aspects of their behaviour, to caricature them as mercilessly as she does the Ascendancy ladies and gentlemen. She seems to think that there is hope for them. Their way of expressing feelings may not fit in with the restraint of the Victorian ethos, but they certainly have a case. Between the country people and the Dubliners of the early chapters of *Hogan MP* there is a social gap—crossed temporarily by Hogan and Dickie Davoren for what they can get out of the situation. Yet the class divisions bedevilling city life are not so marked in rural Munster, nor is sectarian intolerance so evident. What is seen to matter most there is ownership of the land. This is the key to the political future, and the country people, pragmatic to the core, are little concerned about the religious allegiance of anyone who can help them to that key, which they see in the shape of political autonomy.

Following his election, Hogan goes off to Westminster nominally pledged to support Home Rule, Tenant Right, the Catholic University, Fenian Amnesty, Papal Rights—and Lord Brayhead's Railway Bill. He has less than two years in which to make a name.

The *Spectator* review of *Hogan MP* criticised lack of input about Hogan's Parliamentary life. This would be just criticism if Laffan had really intended to write a political novel in the manner of Trollope's *Phineas Finn* (1869), for instance. But we have no evidence that she did. She wanted to illustrate John O'Rooney Hogan's decline and fall, and she could do this very well without bringing in much detail about his inadequate performance in the House. The aspect of an Irish Member's life which Laffan does see fit to dwell on is the relative loneliness, poverty and isolation. That Irish MPs were a class apart, and did not feel at home in the system, has been stated by more than one commentator.[99] Relative to their English counterparts, they were poor, most having no private means; and those who tried to keep a career going found the effort to meet Parliamentary responsibilities as well overwhelming. The failure of Hogan to organize his life sufficiently to make a political mark while meeting his personal financial obligations reflects the experiences of other would-be politicians. Not all members of the Irish Party at the time demonstrated a deep loyalty to that body, or even attended Parliament regularly.[100]

The impression Hogan gives, of being uncertain of what is going on, may have been fairly usual in an age when information was not so widely or easily available. Melmotte, the newly created Conservative MP in *The Way We Live Now*, is humiliated by his series of mistakes on first entering the House. No one has shown him the ropes—it is assumed that he has, like other Members, friends to tell him what to do and what to avoid. But Melmotte, an outsider, has no friends. Like Hogan, he wanted a Parliamentary seat for his own unworthy reasons; and now he pays the price. His personal inadequacy is obvious to all. He is out of place there and is not wanted. Trollope had been a Parliamentary candidate himself and knew very well the scenes he described. He demonstrated, as did Laffan by other means, that some MPs were less welcome than others.

Neither Butt nor his successor Parnell seems to have seen any need to concern themselves about newly elected Irish MPs; in fact, they sometimes appeared to avoid getting to know them. This was probably done to protect the complicated personal lives of both leaders, but it would have had some negative results as far as the novices were concerned, enhancing their feelings of isolation. Hogan avoids taking up Bishop O'Rooney's contacts; he makes no new London friends, and his consequent total reliance on the Bursfords for company makes his entrapment by Diana a foregone conclusion. Hogan's involvement with two women at the same time is probably a polite version of that politician's hazard the work-based "second relationship," in Victorian days kept discreetly hidden from the public eye and until recently ignored by biographers.

How accurate was the general political scene as depicted in *Hogan MP* compared to the way we think things actually were? John O'Rooney Hogan's details and his history do not correspond closely to those of any one real-life Parliamentary candidate in 1871–1874. What does correspond is the attitude and motivation he displays, characteristic of some candidates of the time as described in memoirs and biographies of the period.[101] The shortage of candidates meant that almost any educated man able to attract financial sponsorship and prepared to declare for Home Rule could hope for acceptance as a Liberal candidate. What he would then do—whether he would gravitate towards a National Home Rule party or not was quite another matter. There were various ways of subsidising a needy but useful MP, some methods verging on bribery, while others took the form of the one-off grant or "testimonial." It did not follow either that Catholic candidates always attracted greater clerical support—this circumstance reflected in *Hogan MP*, where we can see that of the four clerics involved at different stages with John Hogan's ambitions, only one, the "mountainy" curate Father Desmond, gives any practical help. Hogan wastes his time trying to present himself as an ardent defender of the faith, but the priest is not fooled any more than the electors are. He will support anyone who, whatever their religion, will press for Tenant Right, and Hogan has undertaken to do this anyway.

Hogan knows there will be a General Election in a year or so, but hopes that by then he will be firmly enough in the saddle to be retained as candidate—he is a Whig (Liberal) insofar as he is anything, and is sure as many were that the Liberals will get in again. He shares the view current in Tipperary at the time that support for the Liberal party under Gladstone offered the best chance Ireland had to achieve some of the people's aims.[102] He does not see Irish MPs having the power to exert great pressure on a British Parliamentary party by interfering with the system—this is to come later, with Parnell. But Hogan, as a barrister, knows that there are rich pickings in the form of office and privilege available to lawyers in return for political services. There is no doubt that he hopes for some of these benefits offered in the past to Irish Members:[103]

> He had set to build a mansion to himself, and he had fixed the top stone of the building first—a well-paid and lofty Government situation, to be the reward of Parliamentary services, to render which services a seat in Parliament must be attained, which seat in Parliament must be obtained by—any means.[104]

In Unionist writings of the time, priests were widely depicted as influencing Catholic voting patterns.[105] Recent research casts doubt on the extent to which this really happened, and calls attention to the lack of consistent policy anyway among Irish bishops and priests on all the important political issues, as well as the tendency of most priests to follow rather than to

initiate political trends.106 The involvement of Catholic clergy in adminis-
tering rural politics, once assumed by their opponents to be due to their
"hold" over a superstitious laity, is now considered to be more likely a result
of other combined factors: the priests' very close identification with the interests of the tenant farmer class from which many of them came, and their
level of education and relevant experience, superior to that of most of the
laymen around them, which made the organizing aspect of an election
campaign relatively easy to them.107 On the other hand, the covert bribery
associated with electioneering certainly sometimes included donations to
priests, as well as to convents and other religious institutions. These contributions raised moral questions, and occasioned some debate at the
time.108

Attitudes of mind depicted in *Hogan MP* as customary in late-nineteenth-century Ireland, with regard to the way people of some education
viewed issues of class and politics, were probably very accurate. Laffan's
panoramic view took in a range of Irish middle-class thinking. She did not
attempt to write of concepts outside her personal scope; but that scope was
wide. As she saw it, all sections of the Irish middle class, whatever their religious allegiance, openly or otherwise attached blame to England for mis-
managing Irish affairs. Socially conservative views were fairly widely held
in the Irish Catholic middle class she described. Most people agreed that
Ireland would benefit from autonomy, but there was no consensus as to
which class should do the governing. Many people believed Home Rule an
impossibility for some time to come, because the electors needed more education before they could choose a government. Radical policies were generally believed to come chiefly from the personal circumstances of unhappy
and frustrated individuals, and were always suspect because of their association with the use of physical force. Hard-line right-wing political views
were held mainly by those who, like Lord Brayhead, took up a position of
superiority and whose religious tolerance was very limited—and most of
the people Laffan showed in this unflattering light were members of the
Protestant Ascendancy. These had of course most to lose by change, which
she thought was bound to come. And when change came about, she implied, the peasantry would take a large part in achieving it.

Hogan MP may be considered as a social and political record, but how far
can it be described as satire? If satire is defined as the holding up to ridicule
of vice and folly, this description would certainly fit all three of the novels
discussed above, and fits *Hogan MP* in fact rather better than it does *A*

Drama in Muslin. The latter work is perceived today more as a feminist, po-lemical novel than a satirical one, presenting as it does alternatives to the vice and folly described by Moore. On the whole, it is a fairly optimistic book. *Hogan MP* and *The Way We Live Now* have in common a far less hope-ful view of their respective worlds, and their happy endings are scarcely convincing. In the case of *Hogan MP*, this aspect was actually identified by the early review in the *Spectator*:

> From rival Lords, Kilboggan and Brayhead, down through Roman Catholic Bish-ops, lawyers, land and financial agents, parish priests, farmers, tradesmen and gossoons, there is not so much wholesome ground as a man may rest his foot on,—nothing but one turbid stream of jobbery, greed, gluttony and truculence, sketched with a cynicism untempered by humour. The stream undoubtedly runs, but it is not a healthy brook, but an open sewer.[109]

One has to allow for the critic's over-reaction to the realism of some of Laffan's descriptive writing, and it is scarcely accurate to accuse her of a lack of humour. However, the anonymous critic goes on to say:

> The reader, unless his appetite is of the strongest, will be nauseated by the monot-onous vulgarity and meanness of the characters. . . . we should have set the book down as the work of some Saxon, banished to the Irish capital, and bent on hav-ing his revenge on all it contains. But the internal evidence is too strong, and we are driven to the conclusion that the writer is an Irishman, who has a keen eye for the meanness and vulgarity of the society in which he lives, but is either blind or indifferent to its good side.[110]

This reviewer has in fact identified one of the most curious elements in Laffan's satire—relative absence of contrast. Her world is darker than that of Trollope. He did introduce some benign characters to point up the nega-tive nature of the others; she does not really do this consistently. Her hero-ine Nellie Davoren lacks cohesion as a character; the dialogue she has been given is critical and slightly carping, somewhat at odds with her oth-erwise naive and trusting personality. Cousin Dorothy is more positive, though incredibly tactless and almost never saying the right thing. Dermot Blake, the rescuer of Nellie, appears insubstantial and perhaps too good to be true. The *Spectator*'s reviewer thought many of the other characters not merely flawed, but distorted—still, there remains a human quality about them. Cosmo Saltasche, Lord Brayhead, and Father Jim Corkran are won-derful caricatures, and they are also more entertaining than their betters.

This imbalance can be explained away by saying that as a novice writer Laffan in *Hogan MP* concentrates on grotesques because she has yet to learn how to make good people interesting; but she also gives the impression that she can scarcely believe there to be any good people left anywhere. She is a pessimist, afraid to hope lest she invite disappointment. Her ridicule has a slightly desperate air; it amuses certainly and also makes one feel uneasy. But perhaps that is exactly what effective satire is intended to do.

It is important to keep in mind that, as novel-reading was the main recreation of literate people in the nineteenth century, filling the space in people's lives now taken up by television and radio, a surprising number of people in Britain and Ireland was able to make a living from writing fiction. The writing population of Ireland was large for such a small country, and May Laffan was one of many. She stands out now because her work was more realtistic and less conventional than the work of most of her literary colleagues, making it still accessible to us today. Few women writers then were issue-driven by the need to write stories with a social and political content, above all in a satirical style which entertained even while it stung.

So there were aspects of *Hogan MP* which were unique. It seems intended to be a book on its own, without a sequel. But where did the impulse to undertake such a book come from?

Before she submitted *Hogan MP*, Laffan could have read Trollope's *The Way We Live Now*, which was published by installments about a year before; but if she did, her first novel holds few echoes of Trollope. *Hogan MP* reminds one instead of Balzac. Just as some of the *Hogan MP* characters seem to blend with those of Moore, others, for example Cosmo Saltasche, Dorothy O'Hegarty, and John O'Rooney Hogan himself, could have come from the series of extraordinary novels which we know as the "Human Comedy." Laffan's gift for characterization, relentless pace, lack of descriptive padding and realistic yet non-judgemental approach were not learnt from English fiction. She may even have dreamed of a series of novels, to present her Ireland in microcosm as Balzac presented his France. It is possible that it was in this way and with this purpose in mind that *Hogan MP* came to be written.

ᘐᘗ CHAPTER 4

Class, Identity and Education
in *Miss Ferrard*

"Wild voices were calling all day long to her. . . ."

T he second of May Laffan's four novels, *The Honorable Miss Ferrard*, was first published by Richard Bentley & Son in 1877. It was reviewed in the same year by the *Saturday Review*, a politically conservative journal noted for the severity of its views on contemporary literature.[1] The anonymous review was on the whole favourable:

> Miss Ferrard [is] showing a very distinct advance on its predecessor, [although there is still] too much of Hibernian politics. . . . It is highly creditable to the skill of the author that he should have made his heroine at once attractive and natural. . . . we should be happy were he to give us a continuation of his novel, containing the sequel of her fortunes.[2]

As was customary in reviews of that time, a very detailed outline of the story was given, emphasising the more entertaining and unusual passages in this record of a momentous year in the life of a forlorn young girl.

The headstrong neglected girl as fictional heroine has a long history, and several Irish nineteenth-century novelists used variants of the character. Some widely differing examples are Giannetta in Rosa Mulholland's novel *Giannetta: A Girl's Story of Herself*, Pheemy in Anthony Trollope's first novel *The Macdermots of Ballycloran*, and Clodagh in Katherine Cecil Thurston's novel *The Gambler*.[3] Sometimes, as in Lady Morgan's *The Wild Irish Girl*, the reader was offered as well a perspective of Ireland seen through the eyes of a visiting stranger, who then fell in love with the girl, a symbol of her country.[4] And, if the girl's once splendid family home could be included in the scene of general desolation, the "Big House" theme emerged.[5]

111

All these elements and more are combined in *The Honorable Miss Ferrard*. Although as a romantic *bildungsroman* it is quite different in nature to the satiric *Hogan MP,* it can be shown that some of the characteristics which made *Hogan* stand out from the generality of fiction of its time are there also in *Miss Ferrard*. The satirical element is present though less noticeable, and two other main features are strongly in evidence: an unusually realistic treatment of both characters and story line, and an even-handed presentation of opposing arguments, related to political and class issues arising in the course of the story. The novel in English had, in the 1870s, scarcely been used as a means to present social and political questions of the day. Victorian romantic novels for the English market tended to be written to formulas and follow certain rules. It is a measure of Laffan's skill that she was able to mock the formula, bend the rules, and still succeed.

Miss Ferrard is set mainly in Ireland in the 1870s. Sixteen-year-old Helena Ferrard lives in Galway lodgings with her ailing father, Lord Darraghmore; her nurse, Cawth McGonigal; and her three wild half-brothers, Clanrickard, Charles and Isidore. The boys help support the family by poteen-making, and by poaching in which "Hel" takes an active part.[6] (She acts as a look-out for them, and also makes their snares.) Cawth, their sole servant, alternately bosses and manipulates the Ferrards, managing their scanty income while at the same time tacitly encouraging them to evade creditors and behave in a generally anti-social way. Family and class pride prevented Helena and her brothers from using the free education available,[7] with the result that they can barely read and write, and Helena's notion of the world is similar to that attributed to the Canadian trappers and "Red Indians" in the pulp fiction she avidly reads. She dreams of living in a remote region where the conventions of middle-class nineteenth-century life, so alien and humiliating to her, do not apply.

Helena's appearance at this time is described in some detail:

> Her hair, thick and black, was plaited in one rough, loose tail, that hung nearly to her waist. It grew low on her forehead, but her temples were wide and clear; the eyebrows black, straight and very close set; her eyes were a long almond shape, and their colour was the rarest, sweetest colour in the world, violet blue. The lashes were long and thick, and turned up at the ends. For the rest, the profile was irregular, the nose the least bit retrousse,[8] and the upper lip rather short; but the teeth were the most beautiful little pearls when she smiled, which Miss Ferrard did not often vouchsafe to do. . . . the expression of her face, grievous to relate, was ill-tempered in the extreme. . . . It was a troubled, anxious little face alto-

gether, and, though forbidding, a face with such a charm of its own that one who saw it once must remember it ever after. Her figure was unformed, or angular. She had . . . fine hands and feet, but . . . their unwashed condition detracted as much from the looks of the one as did the huge coarse brogues and knitted stockings from the other. She wore a skirt of black wool—just what the peasants had—so coarse that it might be taken for bearskin; a hideously made tunic of cheap black material; no collar, no cuffs, no brooch or attempt at girlish decoration of any kind. Such was the attire of Lord Darraghmore's daughter.[9]

The Ulsterwoman Cawth's opinion of her nursling is not high: "Tawney[10].... an' a rale Ferrard, black and dour; gin ye raised her she'd think little o' stickin' ye wi' a knife . . . she canna mair than read a bit, an' she'll be sixteen in a month -a muckle guid-for-naethin' thing, an' ignorant as a kish o' brogues[11]."[12]

As the story opens, Helena's mother (her father's second wife) having just died, Helena is offered a home by spinster aunts, her father's sisters living at Bath in England. Escorted to the port of Bristol by a friendly pig-dealer, she arrives like a being from another world into their luxurious, cluttered house. Overcoming the initial shock, which they do not attempt to hide, her aunts try to get to know Helena, but—

> She was not of a caressing or affectionate nature, her bringing up had been singularly devoid of all softening or loveable influences, and though a physiognomist might trace in her full lips and the ardent deep eyes capabilities of future passion, firey [sic] and wild when once raised, she was as unresponsive and unsympathetic as some strong wild bird, which may crouch under your hand, but has its gleaming eyes fixed on the sky and its pinions straining for flight all the time.[13]

Helena shows some response to one of her aunts, a gentle and patient individual who buys her pretty clothes and books and engages a governess for her. Helena endures for a brief spell the attempts of this aunt to civilize and educate her:

> How Helena suffered . . . no pen could describe. The orderly methodical household, with its clockwork routine and unvarying monotony, galled the young barbarian's wild untamed spirit, and she fretted and chaffed like some caged animal . . . how useless, objectless it all appeared to Helena, brought up in the fatalistic self-indulgent abandon of the Galway tribes.[14]

But Helena cannot adjust to the physically restricted life offered to her, and after a few weeks she makes a plan to escape:

That it was her duty to stay never entered her head. She was stifling in the close warmth of this well-ordered English house. It seemed to her as if wild voices were calling all day long to her from the woods and sea to return to them. A great open space swept by the breeze invited her, and she drew in a deep, broken sigh of longing desire.[15]

She makes her way back to Ireland—to "Darraghstown" (Tipperary) under the Galtee Mountains, where her family has resumed its vagabond life in lodgings near the abandoned ancestral home, which they vandalised on a previous visit. Recent experiences have changed Helena and she now realises the anomaly of her position, a lord's daughter yet penniless, friendless and barely literate—what is to become of her?

Helena fascinates (and torments) the Miss Perrys, daughters of a local solicitor.[16] At their house she meets a wealthy Englishman, John Satterthwaite. A Liberal MP until the recent dissolution, attracted by the natural loveliness of Ireland rather than by its people, he decides to settle in Tipperary and buys an estate formerly part of the Darraghmore ancestral land.[17] He is now using his considerable wealth to restore the house, and to construct a beautiful garden: "Wild and neglected as the place was, it had charmed him."[18]

Quickly he becomes attracted to Helena also: "He felt curious to see more of Miss Ferrard. She was a new experience to him, and her beautiful face and wild troubled eyes as they met his for the first time, seemed somehow constantly before him."[19] He condones the Ferrards' poaching activities, tries to attract Helena's interest, and lends her books. He expresses what he thinks is fatherly concern about her to an enigmatic neighbour, Mrs. Really, who attempts to dissuade him from getting too involved with the family. She gives him her analysis of their situation:

> "You do not know the Ferrards. They are not in their present position for nothing, believe me; they have fallen by their own fault. People are like water, they find their own level sooner or later in this world. . . . Not a Ferrard that ever lived was susceptible of education. They are splendid animals; make excellent soldiers, as I have seen, but that is all."[20]

Satterthwaite is upset by this speech, feeling that it indicates a lack of warmth and goodwill. But Mrs. Really, who lives with her elderly husband in a house overlooking the town, has never actually spoken to Helena. From her beautiful and carefully tended garden Mrs. Really sees through a powerful telescope everything that happens in the streets of Darraghstown, and what she doesn't see, she deduces.

She knows the Ferrards think themselves entitled, because of their aristocratic identity, to live just as they please at the expense of others. Two of Helena's older half-brothers died violent deaths, and there are ugly though undefined rumours about events leading up to the death of Helena's mother. Moreover, the Ferrards are Protestants, and although the Catholic community in which they live is sympathetic to them, it does not intervene in their affairs as readily as it would if they were Catholics. No one has been able to get to know them well; for the young Ferrards, ashamed of their poverty and ignorance, are hostile to outsiders. Mrs. Really describes to Satterthwaite past attempts on the part of the local Church of Ireland rector's wife to offer help:

> "Mrs. Fitz-Ffoulkes went to see them several times. She got in once, and the old man behaved rather nicely. She asked the girl to come to the glebe-house and take lessons from their governess; and she promised to get her a situation as companion or governess in England later. The old man seemed inclined to have the offer accepted; but not a word could Miss Hel be got to say in the matter, and Mrs. Fitz-Ffoulkes was never allowed in again—in fact, the next time she went there, one of the boys threatened to take her life for insulting his sister. She was not gifted with tact, poor lady, and I dare say spoke a little too plainly."[21]

Despite their social isolation, Helena and her youngest brother, Isidore, become friendly with Jim Devereux, a local young farmer and horse-trainer, and he allows Helena to ride his horses. It is to Jim she goes for refuge when her elder brothers threaten her with violence, because she has begun to try to pay some of the family's debts. Jim tells Helena he loves her, and she responds although unsure of her own feelings. When he becomes jealous of John Satterthwaite, Helena then agrees to marry Jim, and as there is opposition from his parents, they keep their engagement secret for the present.

But when Helena shows gratitude to Satterthwaite for saving one of her brothers from the consequences of a poaching foray, he unfortunately misinterprets this as a sign of hope for him: "He stole a quick glance at Helena's face. Her lips were trembling; and though she laughed, her eyes had the softened light of tears in them. He felt sorry to the heart for her, and admired her spirit at the same time."[22]

Shown over the Ferrards' ruined former home by Helena, Isidore and Jim, who now farms the land, Satterthwaite tries to encourage Helena to tell him about the family's past:

> "Where's the use of talking of it now?" And a flush mounted to her cheek as she turned away and stooped over the bunch of roses in her hand.

> The spring sun shone in, lighting up her hair and gleaming in her eyes, and a faint pink shade from the flowers threw its reflection on her pale face. Satterthwaite thought he never saw anyone more beautiful or interesting—almost pathetically so—at that moment.[23]

Gradually, John Satterthwaite begins to feel his possessions to be worthless if he cannot share them with Helena, whom he longs to tame, educate and civilise according to his ideas. However, despite himself he cannot ignore what is going on between her and Jim Devereux: "It seemed to him impossible and wrong that such a union could take place. And now he had a wild hope of being able to enlist Mrs. Really on his side."[24] But that hope is quickly disappointed:

> "If you, my dear sir, were to interfere here between this girl and her lover, you would rue it, and Helena too, the longest day you lived. . . . tell me, do you think Hel Ferrard, as she is at this moment, could ever move in your circle in London? Could you present her to the women of your acquaintance? No, Mr. Satterthwaite, do not wrong yourself and her; don't spoil her life—and she has longer to live than you—leave her to Devereux."[25]

Nevertheless, Mrs. Really reluctantly agrees to talk to Helena, and to assess her commitment to Jim Devereux.

Clanrickard, the eldest Ferrard brother, leaves home, and shortly afterwards Lord Darraghmore dies. Supported by Jim, Helena organizes her father's funeral, confronts Charles, takes control of what money is left and pays off the family's remaining debts. Charles goes off to join the Austrian army in which his eldest half-brother Claud, the new Lord Darraghmore, is now a senior officer. Cawth, sardonic as ever, sees the family breaking up as she has always predicted it will.

Jim tells Helena that his parents will never consent to their marriage, Helena being both a Protestant and dowerless. He plans to emigrate to Canada and asks Helena to go with him—they can marry there. She agrees, on condition that Isidore and Cawth can come too.

Mrs. Really at last visits Helena, is won over by her, offers her help, and involuntarily reveals that she and Helena's officer half-brother were lovers many years ago in Austria. She has never ceased to regret their parting:

> What had the world been to her since? And now here was this creature with Claud's own blue eyes looking at her: certainly if she could help her to what she herself missed, she would do it. She put up her hand to her brow and pressed it hard, and something like a tear—was it regret, or was it envy?—dimmed her bright eyes a moment.26

Mrs. Really tells John Satterthwaite that she will not try to influence Helena at all, because she is sure that the latter would have no future in Ireland or England with her own social class, but has some hope of fulfilment in Canada with Jim Devereux, who loves her as she is. Heartbroken, Satterthwaite tries to accept the situation, and nobly buys Jim's horse, Freney, to make sure the pair will have enough money to start their new life. Satterthwaite accompanies them to the emigrant ship:

> Then a bell rang. The mails were all in, and the floor began to throb significantly under their feet. Helena's eyes, running over with tears, were fixed on Satterthwaite. . . . Satterthwaite had both her hands in his, and was looking his last at Hel. She said not a word, but he could feel the hands he held in his tremble and burn.
>
> "Let go!" screeched the captain, "by the heavens I'll take him!"
>
> The sailors did let go, and the gangway was being pulled in. Satterthwaite cared not: he had lifted Helena in his arms, and was straining her to him in one firm embrace.
>
> "You won't grudge me that," he said as he placed her in Devereux's arms.27

Helena remains to the end of the story ambivalent about her two suitors, seeming not fully aware of what she means to either of them. The story ends with local worthies commenting on the sudden change of plan on the part of the wealthy Englishman—he is leaving Ireland, never to return.

This romantic novel must have been welcomed by Laffan's publishers, since to some extent it appeared to cater to current class-based prejudices. The hero is an Englishman, sensitive, wealthy and cultured, typical of the more acceptable empire builder. He is also faultless in appearance: "a man of about thirty-five, dressed in a shooting-suit of heather-mixture . . . a strongly-built man, with a tanned face and bright English blue eyes, which roved over the landscape incessantly and intelligently."28

To begin with, the situation he perceives is very like the one in Maria Edgeworth's *The Absentee*, or William Allingham's verse novel *Laurence Bloomfield in Ireland*.[29] A benign superior being comes to influence and teach the natives for their own good, sorting out their difficulties for them and creating a model community around himself. The difference in this case is that John Satterthwaite fails—all his efforts are useless. He does not win the beautiful wild girl he thinks he loves, and all his other projects wither. Mrs. Really, cynical chorus for his tragedy, knows it will be so, and predicts the outcome to him. He is applying to Ireland the measures of his own culture; and these will not work. He has expectations which are unreal, and Mrs. Really is quick to let him know it:

> "You English always fancy that you can buy Irish wit as you buy Irish poplins or whisky.[30] It is not so at all, and perhaps it is as well that the wretches have something left that they cannot sell. I don't know why it is that you always expect fun and drollery from an Irishman, and moreover you are angry when you don't get it. . . . Money never yet bought wit. The historical Irishman has a great deal to answer for. . . . The Irishman that all you English have in their mind's eye! A wonderful, impossible animal, extinct, thank Heaven, as the dodo, barefooted and ragged, witty as Voltaire and philosophic as Plato, and ready for a consideration to shower his epigrams and reflections on your eager ears."[31]

Mrs. Really is concerned to make Satterthwaite aware of the gulf between the fantasy world of stage-Irishism, with its stereotypes displayed in well-known novels of the time, and the often sad reality of narrow horizons and hopes, poverty, ignorance and desperation.

It could be said that this is a moral tale about the widespread effects of ignorance. John Satterthwaite shows extreme sensitivity to the beauty of the Irish countryside but does not know the minds of the inhabitants, or even acknowledge the fact that he does not know. Helena Ferrard knows little about anything, including the customs and manners of family life; her ignorance makes her vulnerable, and also more appealing. Her *gaucherie* and avoidance of others are due to acute consciousness of her own ignorance. Her brothers share the same feelings but express them differently, for example, in aggressive behaviour. Helena, by nature more receptive than they, profits from the stay with her aunts by learning some of the formal modes of behaviour expected of women of her class, yet at the same time her awareness of the feelings of others, a quality which should underlie social courtesies, is shown to be pathetically limited. For instance, Satterthwaite's surprisingly generous actions and Mrs. Really's emotional offers to help are observed by Helena with total incomprehension, as she lacks the insight to even begin to make any sense of their motives.

Still, over the year's span of the novel, Helena does become mature, a process shown by her reactions to her own appearance. To begin with, she avoids being placed in the position of seeing herself at all. Here the "original" Helena is shown, buying a hat in Galway to wear to England:

> "A large hat," she said irritably pushing aside a composition of crape and feather flowers presented to her view. "I won't have feathers or flowers, I want nothing but just a hat."

> "Untrimmed hats," said the mistress, sharply. "Be quick, now, Miss Kelly, here's Mrs. Blood coming across the square, and the Miss Persses."[32]

> In a moment a number of large felt hats were placed before Helena. She selected a high-crowned cavalier hat with a broad brim fastened up at one side, which fitted down comfortably on her head. Then unpinning her crape veil, she tried to fasten it on the new purchase.

> "Allow me, Miss," said the attendant, and taking the veil from her customer's clumsy fingers, she fastened it in a becoming wreath round the hat, and then put it on her head. "Very becoming to you, Miss," said she, "very. Like to look at it?" and she handed a toilet mirror.

> But Helena turned her back brusquely.[33]

She speculates before going to her aunts' house about the contrast her appearance would be likely to make with the surroundings of her English relations:

> She had some notion of a different style of living, gathered chiefly from her books, and she pictured to herself surroundings of velvet—which it may be doubted if she would recognise on seeing—silk, lace and mirrors; the last a questionable boon, considering the figure of herself with which any she had encountered presented her—scowling, overhanging brows, tangled hair, and a yellow skin.[34]

And in Bath a week later, "mirrors seemed as if desecrated by the reflection of Helena's wild face."[35]

However, when she has to face the world a year later, after her father's funeral, Helena is able to face the mirror:

> "The fine straight brows were no longer sullen or overhanging, and the beautiful half-melancholy, half-thoughtful eyes were clearer and more serene of look. . . .

Hel seemed to have grown taller. Her long black dress fell gracefully round her slim, well-poised figure, and her face only looked more beautiful for the fatigue and paleness it showed."[36]

A dignified young woman in fashionable mourning wear supplied by her English aunts, her once tangled dark hair dressed in a regal crown of plaits, and her attractive face no longer sulky, but bearing signs of controlled grief, Helena now looks—and is—very different. Helped by Jim Devereux, she has begun to grow up, to take responsibility, to exercise self-control.

It would be tempting though inaccurate to see Helena Ferrard personifying Ireland as perceived by Laffan. Poor in a material sense, Helena is also poor in other ways—untaught, uncivilised, troubled and immature. Her beauty attracts, but it also deceives people into thinking her better than she is, and shutting their eyes to her deficiencies. Impulsive and inarticulate, she is a primitive child of nature rather than of the Established Church.

Her tastes reflect these limitations. We are told Helena reads voraciously, but significantly the one title actually mentioned is Bulwer Lytton's "thesis novel," *Paul Clifford*. This story validates the life of a highwayman by presenting him as a misunderstood victim of society, and it was viewed as highly subversive.[37] Helena is also heard to sing, but what she sings is a grim little ballad about an outlaw who murders the unfaithful lover who betrays him to his enemies.[38] Laffan shows us Helena at her worst: fighting with her brothers over a pint can of beer, being rude to her aunts' maid, jeering at the Perry girls. Under benign influences, it is implied, she may be amenable to change. It is significant that the agent of this change—Jim Devereux—is no aristocratic Protestant, no wealthy outsider, but a young Irish Catholic farmer bearing, like Laffan herself, a Norman-Irish family name. It is Jim Devereux's love and concern for her that are gradually seen to effect the education of Helena Ferrard.

This circumstance illustrates in a striking manner the ambivalence of Laffan towards the religion, culture and class from which her father came, identical in fact to the background of the fictional Devereux family. Jim's is an attractive disposition; he is sensitive, patient and kind in a way Satterthwaite is not and could never be. But he is, we are told, a product of the Catholic education system which Laffan appears to despise, if one takes seriously what she previously wrote, and what she was to write in the future. In the first of her published writings, quoted in chapter two, Laffan is intensely critical of what convent schools have to offer girls.[39] She implies that Catholic belief and general philosophy are responsible for the shortcomings. Yet three years later she creates a Catholic hero, and writes almost wistfully about the advantages a convent upbringing could have had for the beloved Helena:

> Had she been a Catholic, some good-hearted priest would have made interest for the desolate, neglected little girl, and have shipped her across the seas to some quiet Belgian convent, where she would have been tamed and trained into piety and industry, where one day she might have taken the veil, and passed a quiet dream-like life away from the toil and strife of the wild nomads amongst whom her lines had fallen.[40]

Leaving aside Laffan's highly unreal idea of the religious life, it is strange to read a passage which contradicts so markedly her previous views on convents. Perhaps it had been suggested to her that she had been a little sweeping in her original judgements. As it is, she seems almost to suggest that Helena was deliberately excluded from the advantages of convent education because she was a Protestant. This is unlikely to have been so. It was not at all unknown even in the eighteenth and early nineteenth centuries for a Protestant child to be reared in a Catholic convent.[41] But by the 1870s and in the wake of legislation disestablishing the Church of Ireland, resentment against Catholics had evidently become so strong that it scarcely would have been an option to use their education and child-care system for an aristocratic Protestant.

For another, though minor, the theme of *Miss Ferrard* is sectarian discrimination. This is not, as one might expect, discrimination on the part of the Ascendancy against Catholics and Presbyterians but quite the reverse. Irish Catholics, by their growing power and assertiveness—in fact, by their higher profile—are said to be almost deliberately making life difficult for the poorer Protestants, and Laffan exhibits a distinct tendency to dramatise the way in which she alleges the Ferrards were treated:

> Had [Helena] been a Catholic, things would have been different; the common people would have treated the family with more respect, they would have sympathised with them as "belonging to themselves"; their misfortunes would have been ascribed to "the troubles," to their rulers, to the English, just as they laid their own wretched condition to the charge of the aliens and heretics who lorded it over them. . . . [The Ferrards] were treated by the Catholics as in former times the "poor whites" were treated in the slave states of America, despised by the negroes, and almost disowned by their more fortunate fellow-citizens. . . . As poor Protestants, shiftless and dirty as the Catholics themselves, they . . . were an anomaly, an anachronism, and unaccountable.[42]

The key word here is surely *respect.* The Ferrards at some time in the recent past had been wealthy people, large landowners accustomed to an extravagant, lordly way of life with much servile deference paid to them by
their dependants. They seem not to have been Irish or part-Irish, but more
probably part of the Huguenot community that emigrated to Ireland in the
seventeenth century.[43] Their misfortunes, according to their co-religionist
Mrs. Really, were due neither to social wrongs nor to sectarian prejudice,
but to a total inability to adapt to changing circumstances. They thought
they had a perpetual entitlement to demand deference and dutiful assistance from others, that is, from their Catholic neighbours. But that invisi-
ble capital of goodwill diminished year by year, and in fact was almost
exhausted by the period of this story. Laffan hinted that from now on, the
Ferrards and others like them would be accepted by others on the basis of
their personal qualities, rather than their social class.

The genuine emotional distress this change of climate caused to some
has been well expressed by a contemporary of Laffan, Judge William
O'Connor Morris: "I noticed signs of the alienation of class growing up everywhere . . . the peasantry were not what they had been to our family . . .
the people treated us with respect, but their hearts were cold."[44] That benign paternalistic picture which some landowners had of themselves, and
held onto as part of their justification for their control over the country's resources, was in danger of disappearing, and was in fact changing.

The change did not take place suddenly. Nominally it started after Catholic Emancipation in 1829, but for many people it would not have begun to
bite in earnest until the disestablishment of the Church of Ireland in
1869.[45] The reorganization which followed inevitably left less of a
Protestant presence outside of Dublin and the larger towns. Some Church
of Ireland members would have felt, and with reason, extremely isolated.
This situation is alluded to in *Miss Ferrard* when the solicitor, Mr. Perry, tells
Satterthwaite that Fitz-Ffoulkes, the local Church of Ireland rector, has
"commuted, compounded and cut" and has not been replaced. His absence has repercussions for Helena and Isidore, delaying their father's funeral until someone else can be found to officiate.

Disestablishment was seen by most members of the state church as not
only a betrayal by England but an enormous threat to the whole social fabric and the privilege or "Ascendancy" of the Protestant ruling caste. It was
also seen by some authorities to have been an unwise action forced on the
rulers of Ireland by world opinion. Conservatives blamed the Liberal Prime

Minister William Gladstone personally for this, and some even spoke of a Catholic conspiracy. But on the whole, it was admitted to be a just decision. Laffan did not see the situation wholly in that light for, through an exchange between Satterthwaite and the appropriately named Mrs. Really, the Church of Ireland is shown as the chief civilizing influence on Catholics:

> "Roman Catholic society is new; it must be new, for they have only legally existed, so to say, very recently. And since you say the disestablishment removed a means of culture from them, you ought not to be too hard upon their shortcomings."

> "Bah! I'm not. It's their conceit with themselves that I ridicule. They shut their eyes to everything that is aesthetic, that is intellectual. Look at their faces, infallibility is written all over them. If they can play or sing so as to torture everyone within earshot, they are 'highly educated'; if they have a drawing-room, or two or three, crammed full of looking-glass and gilding,—catch them with pictures or books in their possession—they are elegance itself . . . I give them all credit for their good intentions. . . ."

> "Assuming that the Protestants in this country are the exclusive possessors of culture, refinement etc.; do you not think the ecclesiastical prohibition and discouragement of social intercourse has had a certain effect in checking the downward progress of class-improvement?"

> "Well, isn't that what I told you before? . . . Roman Catholics . . . have been consolidating and advancing their claims ever since. It will take half a century to recover the mischief of that measure."[46]

All in all, Protestants generally had been experiencing a progressive loss of privilege and security since the 1840s; there are frequent references to this in writings of the time, and not a little resentment. In *Miss Ferrard,* moreover, we are *told* that the Ferrards suffer actual disadvantage on account of their Protestantism: "The Ferrards were Protestants, stem and branch, consequently their poverty and degradation brought them only contumely. . . ."[47]

But we are never actually *shown* any instance of this happening. Individual Catholics treat the family with respect and a measure of compassion, and are we to assume that this is only due to the air of aristocratic glamour still surrounding them? In Galway a Claddagh fisherman takes the Ferrard boys out with him so that they can earn the cost of their mother's funeral.[48] Later, Jim O'Brien, the Cork pig-dealer to whom Cawth entrusts Helena on the voyage to Bristol, shows real concern for her, extending this from supplying her with a horse rug when the weather gets cold, to protecting her from the unwanted attentions of others. Finally Mr. Perry, Lord Darraghmore's perpetually discontented lawyer, hands back his fees to Helena following his client's death; and his daughters, despised by Helena and her brothers, arrange a warm and tearful leave-taking and readily forgive Helena's occasional unkindness to them. By way of contrast, we are told that when the Ferrards made a brief attempt to settle in Protestant England, they found it very uncongenial. They seem to have found no lasting home in either Ireland or the United Kingdom.

Laffan therefore cannot be said to have put forward convincing arguments to support her statement that the Ferrards were hard-done-by *because* of their religion. They may reasonably, though, have felt themselves to be disadvantaged simply as belonging to a small minority, although there is no direct intimation given of this in the rather limited exchange of ideas apparently taking place within the family. However, they are certainly described by their author in terms which suggest a general sense of grievance: "They received none of the adulation and respect accorded so lavishly to the estated heretic who drives his carriage and pair. As poor Protestants, shiftless and dirty as the Catholics themselves, they were held as creatures with whom even the devil had broken his compact."[49]

It may be queried how far this "adulation and respect" accorded to rich landowners was genuine, if within a few years threats of violence were to replace it. The "compact" referred to seems derived from a belief that Protestants, in return for prosperity in this world, gave up the hope of Heaven in the next. Laffan quotes this belief as one which had clerical sanction and was generally held among the peasantry. It was certainly quoted in the writings of Gerald Fitzgibbon (I) and others, but is not orthodox Catholic teaching, and is likely to be a variant of another idea, common to many religions; that people who are prosperous, as most Irish Protestants were, are not entitled on that account to any greater spiritual advantage.

The comparison of poor Protestants with poor whites is a curious one and rather extreme. Carried to its logical conclusion, it seemed to place the Catholics in the position of negro slaves, on the lowest rung of society and at the mercy of masters who had power of life and death over them—which was certainly not the case in Ireland during the 1870s though it might have been so in the past. It almost seems as if Laffan was trying, a little too hard, to make out a case for some kind of special treatment for the Ferrards and others like them.

The Ferrards, we are also told, were Protestant "stem and branch," a description which, taking into account their French-sounding name, suggests Huguenot origins. Their Continental connections, coat of arms and history of lost grandeur lend support to this idea, as some Huguenot refugees were titled people and very conscious of their class.

It may be questioned how the Ferrards came to be commissioned so readily in the Austrian army, since Austria in the nineteenth century was a Catholic state. Would it not have been easier for them to join the British army? We are told in *Miss Ferrard* that in the eighteenth century Ferrards were among the "Wild Geese" commissioned in continental armies; and this would have supplied a precedent.[50] During the war of the Austrian succession (1740–1748), the Lutheran general Maurice de Saxe, Duke of Courland and commander of the French at Fontenoy, recruited into the Irish Brigade, as officers, Irishmen of all faiths.[51] The one essential qualification for a commission, apparently, was proof of noble lineage, one practical reason why the study of genealogy became very fashionable in seventeenth- and eighteenth-century Ireland. The British Army, on the other hand, would not have been a possible choice for the Ferrards, since the family had no money to pay the price demanded for British commissions.

By the mid-nineteenth century, the Huguenot refugees were absorbed into the Church of Ireland which probably owed part of its Low Church ethos to their Calvinist influence. The Ferrards' infrequent church attendance suggests a measure of religious indifference. But the one notable instance where the Ferrards, or more properly Helena, insist on upholding the tradition of their Church is on the death of their father:

> Had he been a Catholic things would have been differently ordered. There would have been wax candles lighting night and day, and watchers praying, and the house would have been open to all who chose to come and pay their last respects to him in that odd—savage if you will—but intensely human Irish fashion, according to which all joys and sorrows are common property. . . . Helena, however, determined to uphold the colder tradition of her own class, which indeed seemed to her now not only more decent, but more convenient.[52]

Here the reserved approach to death may be a rationalisation. When Helena's father died it was easier to keep people at arm's length, out of the squalid reality of the Ferrard lifestyle, by telling them in one way or another that they were not needed. But Laffan seems to suggest that there is a wide and real class difference as well as a cultural and religious one between Irish Catholics and Irish Protestants, a difference hard to reconcile because founded on the idea of perpetual Protestant superiority.

Helena's personal religious belief is never really stated. The nearest Laffan comes to it is in the following passage. Jim Devereux has just been assuring Helena that he will never expect her to convert to Catholicism:

> Helena looked at him with eyes that spoke only of dumb, loving trustfulness. She hardly understood the drift of what he had been saying. She could appreciate his magnanimity, but was far from conceiving its extent. She knew nothing of the intense religious feeling of the woman who, next to her now, had the best right to him. Hel's own religion had as little meaning to her as the faded crest and motto or empty title of her family, which she hated and felt in a way ashamed of, just as the boys did.53

In this passage, Laffan seems to suggest that membership of the Church of Ireland is linked very closely to the belief in material prosperity and respectability as a visible sign of grace, and therefore it is hardly suitable as a creed for someone marginalised and poor, who is not successful in material terms and cannot always contrive to be "respectable."

Whatever the limits of her understanding about the religious tradition from which he comes, when she is emotionally supported by Jim, Helena is able to assert herself powerfully against her domineering brother Charles. Unfortunately she also turns against the servant Cawth, whom developing self-confidence now leads her to recognise as her social inferior. Throughout some nineteenth-century fiction written in English there seems to run a thread of anxiety about master-servant relationships. The fear seems to be that things would get out of hand, that servants would take advantage of their masters, if the latter were too weak and self-indulgent to exercise strong control. Examples of role confusion actually happening are shown in Maria Edgeworth's *Castle Rackrent*, where the narrator, Thady, while protesting loyalty towards his employers, half-unconsciously brings them down. An even clearer example can be noted in Edith Somerville's novel *The Big House at Inver* (London, 1925). The housekeeper, Shibby Pindy, kills a woman who threatens her plan to restore the fortunes of the Ascendancy family of which she is an illegitimate member. But her crime, which is never discovered, is useless to stop the family's inevitable decline.

So the Ferrard family retainer, Cawth McGonigal, once confronted and threatened by Helena, breaks down and acknowledges Helena's authority, and seems almost relieved in doing so. When a few hours later the new Helena, dressing to receive visitors, inspects herself in the mirror, she also sees "Cawth's wrinkled visage, looking twenty years older, mirrored beside her own in the glass."[54] By the time they sail for Canada the redoubtable Cawth has dwindled into a dependent and ailing old woman.

There are other characters within the story who express their unconscious attitudes verbally, and the most notable of these are Mrs. Really and Mr. Perry, the Ferrards' solicitor. With regard to education, Laffan's constant preoccupation and a main political issue of the time, they present respectively some of the positive and negative approaches to its problems. Through the mouths of these two relatively minor characters, differing views find expression, together with differing estimates of the people for whom the education is needed.

Esther Really is a neighbour of John Satterthwaite who becomes his friend, one of those friends who tells us things we do not want to hear, in fact a Cassandra of a friend.[55] Here she is in her analysis of some reasons why the Irish are not more cultured. "These people," she went on, pointing to the shops they were passing, "are able to afford a better class of instruction for their children, and it is a pity they should be obliged to send their children to the same school with those of mere labourers and paupers...."[56]

Education was highly valued in Ireland, and even poor parents were prepared to make considerable sacrifices to get it for their children, hence the occasional social mixture of pupils of which Mrs. Really complains. Though Laffan does not show awareness of this, Catholic girls' schools in fact fell into groups catering for different social classes.

Mrs. Really herself is a former governess, married to a butter-factor from Cork.[57] Both are Protestant converts, and their name was formerly O'Reilly. According to her husband, this formidable lady has strong Communist sympathies, acquired in Paris during the revolution of 1848: "It wasn't that I sympathised with their mischief," said she; "but there must have been some idea among them—some sentiment, now, and I've got an eye for a sentiment, though you might not believe it of me. . . ."[58]

When speaking to John Satterthwaite, she holds "levelling down" responsible for the absence in Ireland of that educated upper middle class so noticeable and so powerful in England. Her concept of "middle class" is nowhere defined, but seems to be associated with restrained taste in dress, independence of thought, and an interest in literature and the visual arts. By "leveling down" Mrs. Really seems to mean a process whereby the poorer children, rougher and more neglected, influence the middle-class pupils to behave like themselves. At a time when formal "good manners" were socially very important, this was a serious consideration. But the implication was also that Protestants were more aware of the problem than Catholics were. Satterthwaite responds in a predictable manner:

> "I used to think that the reason the Irish are so far behind us in art and literature was, that all their intellectual energy ran to politics. The English think so, anyhow."

> "They are wrong—utterly wrong. If the Irish get anything of a fair chance as regards education, they would soon be—equal to the Scotch, at any rate, and that is saying a good deal."[59]

She goes on to give examples: this artist; that sculptor; a local girl privately studying the English dramatists, who through student-relatives borrows books from the Queen's College in Cork; a local dressmaker who sits up all night reading Carlyle.[60] Under a different system, these girls could become teachers. Surprisingly, Mrs. Really favours on the whole the substitution of a denominational for the secular "national" school system, because the people would support it better. Satterthwaite, the Liberal Protestant Englishman, objects:

> ". . . The Government will never suffer it. What the priests want is to get the money into their hands. The idea of handing over the country to ultramontanism and rebellion![61] . . . you know the school-boards would be under the thumb of the priest all the same."

> "There—begging the question again! If they like to have his thumb upon them, what is it to anybody but themselves? . . . I think the Government, be it Whig or Tory, is in a false and very dubious position when it takes on itself the paternal duty of forcing a nation to accept an uncongenial and lop-sided system of this sort."[62]

And so on, for several pages. Apart from a few side swipes at priestly greed and payment for funeral masses, Laffan makes her character Mrs. Really argue about education almost as nationalists argued, but most of them chose political journals in which to do this, and not the pages of a story written to entertain the English public. That public was not generally interested in Irish political matters, as the reviews of Laffan's books demonstrate, and education was certainly a political issue, in towns and cities the major one, as land tenure was in rural areas. Education, in Laffan's later life, was almost to take on with her the character of an obsession. Today it forms one of the more interesting and complex aspects of her social comment; it is also intriguing for what she leaves out.

At the time when Laffan wrote *Miss Ferrard,* the political debate in Ireland was chiefly about intermediate (secondary) and further education, and what form these should take for the Catholic majority. The Irish Protestant community—about 12% of the entire population—was provided already with schools supported either by the State or by private endowment.[63] Consequently Protestants were more likely to complete their secondary education, and they were over-represented in most professions. Since Emancipation the number of Catholic secondary schools in Ireland set up by religious orders had greatly increased,[64] but these received no state help, and their individual histories reveal how straitened some were financially.[65]

Laffan's strictures on the teaching of "useless" accomplishments in convent schools were valid, but she did not seem to ask herself why this should have been the case. The main reason was probably the one given to John Hogan (in *Hogan MP*) when he asked about it—parental preference. Given that newly rich people wanted better things for their children than had fallen to their own lot, one of these things would have been leisure and another, freedom from drudgery. Why teach a wealthy girl to cook or sew, when she would never need these skills, always being able to pay others to work for her? No, what girls needed were the arts which entertain and please—and if rich enough, they might not need even these to make suitable marriages.

It is interesting in this connection to observe Helena Ferrard's proficiency in skills which she certainly did not learn in any conventional school. She is able to ride, fish, shoot and set rabbit snares, skills which may be of practical use in a frontier land. Laffan herself seems, from her letters, to have enjoyed open air life and valued its skills. Helena Ferrard evidently expresses this side of her creator's personality.

The little formal education Helena does get is from a governess during the brief stay with her aunts in England and this, described in detail, is interesting also because it outlines the general way in which upper-class girls were taught at that time. According to Pat Jalland, who surveyed the way in which girls from fifty upper-class or titled English families were educated in the late nineteenth century, they received only poor and superficial tuition from governesses.[66] The aim was mainly to teach "social graces" like dancing, deportment, etiquette and the simpler forms of music-making. A few academic subjects were learned by rote in a mechanical fashion with little attempt made to expound them. Mathematics and science were not taught. The more intelligent girls educated themselves further by extensive reading, if allowed. Typically, Helena Ferrard's governess, Miss Babcock, sits crocheting by the fire while her pupil memorizes lists of spellings. Her choice of textbooks for Helena depends on which of them attracts the highest bookseller's commission. From Miss Babcock's comments it does not really appear that the depth of Helena's ignorance comes as a surprise to her. She has met semi-literate young noblewomen before, and she feels that little in the way of achievement can be expected from them, since they lack the motivation to learn about anything beyond their own narrow world.

Laffan demonstrates to us that the notion of education for women was hardly more advanced in England than in Ireland. This is borne out by the history of attempts to set up an employment bureau for middle-class women in London during the 1860s.[67] But she has something more to say about the "national schools" which the Ferrard's pride prevented them from using. National school pupils were as a group more homogenous than the convent day-school pupils, but were they any better taught? Mr. Perry, in conversation with John Satterthwaite, does not think so:

> ... the National Schools are a swindle—just a swindle, of no use on earth but to waste the public money. . . . No proper teacher would work for the pay; and the position moreover is too poor a one . . . under the hedge-school system, with its odd scraps of Latin and Greek, they were better off; they had a glimpse, anyhow, that there are fields of knowledge. . . . And they tried to reach them, ay, and some of them did. . . .[68]

Perry is making a case for education in its fullest sense of encouraging, inspiring and developing the individual person, against the narrow view that education is simply about getting people into better-paying jobs. In spite of its inadequacies the hedge-school must have stimulated ambition in some able children (for instance the Fitzgibbons, Laffan's maternal ancestors).[69] This episode reminds us that debates regarding the *real purpose* of education are always with us, but in terms of expressing Laffan's thoughts, it indicates her belief that access to formal education should always be possible to able people. Her strictures on the Catholic University are somewhat wide of the mark—the fact that it survived for as long as it did suggests that many people supported it and wanted it to have a charter. One may also speculate as to whether she realised fully that the Catholic

University's medical school at Cecilia Street was in fact highly successful by comparison with others.

The lengthy passages about education are hardly aimed just at Irish readers, to whom they would have been common knowledge. How did the English reading public react to the implication that the ignorance of the "Sister Isle" could be laid at the door of their own government's lack of empathy and imagination? The English public, unaware of how little control Ireland was allowed to have over its own affairs, blamed Ireland for its own educational deficiencies.

With regard to the topics which Laffan sees fit to leave out, here again as in *Hogan MP,* she almost ignores the subject of higher education for girls—and does not seem to envisage them ever taking any share of university places, although in a few years facilities to train for professions were actually to be open to them.[70] Laffan does not seem either to be supportive of women's technical and vocational training, although she says in the *Recess Committee Notes* that she knew Barbara Corlett, a founder member of the Queen's Institute in Dublin which concentrated on providing such training.

Aside from these omissions, the discussions on education which Esther Really has with John Satterthwaite in the course of *Miss Ferrard* are more wide-ranging than a few quotations from them would suggest. The solutions offered to problems of the time appear to come from a level of knowledge uncommon in a writer of novels. It can be easily understood, though, that reviewers and some readers were unhappy with the amount of time and space given to the political elements in the story, and this was a general complaint about Irish fiction. The need to make the "climate of opinion" clear to English readers, to educate and inform as well as to entertain, was acceptable then as part of the author's role, but had limitations. A novelist might sometimes teach behaviour, but not political activism. The fashion for novels in English with social or political dimensions did not really arrive until the 1890s, so Laffan was writing in advance of her time, and must have been one of the first novelists to seriously introduce social and political themes.

Yet Laffan's Irishmen and Irishwomen *are* political creatures, and would be unrealistic if portrayed otherwise. Even when putting across a point of view representative of the time, Laffan manages to convey the character and antecedents of the person speaking in a way that convinces us that she is expressing genuine opinions. These opinions are more positive than is often the case with Laffan. Here, for example, Mrs. Really demonstrates to Satterthwaite her appreciation of the generosity of her compatriots:

> "Do you see that blue cloak? Well, every Sunday four different women wear that cloak to Mass, going of course at different hours—four wretches poorer than herself."

> "That's like St. Martin of Tours."

> "You have little idea how good these creatures are to each other. It is really pure communism—what one has, the rest have."

> "Ah! That is what keeps them poor. I have not a bit of sympathy with that sort of thing."

> "It keeps them poor. Yes, no doubt of it, but does it not show good-heartedness? I like it, though I see the bad side of it too; and I tell them of it; but 'Where's the good!' they always reply, till I've come to think the same for myself."[71]

Readiness to share was a quality rarely attributed to Protestants or to the English, who were perhaps inclined to see borrowing as an indication of carelessness and lack of thrift. In the same way, Michael J. McCarthy, in *Gallowglass: Life in the Land of the Priests* (1907), looks askance at the time spent lending and borrowing tools and equipment—English people do not do this, he thinks, because they are Protestant and that is why they get so much done, talk so little, and are so industrious.[72] Catholics by comparison are garrulous, lazy and inefficient. It looks as if Laffan, writing twenty years earlier, agrees with him. Her conclusions are often ahead of her time, as when she takes the somewhat unexpected view that setting up school boards of management to include local people would not only improve the schools, but also the people—preparing them for the exercise of greater social and political power, which Mrs. Really knows is bound to come:

> "... I know all their faults, and I have no scruple, as I dare say you know, in telling them; but I know what can be made of the same mere Irishry, and I know the talents that are wasted and lost, and turned to evil use, and in short Mr. Satterthwaite, I have faith in them ... I tell you what you want to do is to give the people some power in their own hands. . . . London is a long way from Darraghstown, though it is *far too near* Dublin."[73]

But at the same time, Mrs. Really has some very hard things to say about her Catholic neighbours, and seems to have readily adopted the classic colonists' viewpoint that members of the native race are lazy, because they do not value activity for its own sake. At the same time she does, speaking now like a Home Ruler, appear to see the dead hand of London on many aspects of Irish life, and she is aware too of the damage that colonial status has done to Irish self-esteem. But she draws no deductions from what she observes, and she still continues to lambast the peasantry for their lack of trust in the local gentry and excessive trust in the parish priest. Her cosmopolitan background and life experience are made to account for her sophistication and her interest in radical and left-wing politics; indeed she represents that European dimension which is one of the features of Laffan's work.

Mr. Perry, on the other hand, represents the professional man educated only in his profession—his horizons are restricted by this. But unlike Satterthwaite, who despises him, Perry is to some extent aware of what he lacks—this half-awareness expressing itself in challenge to people like Satterthwaite and occasional verbal bullying of his wife and daughters. The bullying is clearly an attempt at control, and used at times when Perry seems about to lose it. There is something almost touching about Perry, a realistic Irish type, and one with whom Laffan seems to have felt some innate sympathy. Here he voices his opinion of Ireland to a disgusted Satterthwaite:

> "We're wretched miserable creatures here; lost and wasted entirely. The people here are barbarians—pure barbarians. If I had my will I would not spend an hour in this country. What's the use of making money in such a place? Lord, you live more in one week in London than here! Ireland's so poor, so behind the rest of the world. I'm sure you noticed Dublin yourself—a wretched one-horse place!"[74]

Perry is, of course, reflecting back to Satterthwaite what he knows the latter is too polite to say aloud but really thinks about Ireland and the Irish, Perry included.

Satterthwaite, at first the novel's apparent hero, is gradually and subtly shown to be limited and obtuse, no adventurous thinker at all but a conventional one, and finally the most distinctive features about him are his love of beauty and his acquisitiveness—one could almost say, his greed. He wants Helena Ferrard, but only as another beautiful object capable of improvement to his own exacting standard. We can see that Mrs. Really was wise in her refusal to advance Satterthwaite's interests with Helena. He does in fact supply the focus of the satiric element in the novel, as the clean-cut, Anglo-Saxon hero who is so simpleminded himself that he cannot understand the convoluted thinking of others. He listens to Mrs. Really because she is a "woman of the world" and able to act as his guide to the complex Irish scene. Finally, he does more than listen, he understands and obeys her. Mrs. Really can be seen as the voice of intellectual Ireland attempting to communicate with English Liberalism personified by Satterthwaite. She is given a great deal to say, too much sometimes, and that might be due to the ever-present need for writers of the time to stretch each novel to fit the three-volume format required up until the late 1880s.

It may be said that in *Miss Ferrard* Laffan attempted a critique of the romantic *Wild Irish Girl* type of story, and so arranged a somewhat unconventional and unexpected ending. The treatment of the main issues and the realistic dimension of the story are handled with more confidence and insight than was the case in *Hogan MP*. To a greater extent than in the first novel, too, landscape is used to reflect the emotions of the characters. The story starts in autumn, not spring, as though declaring that growth and change can begin even at an unpropitious time, as in fact they do for Helena Ferrard. That major change of life, emigration, is presented in a positive light, as offering a solution of problems to which the old land has found no answer.

An open question is left with the reader as to whether Helena and Jim will really stay together. They are each carrying with them the burdens of their former lives—the more so in Helena's case, since she is going accompanied by her nurse and younger brother, Isidore. In a scene which shows Helena packing and mentally taking leave of her past life, her ambivalence of feeling is fully shown:

> She crossed the room, and opening the drawer of a queer little old escritoire,[75] took out of it Satterthwaite's pocket Shakespeare. . . . She looked at it, and laid it back again. Helena intended to keep that book always. Then she took out a tiny packet of silver paper, much crumpled, and a little dirty. She unrolled it by degrees, and then laid the enclosure in the palm of her hand, turning and looking at it almost reverently. It was a gold ring—a thick circlet of frosted gold. Helena slipped it on her long white finger, and holding her hand a little way from her looked at it again. A long thin ray of sunlight had crept through the shutters of the front window, and as it fell on the outstretched hand the new gold frosting glittered and shone like particles of diamonds. She smiled and gave her head a little determined shake, then hastily pulled off the ring, and folding it up in the silver paper again, turned away and down the stairs.[76]

We are not told anything more about that ring, or what Helena meant when she shook her head over it. We are left feeling that the paths of Helena and John Satterthwaite might cross again in the future. Perhaps Laffan intended a sequel to her story, or at least wanted to leave open the possibility of this.

On either side of Laffan's family there were people who emigrated to Canada; in fact her granduncle James Fitzgibbon had spent most of his life there. In the light of successive famines and risings, we are inclined to see emigration from Ireland as a response only to desperate economic or political need, but Laffan helps to correct that view. Emigration was not totally confined to one social class in nineteenth-century Ireland. Helena and Jim are looking for a more tolerant society, where the social rules will not penalise them. If they remain in Ireland, or for that matter most European countries, the class system would be hostile to them. Also, it is implied, the Catholic community would not accept their mixed marriage. Isidore, on the other hand, seeks the opportunities denied to him in Ireland, where he is marginalised. Other emigrants, like Laffan's own brothers, appear to have gone to seek adventure, or simply a wider field in which their talents could develop.

Laffan was, as a matter of deliberate policy, able to present more than one aspect of a complex and contentious issue—one of the few Irish writers of her time to attempt this. It seems that she did it because she felt she owed it to her aim of giving a true picture of human life, which is rarely so clear-cut and focused as in a fictional presentation. It is this quality in her writing which gives it such an air of illuminated reality, like a tiny vivid window through which we can perceive aspects of the past.

Hogan MP had been a successful novel, in that it sold well and ran into several editions, and *The Honorable Miss Ferrard* did likewise. Both were reprinted by Macmillan in 1881, first in classic three-volume format and then, later in the same year, in the popular cheap one-volume editions which Laffan's contemporary George Moore, intent on breaking the monopoly of the circulating libraries, was instrumental in promoting. A brief review in *Academy* approving the new policy, says of Laffan—whose female identity seemed by then to have been acknowledged:

> Amongst the younger generation of novelists we know none who writes so manifestly from the heart, and at the same time fully satisfies the demands of the critic for literary grace, whether in her longer or her shorter pieces. To become popular a writer must be in the houses of the people, to be read more than once, and to pass from hand to hand. On this ground, we welcome a cheap edition more cordially than an edition de luxe.[77]

As far as this reviewer and Laffan's publishers were concerned, political content did not seem to have adversely affected the quality of the novel. The reason probably lay in the skill and relative objectivity of the author, who managed to present differing viewpoints without detracting from the story or seeming to threaten any one group in her readership. Her picture of a decadent and impoverished family in provincial Ireland of the 1870s convinces. The insight it provides with regard to the class and certain political issues then current is therefore striking, and probably unique.

In *The Honourable Miss Ferrard*, as earlier in *Hogan MP*, the class dimension is still strongly linked to religious affiliation, and the political dimension to the major issue current at the time: namely education for Catholics. Contrasting aspects of these two factors are shown by people representing different groups within the society as it then is, a society in a state of change. We recognise in turn the confident representative of the ruling race, John Satterthwaite; the less confident members of the former Ascendancy in the Ferrard family; the unsatisfying present described by Esther Really and the self-denigrating Perry; and the rising generation, Helena, Jim and Isidore, preparing to try to get away from all that. A recurring theme is the stultifying effect on the human spirit of poverty, of lack of self-esteem, and above all, of ignorance, for those who are:

> *Lost like a wind within a summer wood,*
> *From little knowledge, where great sorrows brood.* [78]

Francis Ledwidge (1891–1917)

ᘒ᷒ᐢᐟ **CHAPTER 5**

Conflicting Values,
Class and Religion in *Christy Carew*

"The more he tried to summon up, feature by feature, Esther's
face before his own, the more it seemed to elude him."

L affan's third novel, *Christy Carew,* was published by Holt in New York
in 1878, and by Macmillan in London in 1880. It seems to have been
reviewed less extensively than were her other books, and even the
anonymous reviewer in *The Cabinet of Irish Literature* disposes of it in a few
lines: "In Christy Carew, which is the last book the authoress has produced—she is back once again among the middle classes of Dublin, and
her biting satire of some of the meannesses of metropolitan life cannot be
read without a certain degree of sadness."[1] Though curt, the statement is
accurate as to the novel's quality of sadness, but not as to the satire. *Christy
Carew* is sometimes an angry novel but lacks the fantasy element of a
purely satiric one. It is a realistic study of middle-class Dublin life in the
1870s, the relatively small Anglo-Irish Protestant Ascendancy feeling
threatened by the growing Catholic middle class[2] and the latter dominated, according to Laffan, by narrow-minded *ultramontane* clerics and
their bigoted supporters.[3]

A story of two young women from subdivisions within that Catholic
middle class, *Christy Carew* explores differences beginning to emerge in the
last quarter of the nineteenth century between the new professionals and
managers, some of whom—the "Castle Catholics"—regarded themselves
as belonging to the British Empire and imitated the Ascendancy lifestyle as
far as their means allowed, and the merchant class, richer but less sophisticated and more accepting of an Irish identity, religiously devout and still in
touch with their peasant origins. This story is disconcerting in its harsher
aspects: for instance, in its treatment of death and bereavement. The sense

137

of a society in uncomfortable transition from one colonial system to another is conveyed to us, and we are made aware that James Joyce was not the first skilled recorder of that period of unease, which he was to portray thirty years later in *Dubliners*.[4] Frustration and boredom, lost hopes and empty futures, a sense of powerlessness which nothing, apparently, has the capacity to remove—these sensations are, in *Christy Carew* as in Joyce's stories, transmitted to us realistically and entertainingly, but through a different mind, that of an intelligent young woman. Laffan as the child of two traditions was accustomed to criticise both. Her ambivalence of feeling is obvious at times, and nowhere more than in this novel. Upper-class Irish Protestants, she seems to say, are riddled with snobbery, bigotry and contempt for anyone not like them—but perhaps they are justified, perhaps they really are superior in many ways and this fails to be acknowledged by the majority. Middle-class Irish Catholics on the other hand are volatile and ignorant, their way of life often chaotic, squalid and unattractive. They do not know how to behave in polite, that is, English society. But then sometimes they can surprise one into the realisation that the difference between them and the Ascendancy or would-be Ascendancy is not simple, but complex and many-layered; not a class difference, then, so much as a difference of values.

The young Laffan was a Dubliner, one who enjoyed cities as much as Joyce apparently did. In *Christy Carew* she brings the more engaging and intimate aspects of late nineteenth-century Dublin to life in affectionate detail, as here, when Christy and her friend Esther are taking a walk through the Liberties:[5]

> They plunged . . . into the labyrinth of dirty tortuous streets that run behind Dublin Castle . . . from the windows, which were set almost level with the walls, were hung lines and poles, from which depended ragged garments of very dubious colouring and texture. Underfoot was a soft greasy mud—the frost had long disappeared—so slippery that the girls had to be careful of their footing. . . . the public-houses, terribly frequent, were surrounded by the usual gangs of hangers-on. They were civil, however. Even a tipsy workman lurched off the footway to let the ladies pass, and a huge drayman stopped his horse and cart at a crossing and roared some complimentary remark concerning their appearance to a friend farther back. Two small boys at the same time, who were amusing themselves on a doorstop catching the sun's rays on fragments of broken looking-glass, did not hesitate to direct the little yellow willow-the-wisp-like reflection into the young ladies' eyes.

"Look at the urchins," cried Christy, "casting reflections upon us!"[6]

The story begins very precisely in August of 1873 and finishes in October of the following year. In what seems at first to be simply a novel of urban life and manners, we are shown the contrasting fortunes of the "liberal" Carews and the "conservative" O'Neills. Early in the story, Edward Carew, Crown Solicitor, confides his financial worries to his clerk, Anthony Sugrue:

> "'Clare to heaven, I never was so hard run, and there's that bill of Rochford's renewed and renewed. It's most unpleasant, and indeed I confess to you they go altogether too fast at home for my purse. I don't like to say stop, for if a man can't have peace in his own house, what is he to do? . . . It's a terrible anxiety to think of those young children and—I don't mind saying it to you—no provision whatever for them. Let me once out of this wood and I'll turn over a new leaf. I will have economy. My wife has no more notion than a child of taking care of money, poor thing. She has an idea that it serves a good purpose, and I haven't it in my heart to undeceive her. . . ."[7]

Edward is portrayed as a typical "Castle Catholic." He is seriously in debt to his brother-in-law, John Rochford, among others, and is living well beyond his means, with a rented house in Mountjoy Square, a staff of servants, formal entertaining, and at least a month in a seaside villa every year. There are two adolescent children from Edward's first marriage, Christina (Christy of the title) and Leonard (Lanty), and two infant girls, Minna and Elsie, by his much younger second wife, Caroline—"a pretty woman of thirty who had perfectly the air of being aware of her good looks"[8] and who comes from an impoverished Ascendancy family, the Poyntsetts. Her eldest sister Harriet married John Rochford, a wealthy landowner; her second sister married an Englishman and severed connection with her own family to please his; and her youngest sister Susan married an Army officer, Wentworth Almond. Her sisters unite in despising Caroline as a "vert"—a genteel though insulting term for a member of their class who has "gone over to Rome." When she married the much older Edward Carew, Caroline became a Catholic, and Catholics, particularly Irish ones, are not highly regarded by this Ascendancy family: "'One does know them somehow always,' went on Mrs. Rochford. She had a full, rich voice, and liked to hear herself talk. 'Look at their women—superbly dressed, are they not? and look at their faces—overeating, thats what makes them so ugly and coarse-looking. They have all more money than is good for them. Ugh! I never could bear them except as servants. I'll allow R.C. servants can't be done without.'"[9] At the same time, Harriet Rochford is kind and

generous in her actual dealings with her Catholic kin, unlike Susan's hus-
band, the alcoholic Wentworth Almond, who while drinking Edward
Carew's wine refers to him behind his back in uncomplimentary terms:
"'Fernal old attorney! Low old—"Captain Almond could not find a word
strong enough to embody his feelings of reprobation towards the Crown
Solicitor. "Nice party! A nice collection of your low-lived relations, Susan,
I'm asked to meet! Rubbish and trash of people!"[10]

The Carews are nominally part of the Catholic community, but tend to
avoid being identified with it socially. They are embarrassed, for instance,
by recent publicity about the doctrine of Papal Infallibility;[11] finding the
concept impossible to explain to their Church of Ireland associates, probably because they do not know much about it themselves. But then to them
the whole idea of any religious dogma is incomprehensible:

> As a rule it was only from among the ranks of the professionals—doctors and
> lawyers, and those of kindred followings—that the great dogma found oppo-
> nents. But there were others who maintained . . . that Infallibility was a mischie-
> vous and useless graft on a stock already overloaded; a novelty, the outcome of
> senile vanity; and a wanton flourish of defiance from impotence discontented
> with its insignificance . . . a manifesto which avowedly widened the breach be-
> tween them and the class representing that culture and refinement towards
> which the most fervent Ultramontane unconsciously strives . . . the massive in-
> difference or docile acquiescence of the unreasoning mob, trained to passive re-
> ceptivity, soon imposed its will upon the dissidents.[12]

Laffan seems to be indicating here that the Irish Catholic community
consists of a small class of educated people cynically making pretence to
believe what that faith requires of them, and a huge passive majority deliberately kept in ignorance, too spiritless to question anything at all but exercising some long-term influence by reason of their numbers. Irish
Protestants, meanwhile, are the fortunate possessors of whatever morality,
culture and discernment actually exist in Ireland. This, anyway, is what
Laffan wrote first, but what she shows us throughout the course of her
novel *Christy Carew* appears to contradict what she wrote at the start.

Christy herself, the story's nominal heroine, although convent-edu-
cated is not devout. She disbelieves in the genuineness of her stepmother's
conversion, and sees herself as resistant to all religion: "'I am not religious,
it was left out of me, and that's no fault of mine.'"[13] In fact, she seems to
confuse religion with pious emotion, a not uncommon mistake. When
Dawson, a wealthy agnostic Englishman more than twice her age, begins

to pay court to Christy, Edward and Caroline think they see an end to their financial difficulties. The *naïf* Dawson, an admirer of Darwin, has been already turned down once, as a suitor for Christy's friend Esther O'Neill. But he still wants to marry an Irish girl: "He approved of religion for women—it kept them in order, and made one sure of them. He had intellect enough for two, and a wife of that sort is always a pleasant and stimulating term of comparison—a grindstone always ready to whet the blade of a superior masculine reasoning intelligence. . . ."[14] Dawson threads his way through the Dublin social maze in a perpetual state of bewilderment. Most of the time he does not understand what is going on, or why people laugh at the things he says: "He liked the Irish thoroughly and despised them about equally—they were congenitally inferior to him and to any or all Englishmen. He was willing to make allowances for them, as he might for the inhabitants of Congo. They could not help themselves—they were Irish: a comprehensive term, explaining and accounting for everything—rain, poverty, piety and all included, even to jokes which he could not understand."[15]

With all of these attitudinal disadvantages, it is no wonder that Christy finds him unattractive. But his attentions to her bring material rewards, which she is not above accepting. Her stepmother, Caroline Carew, who after coming from a shabby-genteel family is now very extravagant, tries to bribe her stepdaughter with new clothes to look favourably on Dawson: "Mrs. Carew preached hour-long sermons on the text of poverty, lamented the family embarrassments, and discussed ways and means in detail in a manner that was perfectly new to her. . . . but there was not the slightest use attempting to drive Miss Carew into anything, and the subject (of marriage) was carefully avoided between them. . . ."[16]

Christy has her own plans. She has many admirers, but feels attracted to only one—the penniless barrister Anthony Sugrue, who in addition to working with her father tutors her brother, Lanty. To Sugrue alone she confides her boredom and dissatisfaction with her empty life, a life focused, though she does not need to be explicit about this, on making a wealthy marriage. Sugrue listens to her and lends her books, but then feeling himself drawn to her begins to keep her at a distance, aware that he would not be acceptable to her family because he is too poor. Sugrue, a Dissenter of Huguenot origin, is ambitious and hardworking. Laffan always characterises Protestants as industrious, Catholics as the reverse; and her occasional stereotyping extends to the facial features of her characters. She considers that Irish Catholics lack "strong" faces: "The chief characteristic of [Sugrue's] face was indeed its utter un-Irishness. The mouth was certainly the best and most expressive feature; mobile and clear cut, and thin rather than thick-lipped, its silence to those who could read it had a language of its own, that spoke of strength and patience waiting on the intellect that sat enthroned on the broad well-filled brow above."[17] This detailed description reminds us of the keen interest which the Victorians had in phrenology, in the supposed close relationship between skull conformation, facial features, and personality type.

Impulsive and acquisitive by nature, Christy Carew lives for the moment. She despises her stepmother, but humours her so that she can get Caroline to go on buying her new dresses, and she makes fun of Dawson but continues to accept his expensive flowers. Caroline, deliberately childish in behaviour, uses indirect means to control the situation, telling Dawson that Christy favours him when this is not the case, and later, intercepting and hiding a letter to Christy from Anthony Sugrue. The implication is that Christy needs good example and a structure in her life, neither of which Caroline is able to supply.

The Carew family would accept a rich suitor, whatever his religion, although there are practical difficulties, Cardinal Cullen, the Archbishop of Dublin, having forbidden the celebration of Catholic-Protestant marriages in the Dublin diocese. Wealthy couples sidestep the problem by going to London or to Paris, obtaining the necessary dispensation through a parish priest and marrying in a Catholic church there. People who cannot afford this solution make do with a civil marriage, recognised as valid by the state but not by the Catholic Church.

The action of Cardinal Cullen was undertaken for reasons which appeared more understandable at the time than later. It was then still usual in most societies, and not only Catholic ones, for parents to arrange to a greater or lesser extent the marriages of their children. By the 1870s actual overt pressure to marry was frowned on, but young people were still expected, particularly in rural communities, to find partners among their own friends and family connections, and to avoid matches of which their family would disapprove. Girls were of course particularly aware of their lives being subject to parental wishes, and most accepted the idea. To marry someone of a different race or culture and above all of a different religion without parental backing was very unusual and effectively meant encountering difficulties which handicapped the marriage from the outset.

Additionally, it was believed that children of a "mixed marriage" usually grew up to reject the religions of both parents.

In nineteenth-century Ireland, there were, until 1870, special circumstances relating to Catholic-Protestant marriages. As stated earlier, a Catholic who wanted to marry a Protestant had to do so according to the rite of the Church of Ireland. By any other rite the marriage would be legally invalid, with obvious serious consequences regarding legitimacy of children and inheritance rights of spouses under the law. In fact, originally the law had been even more severe, charging Catholic priests who performed the marriage ceremonies for Catholic-Protestant couples with a criminal offence, punishable by death. To Catholics (and to Presbyterians to whom it applied up to 1850), this law was an insulting relic of the old penal code and colonial domination.[18] Its real purpose is likely to have been, not religious conversion, but prevention of the transfer through marriage of Protestant property to Catholic hands.

Unfortunately its retention on the statute-book led to a number of conspicuous lapses of justice as well as to painful and scandalous lawsuits. Probably the most significant of these was the Yelverton case, a *cause célèbre* which precipitated long overdue changes in the law.[19] Laffan would have known of it, and she certainly borrowed aspects of it to use both in *Christy Carew* and her last novel, *Ismay's Children,* so for these reasons it seems appropriate to give an outline of the circumstances.

William Charles Yelverton was a member of the Irish Protestant Ascendancy, and a British Army Major. On active service in the Crimea in 1855, he met Theresa Longworth, who was nursing with a group of French nuns. Theresa, an English Catholic and an independent spirit, was an orphan with a small private income. She and Yelverton fell in love. She was later to testify that he suggested they marry in the local Russian Orthodox Church, but she insisted on a Catholic ceremony, which took place near Rostrevor in Co. Down in 1858, but not before Yelverton had tried to get her to accept an un-witnessed "Scotch marriage" instead.[20] He said that his family would disinherit him if they found out, hence the need for absolute secrecy.

The couple lived together in Ireland, Scotland and France. Theresa, now pregnant, wanted to make the marriage public. Yelverton refused, insisting that although he had to go to Edinburgh to rejoin his regiment, she must stay out of the country. Alone, Theresa became ill, miscarried, and returned to Yelverton only to find him about to marry again. Theresa then

sought a declaration that the first marriage was valid and the second biga-
mous.

Yelverton said in court that he saw Theresa as his mistress, and only
went through with a Catholic marriage to please her, knowing it did not
bind him legally. He implied he would scarcely consider marrying Theresa
in earnest, since *she*, as a Catholic, could never be his social equal. The arrogance of this statement was underlined by common Dublin knowledge
that the Yelverton family was of plebeian English origin and moreover the
Major's grandfather Barry Yelverton had changed political sides in 1800
for a union peerage. He had also in early life contracted and later set aside
a marriage with a Catholic.[21]

In a society where members of one faith regarded members of another as
intrinsically inferior, "mixed marriage" under such conditions frequently
served to exploit women. The typical course of events involved, as in this
instance, a girl who agreed to a Catholic marriage without knowing that it
would not bind her Protestant lover. The typical victim of these events
would be a peasant girl whose lover was of a higher social class, for example, a son of her family's landlord. When he tired of her or wanted to make
a legal marriage, she would be pensioned off and encouraged to leave the
country. Usually she would lack the confidence to resist. But Theresa
Longworth was an educated and articulate woman, who maintained her
marriage to be valid and fought attempts to denigrate or manipulate her.
It could be said that in one way she failed but in another she succeeded,
whether she realized it or not, in changing the marriage laws positively.
The Yelverton case caused a sensation, being widely attended by the public
and reported on in contemporary newspapers—it was even made the subject of a ballad.[22] The significance of the case appears to have been symbolic as well as sensational. Theresa's courage and spirit impressed the
public in Ireland as well as in her native Manchester; they—especially
women—identified strongly with her, contributed to her legal expenses, re-
joiced when she seemed about to win her case, and then had to realize that
it would go against her, essentially because she refused to accept a lowering
of her social and moral status from wife to mistress. Yelverton attempted to
prove in court that Theresa knew and accepted the temporary nature of her
relationship to him. When the courts found against him in Ireland and
Scotland, Major Yelverton, now Viscount Avonmore following the death of
an elder brother, took the case to the House of Lords which decided in his fa-

vour by one vote. Theresa according to the civil law was not, and never had been, his wife.

Stories about the hazards of irregular marriage are many.[23] The Carew family in *Christy Carew* seems unaffected by the socio-legal drawbacks to mixed marriages, for this is never mentioned as a factor in their discussion of Cardinal Cullen's decision to tighten the rules and make mixed marriages difficult. The O'Neill family's harder peasant background seems to have ensured they know about the often tragic results of such unions, and accordingly they are against them.

Hugh O'Neill, the wealthy merchant father of Christy's friend Esther, is a determined opponent of mixed marriages. His motives are less religious than based on a deep distrust of the ruling caste which, taken in the social context of the time, is probably well founded. This prejudice of O'Neill's is to have a bearing on the course of the story. In the meantime, to pay urgent debts, Edward Carew borrows a large sum of money from O'Neill.

Hugh O'Neill is a complex individual, a successful business man who is also over-sensitive and deeply, if narrowly, religious and patriotic: "O'Neill's face was pale, lean and hard; the forehead high and narrow at the brows; the lips thin, close-locked and severe. The nose, at a distance, looked large and bold of outline; nearer, the nostrils were narrow and their curves unfinished, and the bridge flattened and, so to say, deformed. His head, thickly covered with iron-grey hair, was slightly stooped between the square, lean shoulders."[24] Hugh is portrayed as a severe and anxious man, but one with a natural dignity and self-respect: "the descendant of a line of famous chieftains, . . . hardly likely to allow that any heretic could have social ascendancy over him. . . ."[25]

O'Neill's descent is notionally from the family of his namesake the chieftain Hugh O'Neill (1550–1616); and this would suggest him to be an Ulsterman. Hugh, in his single-mindedness and intensiveness, reminds one strongly of the main character in William Carleton's famous creation *Fardorougha the Miser* (1839), and Fardorougha is also from Ulster.

Hugh O'Neill is not interested in show, and is portrayed as a reluctant Lord Mayor of Dublin. That office being about the only influential and public one open to an Irish Catholic, Hugh accepts it when offered, as a matter of principle. He reacts to the petty snobbery which labels him—and other Catholics—as second-class citizens by deciding to have no more social contact with Protestants than he can help. Hugh has a devoted, motherly wife, Mary Josephine, and a large family which he rules strictly. The eldest, Esther, went to school with Christy, and the action of the story arises from the way in which each girl deals with the challenge of loving someone from a different culture and faith.

Esther O'Neill has grown up in a very protective family with parents who are fond and proud of her. Her mother Mary Josephine dreams of a brilliant—arranged—marriage. But Esther, unlike Christy, is emotionally dependent on her family, their approval meaning so much to her that she cannot go against it. When Neville Jocelyn, an Army officer from an Ascendancy background, pays court to Esther, she responds wholeheartedly to him but is then unable to cope with her father's refusal of consent to their marriage. Ostensibly this refusal is made on the grounds of religious difference, but Hugh O'Neill clearly has a more personal distrust and dislike of Neville. He is not prepared to let Neville even see his daughter again, much less marry her, because of who Neville Jocelyn is and what he represents.

The surname Jocelyn is that of an actual Ulster family, arrogant in their Ascendancy status, leading supporters of the Orange Order and notoriously anti-Catholic.[26] It is implied, though not stated, that the Jocelyn and O'Neill families have crossed swords at some time in the past. We are told that Hugh "[c]onsidered his family infinitely older and incomparably more noble than the Jocelyns. Lord de Blacquiere was only a 'union lord'; and moreover the family was of a very recent English origin. . . ."[27] If Esther married Neville, there would be no possibility of the Jocelyns accepting her as his wife. Neville would have to exchange to an Indian regiment, losing social and career status by doing so, and the couple would have to live abroad. They would both in fact be rejected and exiled. Esther is seventeen, gentle, idealistic, dependant on others, and not a resourceful character. How would she and Neville deal with the hostility and isolation they would have to undergo?

So Hugh O'Neill forbids the lovers to meet, but Christy and Lanty Carew, at the request of Neville, set up a meeting between him and Esther in the Phoenix Park, Christy overcoming any doubts she has about doing this by resolving to see O'Neill simply as the oppressor of his daughter. In the meantime, Esther approaches two priest friends to beg each to use his influence to get a marriage dispensation. She feels, illogically, that if this were only granted her father would withdraw his opposition, seeing that the Catholic Church approved the match. It is notable that Esther does this by herself. It does not apparently occur to Neville to help, or indeed to make any move towards persuasion or conciliation.

Father Paddy Macklin is a dedicated and well-known social activist, but when Esther approaches him he refuses to become involved, mentally contrasting Esther's privileged background with the miserable circumstances of the abused women he is currently trying to help. He can feel little sympathy for Esther: "To understand her was altogether beyond him. . . .What could she mean by assuming the woe and wretchedness to which experience led him to believe poverty alone is entitled?"28

His response shows, most unusually for the time, the all-too-real hazard affecting those whose work involves helping distressed people—the danger of blunting of sympathy, an early stage of "burn-out." Fr. Macklin has always sublimated his own feelings and desires anyway, and all he can do is to counsel the unhappy girl to do the same: "'I was just thinking how short a time it is since you were a tiny little girl at the convent; it is as if it were only the other day, and here you are a grown woman now, and fretting yourself over something that as many years hence will be no more to you than the playthings you had when you were a child. How can anyone trouble themselves about this world, or set their heart upon anything in it!'"29

The character of Fr. Macklin seems based on that of Fr. Charles P. Meehan, the former Young Irelander and writer for the *Nation* newspaper, who during the 1870s was a curate in the Liberties.30 The befriender of Anne Devlin31 and of James Clarence Mangan,32 he dedicated much of his considerable energy to helping the Dublin poor. Fr. Meehan was hot tempered and outspoken; he made himself unpopular by openly opposing the drink culture, but there is no indication that he believed in a hierarchy of need discriminating against the middle-classes. Fr. Charles P. Meehan/Paddy Macklin was a well-known person in a small city. The amount of detail Laffan gives about him, his philosophy, and his unorthodox lifestyle, both in *Christy Carew* and in the *Recess Committee Notes* referred to earlier, suggests that she got to know him personally. There would have been no difficulty in doing this; he was an approachable person. But Laffan readily became annoyed with people in caring professions when, in self-defense, they practiced detachment. Unable to understand their need to control emotion, Laffan considered they left themselves open to the charge of lacking empathy with distressed people. It seems likely from the amount of detail she gives about him that Laffan actually knew him; she could well have been one of the voluntary helpers he recruited to teach poor girls.

Esther's godfather, Father Considine, an eccentric bibliophile, is far more sympathetic. After hearing Esther, he goes to see Canon Caffrey, D.

D., Dublin diocesan administrator. The Canon, at first revealing himself as a social snob, declares it is nonsensical to contemplate a marriage between a "mere publican's daughter out of Bride Street"[33] and the possible heir to a peerage—anyway, the Jocelyns of Mourne wouldn't even hear of such a thing. Fr. Considine, not to be sidetracked, asks why the marriage laws of the Universal Church seem to be interpreted more strictly for Ireland than in other Catholic countries.[34] The canon replies:

> "Ireland is not a Catholic country—nominally at least—though it ought to be so. . . . The Protestant Church retains at any rate a part of its endowments. It may have been disestablished, certainly; but while they retain the supremacy in education, and Trinity College its endowments, you cannot maintain that the Catholics are on an equality with the Protestants in this country. . . . we only desire to see their educational monopoly treated like their religious monopoly, the Establishment."

> "I do not like this reopening of old wounds. They have been just; they have been generous to this country, and why always foment dissension and distrust?"

> "Just—generous? Why, will you tell me if one single act of justice was ever rendered to Ireland, save by way of a quietus to agitation? Fenianism got this same Disestablishment; Home Rule got the Land Act, and will, I hope, get the University for us. No. History teaches that every just concession made by England was wrung from her by force—by violence. I maintain it!—disprove it who can!"[35]

The implication is that Protestants, who mainly identify with the British Government and British interests, are being deliberately paid back for this by local church regulations making it harder for them to marry Catholics—anyway, this is the way Laffan appears to interpret the situation. She does not consider the additional possibility that Cardinal Cullen may have been too well aware of the drawbacks of mixed marriages (for instance, in cases such as Longworth v. Yelverton) to want to facilitate them. Crushed by the realisation of his failure to help his goddaughter, Fr. Considine retreats to his isolated parish in the Dublin mountains, where Esther has to seek him out to learn the result of his attempts.

Meanwhile, the arranged meeting between the lovers does not go well:

> "Have you chosen between your friends and me? Am I to be given up for them? For that priestridden—"

> "Stop"! she almost screamed, putting her hand over his mouth. . . .

"I did not mean to hurt you, but who could have patience with those people? And your father, Esther, spoke to me in a manner I never in all my life heard. I never listened to such insults, and only for you—that he was your father—" A pause ensued, then: "I will take you away from them, my darling, far far away, for ever. Only say you will—say you will trust me, Esther. Will you leave them for me—with me?"

"Oh, Neville, but we cannot be married before going away."

"Child! That is not necessary, not at all necessary. We can be married by the registrar, you know, and afterwards in London, or in Paris, in church—chapel, rather—and by one of your priests. We could not be married here, I know that well enough."

She heaved a deep sigh, and looked away from him.

"Esther," he went on, "you know very well I am in earnest. I am not like plenty of other fellows—fellows I know, too. I never cared for a single human being but you. Yes, I mean to marry you" (if it were only to pay out old O'Neill, he added to himself). "I will never marry anyone else, Esther, I have made my mind up to it. What makes you look so sad?" he demanded almost angrily.

"Nothing, nothing!" hastily answered poor Esther, and she could not have told him had she tried to.

She was in a maze of astonishment and fear. . . . to run away with him . . . to have them all far away. . . . Her brain seemed to be boiling. She caught the arm of the seat and gripped it hard in her hand, as if to reassure herself that she was really awake and not dreaming. . . .[36]

As Esther cannot face an elopement, the couple part in the rain. Unfortunately Hugh O'Neill hears about their meeting and the Carew family's share in it. He reacts by instantly cutting off communication with the Carews, and recalling Edward Carew's loan, causing the latter to respond predictably: "'That religious sort is never to be trusted! He is just making a great blow over the girl's love affair for an advertisement—deuce a more! That sort of thing always goes down with the priests, and will bring him lots of custom.'"[37] Still, Edward confronts his son and eldest daughter. Lanty cleverly equivocates and so escapes blame, but Christy owns up, is told she has ruined her family, and is sent in tears to her room. An hour later she hears laughter in the street outside. Edward and Caroline, on the strength of a new loan from a moneylender, are taking the little ones off to a picnic at the zoo.

We can see already how very different this novel is from the conventional "family story" of the time, which upheld values of obedience to parents, self-sacrifice and patience under adversity, with the prospect that virtue would be rewarded in this life as well as in the next. In *Christy Carew* Esther, the angelic, good and obedient daughter, dies a tragic death. Christy, on the other hand, succeeds in her aims not because she is "good" in Victorian terms, but because she is disobedient, selfish and rebellious. Christy shows little concern for others. Some feeling for her stepmother and little half-sister Elsie develops, but too late to help the unfortunate Elsie. With her quick wit and strong sense of self-preservation keeping her out of serious trouble, whoever suffers it will not be Christy. As a heroine she is interesting, alive, yet somehow unappealing—there is more than a touch in her of Becky Sharpe,[38] or even of Hedda Gabler,[39] and like the latter, she has fantasies of escape to a more stimulating life.

Not much more attractive is her lover, Anthony Sugrue. For some reason, his affection for Christy does not catch fire—does not convince. Christy sees him as her intellectual superior, seeking his advice about her life and occupations, reading books he recommends, and even fearing to displease him, for Anthony Sugrue is a grim young man, and quick to judge others, even those he has not yet met. Here he is, on the subject of a nun who is a confidant of Esther's:

> "Well, I say this . . . if ever you go to her in trouble and perplexity, real serious trouble, anything that is likely to affect your happiness for life, you'll be disappointed. First, because she is a general favourite. That limpid transparency of nature that mirrors pleasantly the mood and shadow of everyone that chooses to project their shadow on it, has never body or depth enough to hold an entire soul—no, no. . . . I like people that are not 'too good,' as somebody says, 'for human nature's daily food.' People with redeeming vices please me best."[40]

The admired forcefulness of Sugrue's character is put down to his Huguenot ancestry; his arrogance is taken as an indication of his honesty. Now he is talking to Esther O'Neill about another of her circle, her musical cousin Philomena Dunne: "'Well, it's my experience of musicians, they are just that and nothing else. It must be a wonderful absorbent, music. It seems to suck up brain and heart and all into itself. Musicians are always egotistic, always conceited, and never good for anything but music.'"[41] It is not easy to imagine Christy and Anthony finding happiness together.

Esther O'Neill is Christy's opposite, so different that they have nothing in common, except that Esther is also an eldest child. The conventional Victorian daughter in most respects, she is docile, devout and self-abnegating. But unlike Christy she is compassionate:

> There was some charm about this girl. The little Elsie looked up with a smile through her tears, and Minna released an imprisoned fly from an empty match-box, and came over to rub herself against Esther's fresh holland dress.[42]

> "What ails this little old woman?" said she, sitting down on the floor in front of Elsie, and, taking the tiny chin between her finger and thumb, she turned up the smudged little face and looked at it sympathisingly.[43]

Esther does not question authority, and is not rebellious by nature. The implication is that people like her are not intellectually able either. Asked by Dawson her opinion of the Old Testament story of Jael and Sisera, Esther is at a loss to reply, having no idea what he is talking about. She does not know her Old Testament, because Catholics were not encouraged to study it in depth; this circumstance is seen by Laffan as a great educational deficiency, and Esther is made to appear on that account a lesser person: "a convent-trained Roman Catholic, whose acquaintance with Old Testament lore is confined usually to the leading facts of the first chapters, or so, of Genesis, and a few anecdotes, chronologically arranged. . . ."[44]

Yet in other ways, it appears Esther is actually an object of envy to her friend. Laffan can sometimes acknowledge that there exist other advantages than purely intellectual ones. Mrs. O'Neill, Esther's mother, unlike the Carews, is by nature affectionate and demonstrative: Christy "had seen Esther's mother stroke and adjust her daughter's attire merely from the love of doing it. Every touch seemed a caress, and Christy had envied her friend each of them. For her there were no such loving cares and watchfulness; no mother took a pride in her good looks."[45]

Having received loving attention, Esther can bestow it on others without needing to acquire Christy's defensive and self-protective attitude. By way of contrast to Christy, who is perpetually bored and mischief-making, Esther belongs to a group that makes clothes for poor children, and helps with a literacy scheme for servant girls, projects in which she tries to involve the reluctant Christy. But above all, Esther is a musician, her imagination and emotions finding ample expression when she plays and sings. She has a beautiful, expressive voice, and it is this that enchants Neville Jocelyn:

> Never in his life had he heard such pathos of tone, such a simple and unaffected expression of sadness. There was no posing, no affectation, and the words were each spoken distinctly. He followed them each one—

"I will fly with my Coulin and think the rough wind
Less rude than the foes we leave frowning behind."

The transient burst of strength and resolve of these words died away in a melancholy minor cadence that was followed by the forecast of promised, but sadly uncertain, tenderness and safety . . . the last soft modulation had died away before any of the listeners spoke . . . he could scarcely bear to hear their voices, even Esther's, as he said goodbye and took his leave as hurriedly as possible. To stay longer would have been unbearable. . . . He wanted to keep that shadow picture of her and her weird singing, and in the mist and mud of the streets as he rode back to the Castle the vision of her fair, sweet face, set in its framing of blonde hair, seemed to float before his eyes. And yet, strange enough, the more he became enamoured of this recollection, the more he tried to summon up, feature by feature, Esther's face before his own, the more it seemed to elude him.[46]

The instant and intense emotional response of Neville to the song is significant in terms both of his character and what is going to happen to their relationship, and the message of courageous help and love conveyed by Esther's singing is never destined to be actual. This episode foreshadows closely the climax scene of Joyce's story "The Dead," in which Gretta Conroy hears another guest sing a few bars of a traditional lament *The Lass of Aughrim* and is at once carried back in time to half-forgotten first love of Michael Furey, all through the evocative power of music.[47]

That Laffan was personally very fond of music is clear from the frequency with which she introduces music and musicians into her stories, and she was also aware of its power. In this she shows resemblance to an earlier writer Charles Kickham (1828–1882) who shares her readiness to use music and song to heighten atmosphere. Accordingly, her choice of the music and song lyrics used in her fiction is always significant, telling us something about the performer, as with Helena in *Miss Ferrard*. The song, quoted above, which Esther sings is one of Thomas Moore's lesser-known lyrics set to a well-known traditional air. It is a love-song addressed to a man—a harpist exiled by Elizabethan law for wearing his hair (*coulin*) long in traditional Gaelic fashion. His love assures him of her readiness to go with him:

> Though the last glimpse of Erin with sorrow I see
> Wherever thou art shall seem Erin to me,
> In exile this bosom shall still be thy home
> And thine eyes make my climate, wherever we roam. . . .[48]

Neville, the recipient of the message, is not possessed of the ability to feel to any depth, or the resolution to overcome difficulties—but here the girl is expressing her willingness to do this for both of them! Therefore, he is quickly and easily moved, but only for a time. He wants her, but only on his terms, not hers. And part of the attraction which pursuit of Esther holds for Neville is the possibility for him, through her, of getting the better of Hugh O'Neill, whom, from the evidence of the lovers' last conversation together he despises and dislikes.

What does seem beyond question also is that the seventeen-year-old Esther is more deeply attracted to Neville than he to her; but she is also much less able to admit the possibility that their love may have no future. The attraction which Esther feels for Neville is expressed as her acute awareness of his difference from the other young men she knows: "He was cultivated and refined; he had all those outward graces of manner and appearance that go so far to captivate a girl's fancy; a man of a totally different stamp, in short, to the men of Esther's own circle. She never would be able to marry one of them—never, it would be impossible."[49] This statement also, if taken literally, implies a trenchant criticism of the young men from Esther's own social group. As coming from the Irish Catholic middle class, they lack the polish and social ease of the educated Anglo-Irishman. But it is not certain whether Laffan speaks ironically here or not. Her much later summing up of Neville, presented during the set-piece which ends the novel, suggests a degree of irony: "He was feather-headed enough, this youth, but in no way vicious; all there was in him to give of love and passion Esther really had had. . . . Esther was now but faintly imaged in his memory, the shallow pool of his mind being occupied with his own image solely."[50]

It is significant that Esther, and not Neville, fails to adapt to reality. However, her disposition is described in terms which suggest a too-ready acceptance of appearances: Esther had "one of those rare, sweet natures that could never see below the surface of things, and took everything literally and unquestioningly: gilt gingerbread was always solid gold to her."[51] This description is not complimentary at all, for it implies that Esther is not very perceptive and is unable to be decisive or independent in her thinking. Laffan seems in this part of the story to want to say that "weak" characters like Esther O'Neill are foredoomed to fail in what they undertake, whereas "strong" ones like Christy succeed and in fact ought to do so; they are intrinsically more efficient, more practical and single-minded, do not need help from others, have an eye to the main chance and are therefore, somehow, better people. We touch here on the aspect of the prejudice towards anyone who, dependant by nature, could be seen as racially inferior. It must be borne in mind that even in the 1870s the idea of a social hierarchy of races within the British Empire—some born to rule, others to be ruled—was still widely held and in literary terms influential. Novels in which family life was depicted would have taken this into account, as they reflected the ideas and assumptions of their time.

In *Christy Carew* the main indicator of Irish social class is still religion, as in *Hogan MP,* but there are indications of change, the merchants of the Irish Catholic middle class being not quite the figures of fun portrayed in *Hogan MP,* where, for example, Mr. Rafferty the Lord Mayor and his associates are comic figures, whose formal clothes look all wrong on them; in *Christy Carew* Lord Mayor Hugh O'Neill and his entourage show a certain dignity remarked on by spectators, who compare O'Neill to the Lord Lieutenant, to the disadvantage of the latter. Accent and level of education are added to religious faith as definite class indicators. The comic and complex aspect of snobbery is well in evidence, for instance when the Catholic convert Caroline Carew forgets about her change of allegiance and starts to make snide remarks about "R.C.s"—then remembers, stops in confusion, and quickly switches to equally catty remarks about "trades-people." The passage mirrors one in Carleton's novel *The Black Prophet,* in which two converts at loggerheads forget their newly assumed faiths and return temporarily to their old ones, the better to express themselves freely. Another, and very deliberately chosen, aspect of the minefield of nineteenth-century social and class nuance is shown in the following exchange, which takes place early in the story during a meeting on Kingstown Pier:

> The manner of each lady was peculiar and worth studying. The lady mayoress elect, conscious of her prospective dignity, in addition to the heavy bill due by the Carews, was the least possible shade—not patronising, for that would have been impossible,—but perhaps, independent in manner. She did not turn her head towards her companion as she addressed her; she put more questions to her, and in a broader accent, than she usually did in conversation, and she barely gave her interlocutor time to finish the rather curt contributions which she vouchsafed towards the conversation. On her side, Mrs. Carew, mindful of her position and her superior accent, which implies even more, wanting to be condescending and patronising, and half afraid to be openly impertinent, was calm and self-possessed. She grew more freezingly courteous as the other lady grew less formal. The conversation ran upon their respective sons.

"'Ah!" Mrs. O'Neill said, "I don't know what his father is thinking of for Nicholas John. I declare the Bar is that expensive: it's all very well if you have relations judges or attorneys, but edication [*sic*] nowadays is no joke. I declare his bills were enough to frighten you; and oh dear! but they have sent him home that rough and unrefined!'"

"Ah! Indeed!"

"Yes. Now your Lanty, look at him; oh, he's lovely! Those Protestant schools are so different, but then there's the awful danger of him losing his faith. I wonder you were not afraid of that: oh, I wouldn't risk it for anything. I wanted his father to send Nicholas John to one of the English colleges, but 'no' says he; 'he's an Irishman and so am I, and let him not be ashamed of speaking his native tongue.'"

"I really think Mr. O'Neill is quite right—quite right; you see, so much more is expected from Leon—"

"Yes," interrupted the lady mayoress elect, "I know we could hardly pass by St Patrick's College; but all the same I can't help wishing Nicholas John had got Lanty's ahxent [*sic*]."

Mrs. Carew was laughing to herself, and waited a moment before replying, lest the laugh should betray itself in her voice.

"Yes," she said, "Leonard has not much accent, all things considered."

Mrs. O'Neill was not so obtuse as not to notice the implied correction.[52]

It is significant that Mrs. O'Neill openly refers to the practical advantages, when it comes to the need for patronage for a son, possessed by people like the Carews and their Ascendancy connections who already have relatives in the legal profession. Lacking this patronage, it was virtually impossible for anyone in Ireland of the period to develop a career. But she also hints at the price to be paid, in terms of religious indifference and confusion of identity, if children are not educated in compliance with the religion to which their family gives nominal allegiance.

This brings us to a curious and unique aspect of *Christy Carew*, almost a literary *trompe d'oeil*.[53] On the face of it, the liberal Carews contrast very favourably with the reactionary O'Neills. The former are carefree and tolerant, therefore appear right, the latter are less easy and less tolerant, therefore appear wrong; and the narrator seems concerned to tell us so in several different ways. Yet upon reflection, and as the story develops, this picture does not appear to be quite whole or quite real, and the issues are by no means as clear as they first appeared to be.

For the Carews, educated, enlightened, non-bigoted as they are, are also a loose-knit family where each single member appears to ignore the needs of the others. Edward Carew is *laissez-faire* to the extent of simply not being involved; he prefers to ignore what his wife and eldest daughter do; and the freedom he gives them is based on indifference. Caroline Carew, similarly, ignores and neglects both her own and her husband's children, only attending to them when they misbehave, with obvious results. Caroline assumes, moreover, that others share her value system, and she sees nothing amiss in using her stepdaughter as the means to get out of money difficulties. By any standards, her attempts to sell seventeen-year-old Christy to the boorish Dawson are indefensible—only Christy's native intransigence saves her.

Christy, for her part, spends her mental energy on the criticism of others, and supports Lanty even when he treats their stepmother with a rudeness not a usual feature in novels of the time—though no doubt it did take place often in private life. Caroline Carew in her turn is treated by her husband as a child, and seems to prefer to be so treated. Lanty, who is supposed to be studying for university entrance, passes his days in smoking, gambling, and taking potshots at cats from the study window, and no one—apart from Anthony Sugrue—ever seems even to notice what he does, much less to care. Of the little ones, Caroline's elder child Minna, always referred to as "the pretty one," is a vain little girl, spoiled by her mother in contrast to Elsie, the youngest child, who is neglected and appears unloved.

The overall impression, beneath the humour, is of lack of tolerance. The Carews "wind each other up," but never express more positive feeling towards each other. And nobody has time to listen to anyone else. But the most poignant and disturbing evidence of the family's dysfunction is seen in Elsie. She is supposed to be about four years old, and is not pretty but *gauche*, unlike Minna whom Caroline dresses up and takes with her to social occasions as a sort of human fashion accessory.

The most telling remark made about Elsie is the narrator's statement that she is "a plain baby-girl, who should have been a boy. . . ."[54] Elsie is superfluous. Caroline largely ignores her, and the child is left to the occasional attentions of Christy and the careless nursemaid, Hannah. Craving affection, Elsie adores Esther, who treats her with real understanding. Otherwise Elsie consoles herself by obsessively collecting sea creatures. On the day of the picnic on Dalkey Island, a set-piece of the kind which Laffan did very well, generally including one such in each novel to assemble all the main characters and draw the narrative threads together, Elsie tries to get attention in turn from Hannah, from Christy and from her mother Caroline. Each one pushes her away; her aunts too are preoccupied, one with the catering and the other with keeping her husband from the drink supplies. When Elsie is first realised to be missing, Christy and the nursemaid each try to blame the other:

> "Hannah!" cried Christy, ". . . I left the place last of all, and sent her to you to keep her, as her mamma said. You know very well I did not take her with me."

> "Go' bless us, miss," vociferated Hannah, "you needn't be talking to me, for I haven't wan bit of the child, nor hadn't since she went off after yourself. Didn't she, Matthew?"

> "My God!" cried Christy, whose very lips were white with terror, "if she has gone down among those rocks! Hannah, where are—"

> "Tis yourself ye have to ask," roared Hannah tempestuously, whose sole thought was to exculpate herself. "She went off with you. I never had her nor seen her since dinner at all."[55]

The neglected Elsie is later found drowned in one of the rock pools. The Carews take her death with a certain degree of insouciance, apart from Lanty who finds the body and Caroline who is afraid that the shock will cause her to miscarry. The whole event leaves a sense of chill behind it, but no deep sense of any loss, much less any implication of responsibility for that loss. It is instructive to contrast the real anguish of the O'Neill family at the death of Esther, which follows shortly after that of Elsie, and it is not clear how deliberate that contrast was meant to be, or how consciously it was arranged.

One is reminded in this connection of the term "moral absenteeism" used by Julian Moynahan to describe that callous disregard of responsibility for others which he perceives as a unique feature of the Anglo-Irish gentry and their imitators, examples of which he found in Somerville and Ross's novel *The Real Charlotte*. In his estimation, "the class most admired for its social grace—its fine manners and speech and mellow way of life—is also the most deficient in meeting moral responsibilities. . . ."[56] The striking portrayal of an unwanted little girl, physically cared for but not loved or protected, adds an unexpected and harsh note to *Christy Carew* which brings it nearer to our own time. The same unconcerned attitude can be found in some of the stories of Molly Keane (1905–1998), arising from the

same aspect of Anglo-Irish culture, apparently unchanged over generations.

Emotionally deprived orphans were not uncommon in Victorian times,
for with comparatively low standards of maternity care, mothers were
more likely to die young, leaving infants whom other adults might well
view as burdensome and whose life expectancy was often shortened if they
did not receive the individual loving care they needed. Elsie Carew, though,
is not an orphan. She is neglected by a family who put their own interests
first. Elsie's presence in this novel of manners lifts the whole story into a different dimension, suggesting as it does that libertarian views have a high
price, and that a conventionally progressive family can also be destructive
to its weakest member.

Comparing, then, each family's actions towards its own vulnerable
child, the Carews appear motivated by material considerations, by self-in-
terest and expediency; and the O'Neills by moral considerations, that is to
say, they do what they think to be right, only—they do not do it with much
skill. Their instinct regarding Neville Jocelyn is, on the evidence, quite reasonable. He is hardly to be considered sincere in his attachment to Esther,
for he does not respect her or her family sufficiently to try to win them over,
or try to see their point of view. Hugh O'Neill, sensing this, is rude to Neville,
whereas some weeks earlier when he turned down the agnostic Dawson as
a suitor for his daughter, he did so in a tactful and sensitive manner.

Hugh personally distrusts Neville, more because of the latter's family
background than for any reason of religious difference. Hugh and his wife
seem aware that Esther would not make a success of a difficult marriage.
The unexpectedly destructive way in which she takes her reversal in love
actually proves them right. Esther becomes depressed, cannot sleep or concentrate, refuses food and eventually succumbs to tuberculosis. Effectively,
she may be said to choose to die because she cannot have what she wants,
and she is unable to see past present loss and into the future. Whatever the
O'Neills thought might be the result of their intervention, they never anticipated this, and are horrified and scarcely able to believe what is happening. From the level of today's knowledge, it seems likely that the outcome of
Esther's adolescent crisis could well have been the same whatever steps her
family took.

But there is also a suggestion that, whereas some people blamed the
Carews for the part Christy and Lanty had played in Esther's romance,
"their position secured them against any disagreeable consequences."[57]

This statement calls our attention to the important place, despite his financial insecurity, that Edward Carew holds in Dublin society. It is also mentioned that, although poor, he comes from an old Irish family and received a good education at a Church of Ireland grammar school, these being factors which helped him to reach his relatively high status. Perhaps he may be compared to Laffan's father, Michael Laffan, a token Catholic in a Protestant Ascendancy world.

Hugh O'Neill's background, we may assume to have been very different to that of Carew. Now a middle-aged man, he would have memories of the famine. As a rigid, rather anxious personality, it would be natural for him to seek to safeguard his family from a repetition of the horrors of the past by controlling and organizing their lives, something he has a gift for, just as also he piles up his material resources because he cannot bear the possibility that his children should want. Mary Josephine does not altogether agree with his views, but understands why he holds them. She, for her part, copes ably with her hostess role at the Mansion House, official residence of the Lord Mayor of Dublin during his year of office, but occasionally she feels she has lost something: "She could not, as a good housekeeper and manager, reconcile herself to that self-effacement as to the commissariat and maintaining of the household which was required of her by the functionaries whose province it was to look after these departments. . . .that made her feel, as she said to her confidant Mrs. Dunne, 'as if she were a guest in her own house.'"[58]

Esther is lonely once the novelty of the Mansion House begins to wear off. Her brothers and sisters are away at school, and Christy is no longer living around the corner. She has nothing to do but take part in the soul-destroying social round, which takes up so much time that it cuts out her voluntary work, and she has no one to confide in, except her bird-witted cousin Philomena Dunne. In such circumstances, the impact of Neville Jocelyn is all the greater. The decision Esther has to make, to go with him or not, appalls her; we are reminded of the similarly circumstanced Eveline in Joyce's short story of that name, who at the last moment lacks courage to join her lover.[59] Esther does not come from a social class, it is implied, where she can exercise choice even in a matter as important as this. She has been trained to obey and she cannot do anything else, even though it may kill her. Meanwhile, her mother, Mary Josephine, experiences distress and foreboding:

She felt at once confused and grieved, injured and indignant; and she had too an unceasing consciousness, gnawing like a pain, that Esther was suffering and ill ... a sad, sore sigh of complaining and helplessness rose from her very heart ... and a tear ran down her nose and off the end of it onto her rich silk dress. . . .

Opposite to her sat Hugh O'Neill, immoveable and grey as ever. His elbows rested on the cushioned arms of the chair and his hands were clasped together before him. . . .

"Mary Josephine," said her husband in his usual low voice, only harsher than usual, "it is useless your troubling yourself."

She only groaned deprecatingly, and again wiped her face.

"No, it is useless. She must repent her folly—her—her misconduct, and make amends."

"She's not to blame, Hugh O'Neill. I'll not sit here and let that be said."

"I say she is, and the mischief is now done; but it must be suffered to go no further. I am responsible—I am answerable,—and it shall not."

She made no answer; his words—"the mischief is now done"—rang in her head.[60]

The O'Neills' method of strict family control has failed them, and they have no knowledge of any other resource to fall back on: "They both belonged to the peasant class, or were but one remove from it, and both shared the peasant feeling, that no [social] intercourse between a young man and a girl is permissible unless with matrimonial intent."[61]

They know that Esther's ready and obvious response to Neville's overtures has already compromised her in many eyes, even to the extent of possibly spoiling her future chances of marriage, but they have yet to find out that they are also condemned, for making no secret of the whole affair. Dublin society liked at least the pretence of discretion. Their acceptance of an honour they thought would advance both their class and their family—for Hugh is described, erroneously, as the first Catholic Lord Mayor of Dublin since the seventeenth century—has only drawn tragedy on them and disgraced them.[62] Their sufferings, too, are worse for having to be borne publicly.

The O'Neills seek medical advice for Esther, and are recommended to take her for the winter to the milder climate of the South of France. This was the usual resource for well-to-do people susceptible to disease of the lungs.

When Mary Josephine brings the seriously ill Esther back to Ireland some months later, the latter insists on returning to their own home, rather than the Mansion House: "She felt it impossible for her to enter again the abode where she had suffered so much, and the mere name of which was to her associated with pain and affliction."[63]

Back in her old room, with all her childhood belongings about her, Esther at last makes her confession and accepts absolution which, up to now, she has refused to do. Her mother begins to realise that this means Esther knows she is dying: "Mrs. O'Neill . . . held the curtain forward with one hand, so as to keep from Esther's view her tear-stained, despairing face, which was every now and again convulsed by a sob, which she could not, with all her efforts, keep back ."[64]

Hugh O'Neill waits downstairs, alone:

The gas had not yet been lighted, and the neglected fire burned dim in an unswept grate: not a sound penetrated the room from without or within, and O'Neill could hear his own hoarse breathing. What was he thinking of as he sat there, his massive grey head bent, and his hard hands clasped on his knees? A cinder fell from the bars, and it startled him. He fancied he heard someone cry out, and he leaped up and listened. No, it was only his fancy; then he began to pace up and down the room, his hands still clasped. A chair was in his way, he pushed it aside roughly with his foot. As he did so, something that was lying on the seat fell heavily on the floor.

It was a large, heavy book. O'Neill picked it up and took it over to the fire to see what it might be. Esther's book of songs, which Philomena had unpacked and left there. There was her name written in gold letters across the cover. He held it in his hands and gazed vacantly at it. Then something stirred within him that gave him a sore pain. Never again would that book be opened, and he let himself fall on his knees on the floor, and bitter sobs, that seemed to wrench his whole frame, shook the very room. So loud were they that the watchers above might have heard them.[65]

Laffan almost seems to hold the O'Neills responsible for their daughter's death, in the sense that a few weeks previously the Carews were for the death of Elsie. If this was what truly was in the writer's mind, it is interesting to speculate on how she justified such a conclusion. A likely hypothesis is that Esther is too weak-minded to challenge her parents, because she is the victim of their "repressive" Catholic upbringing and education. Laffan's ideas regarding Catholic education, expressed throughout all her writings, are extremely negative. She seems to have shared the belief, commonly held and expressed in English fiction of the time, that of all systems the English education system was the best possible, and anything differing from that must of necessity be inferior. In *Hogan MP*, for example, the downfall of that hapless politician is put down to his education at a Catholic college where he was taught by priests.

Priests generally are exceptions to the usually even-handed Laffan approach, being presented as at best weak-minded, at worst overbearing, especially in scenes in which current political opinions are aired. The first of these scenes, early in the story, arises during a party at the O'Neill's. There is a discussion about the results of recent by-elections, and local issues generally. The group hears that a barrister friend of Sugrue's, Farrell O'Gorman, has just been elected for a Mayo constituency:

> "How can he afford to give up his profession, eh?" asked the Canon in a sneering tone, "expects to make something by his patriotism!"

> "He has some private means," hastily rejoined Sugrue, "I think, for the rest, he is thoroughly sincere and honest; in fact, I know he is—an utter visionary." He added the last words, in a lower tone, to himself.

> "Well, we'll live to see how long it will last, once he gets to the other side of the water. There's something in the air there that changes them all, once they get into it."[66]

There was a general belief that, once elected, Irish MPs lost motivation and simply feathered their own nests, and this seems to have been true in some instances. Many of those elected on a Home Rule ticket did not even attend the House regularly. The character Farrell O'Gorman seems to have been a mixture of Frank Hugh O'Donnell[67] and John O'Connor Power,[68] the former of whom shared Laffan's anti-clerical views and was equally critical of Catholic education.

The group continues to speculate about the choice of a dubious political candidate, a "stray bird," in place of a more deserving man who is also a local employer.

"A-a-h! but MacSheehan is a Catholic," said the host, "and Mr. Laurence was a Presbyterian." As O'Neill said this, he compressed his thin, hard mouth, and half-closed his eyes.

> "Aye, aye," said the Canon, taking an enormous pinch of snuff; "no doubt Laurence is a worthy man, and liberal too; oh very, gave a handsome donation to the church there some years ago—a hundred and fifty, indeed!"

"That was very fair," said O'Neill, "I know he was anything but bigoted, rather tolerant, on the contrary. . . . I don't know why it is so, but Dissenters from that church are usually less bigoted than the regular Protestants."

"Because they have a sort of fellow-feeling for your party," put in Sugrue. "They are looked down on and have been ill-treated themselves. . . . they have not the social ascendancy to maintain which the others have—or fancy they have." Sugrue added hastily, for he remembered suddenly that his listeners would probably cavil at that assertion. "Aye—true, true," assented the host, in a constrained tone.[69]

The attempts to achieve a "Union of Hearts" between Catholics and Dissenters, most of whom were supporters of Gladstone and voted Liberal, were being made at this time (1873) but apparently to little long-term effect. Laffan thought that most Catholic clergy though nominally Liberal were really both politically conservative and greedy, and that they would support anyone however corrupt who was likely to make it worth their while. She was bitterly critical also of attempts to ring-fence jobs for Catholics, but ignored the fact that patronage excluded Catholics from many kinds of employment already.[70] Her view is demonstrated when Canon Caffrey is heard to ask O'Neill to use his influence to get a Catholic into the position of doctor to one of the city workhouses. Laffan felt such posts should be allocated on a strictly merit basis to the best person qualified irrespective of religion. But the use of public appointments for political ends is justified by O'Neill, in terms of the need for "positive discrimination," as well as to unite Catholics openly under the same constitutional banner. It is notable that he is prepared to take an active part in local politics, which may not have been strictly in accord with his role as Lord Mayor.

The way in which religious and political issues in *Christy Carew* are dealt with suggests some confusion in Laffan's thinking. On the one hand she seems to argue like an Irish Whig, or Liberal, and feel sympathetic to Presbyterians who tended to be Whigs also, as opposed to members of the Church of Ireland, who were traditionally Conservative. On the other hand she seems to be uncritical of the Imperialist stance taken up mainly by political conservatives. She rarely hints that colonial rule can damage not only the ruled, but the rulers.

There is no doubt that growing up in a family of mixed traditions could account for her unease and ambivalence. It could have the effect of making it impossible to take anything for granted; and sometimes people need to be able to do this. We cannot assume that May Laffan had the security of knowing that her parents were in agreement on the most important aspects of her care and upbringing. We do not know if the religious difference between the Laffan parents led to quarrelling, but it may well have done so. It would be surprising if there was not much disagreement and argument about the children's education, for instance. The class aspect of the religious divide would also have been a factor, and Laffan and her siblings must have contrasted the comfortable, even luxurious lifestyle of one side of the family with the rural simplicity and austerity of the other. At times it would have been hard not to take sides; to see one tradition as totally good and the other as all bad.

This is probably why Laffan contradicts herself occasionally, and why although she disapproves of them, she cannot dislike or castigate the marginalised individuals who appear from time to time in her work. If they do not fit one tradition, the other must have a place for them. In the same way, if she later has difficulty in reconciling her intellectual and literary aspirations with her role as a housewife—she may regard her mother's individualistic tradition as being historically more sympathetic to women who want careers.

The death of Esther is the climax of the novel. Shortly before it happens, Anthony Sugrue goes to London. During this stay he reencounters his friend Farrell O'Gorman MP, and discovers Canon Caffrey's prediction about the latter to be fulfilled: "'My principles, as you are pleased to call the crude ideas with which I started in the political world, have suffered a "sea change". . . . there's an awful fascination about Parliamentary life; there's some fierce magnetism in Westminster that draws and holds a man in spite of himself; conscience, duty, rectitude, all go down before it, you can't help it. Once you have been in, you'll never rest again while without.'"[71]

Sugrue is introduced to the party political scene by Rebutter MP, a Q.C., to whom he has been lent by Carew to help with several tricky cases. A veteran politician and a barrister of great talent, Rebutter leads the Irish party in Parliament but neglects his own law practice. An instance is given of him making lying excuses, and he is pictured as a shifty demagogue flashily dressed and sporting an emerald shamrock tiepin. This character, whose first name is not given, is clearly modeled on Isaac Butt (1813–1879). A lawyer and politician, he was one of the founders of the Home Rule movement and led the Irish Party at Westminster (1870–1879). A flamboyant, warmhearted and popular individual, Butt was a constitutional nationalist and conservative by nature, and he saw Ireland's future as continuing within the British Empire. With declining health, he was unable to be assertive enough to attempt to pursue Home Rule to its limits. Butt was superseded by Charles Stewart Parnell, like himself a member of the Church of Ireland community, but a far harder, more ambitious and forceful man.

Laffan rather unkindly focuses on Butt's weaknesses. He was perpetually in financial difficulties, partly because he had two families to support, one legitimate, one not. Sugrue, whose faults lie not so near the surface, despises Rebutter yet acquits himself so well as his junior that he attracts the attention of a famous Anglo-Irish Q.C., Mr. Sargent, who offers him a permanent job as his assistant—first making sure that he is not a Catholic. Mr. Sargent dislikes Catholics, since his only son has just "gone over to Rome" and been disowned in consequence: "It was a treachery—an abandonment of loyalty, of social position—a degradation in every way."[72] Sargent clearly sees Sugrue as in some sense a replacement for the errant son. His views on Catholicism are given as typical of those held at the time by some Evangelical Protestants; they would appear to be based less on doctrine, than on the felt necessity to have inferiors.

Sugrue's disillusion with party politics is confirmed by what he sees of Westminster. He views the scene with a cynical detachment probably shared by Laffan. Rebutter is lazy, dishonest and the tool of unscrupulous Conservatives. Home Rule is a chimera, just something else with which to deceive the ignorant electorate. The Irish politicians are disorientated for the most part, and no consistent line for them to follow exists. They lack an energetic leader. Parochial issues about petty religious discrimination and the financing of local projects take up all the time of Irish MPs, who should, it is implied, be devoting themselves instead to wider and more weighty matters involving the British Empire and its imperial policy.

An actual example of such an issue is mentioned: the threatened famine at Behar in India, mismanagement of which occasioned an acrimonious debate in the House during April 1874.[73] The debate was one in which Irish MPs—principally Frank Hugh O'Donnell—took an active part not only because the subject had a natural emotional appeal for them; but because one of the officials involved, Sir George Campbell, was well known to have had experience working in Irish famine relief, and to have learned from that experience. The inclusion of this example shows how thorough Laffan could be in setting up an authentic background to a story.

But her general opinion presented in these chapters is that Irish politicians are too inward-looking. They should identify more strongly with the Empire, which after all they had helped to create, and work within the colonial system instead of opposing it. They behave as they do, according to Laffan, because they are educated by the Catholic Church to be passive, resigned, and neglectful of worldly affairs: "'They are asleep over there. They are looking to God and to Parliament for what lies under their own hands to do for themselves, and its the same all through with everything. Their heads are in the clouds. . . . none of the Irish have any energy, have any ambition.'"[74]

None of this applies to Sugrue, of course, because he is a Presbyterian of Huguenot descent, not a degenerate Hibernian. When O'Gorman makes the statement just quoted above, Sugrue remarks that only when MPs are paid a salary will they truly be enabled to represent their constituents. Such men as he, high-principled and tough-minded but without private means, cannot yet aspire to a political career.

Sugrue is shown as one completely disillusioned with Ireland and the Irish—no wonder that, once given a chance, he makes a firm decision to seek his future in London. The political scene as revealed in *Christy Carew* is at about that period in Irish history when a lack of confidence was developing in Isaac Butt's ability to deliver any measure of independence. This feeling had already found expression in November 1873, when the Home Government Association became the Home Rule League, and Fenian influence, resisted by Butt, gradually became more apparent within it.[75]

Apart from the character of O'Gorman, and that of Rebutter who is clearly meant for Isaac Butt, Laffan does not use identifiable models for her parliamentarians in the London scenes. Nor is there as much clerical involvement as in *Hogan MP*. Changes have taken place in Ireland since the by-election which returned Hogan. Lay people are now able to take administrative roles, and they no longer need to use priests as canvassers and election facilitators.[76] Indeed, since the advent of Cardinal Cullen they are discouraged from doing so. But there are still some clerics involved at a higher level, and Canon Caffrey is probably a blend of several who were politically active behind the scenes.[77] Laffan did not approve of priests in politics; it was about the only opinion she shared with Cardinal Cullen.

As usual with Laffan's novels, class, politics and religion are closely intertwined. *Christy Carew* is, however, darker than the other novels, and seems less balanced and impartial, perhaps on that account. The

Protestant Ascendancy, already experiencing removal of the privileges associated with the established church, is growing uneasy at the increasing wealth, size and power of the Catholic majority. Discrimination, insult and snobbery, therefore, can be seen as not very adequate defensive reactions. The Catholic middle class has its divisions also, represented by Edward Carew and Hugh O'Neill. The former has made peace, so to speak, with the Ascendancy, by marrying into it. But he was eligible to do this because of his professional status as a solicitor and because he is pragmatically indifferent to both politics and religion. Hugh O'Neill, devout and patriotic, appears by contrast a fanatic, and is portrayed in terms suggesting seventeenth-century Spain rather than nineteenth-century Ireland:

> Hugh O'Neill had risen from his chair, and was striding up and down the room with stiff measured paces. At the other end, the long stooped black figure was reflected in the great looking-glasses. He stopped suddenly, and casting a look at his wife as if he thought he had heard her say something, said in a hoarse mutter: "Never, never, never!" then resumed his pacing to and fro. What could have been running in his head? There was not room for much imagination to work and ferment among all the prejudices that cumbered that not too spacious receptacle, else one might have thought that the worthy chief-magistrate was rehearsing a role for himself to play later on in some terrible religious and political drama.[78]

In reality O'Neill *is* called later on to play a tragic role, that of a grieving father.

From being a novel of manners, that is, a story which mirrors the society of a particular time and place, *Christy Carew* almost becomes something more—a psychological novel in the harsh tradition of Samuel Richardson's *Clarissa*.[79] By the term "psychological novel" is meant a story in which the personalities of the characters rather than external circumstances decide their fortunes. Clarissa, rashly trusting a man she does not know, ends by willing herself to die because no alternative seems to be left her. In almost the same way Esther O'Neill, accidentally witnessing Neville courting another girl, realises that he has forgotten her and the suffering he caused her, and gives up the will to live.

Christy Carew, the book's nominal heroine, goes on to make a prosperous life with Sugrue in London. She tries to leave behind in the past, along with her memories of Elsie, her memories of Esther who was unable to escape those nets of family and tradition memorably referred to by Joyce, but was caught in them and died in their tangles. Yet, true to her art, Laffan leaves no more poignant and persistent image with us than that of the

O'Neill parents mourning their daughter. Their dignity and tragic grief make a comment on the greed and superficiality displayed by the other characters taking part in the fashionable society of Dublin, the limitations of which are now shown all too clearly.

Reading this curious book it is possible to see why so much was hoped for from Laffan as a writer. It is difficult to think of one other Irish novelist of her time with the same sureness of touch on social class or informed interest in politics, possessing the ability to combine them with a gift for characterization, and a tantalizingly ambivalent approach. Like *Hogan MP, Christy Carew* presents a view of late nineteenth-century Dublin life not always attractive, and certainly not comfortable, but always vivid, interesting and real because it endeavours to give us a three-dimensional picture and displays more than one side to each question.

꧁꧂ CHAPTER 6

Stories of Poverty and Hope

She never thought . . . of the cold, the day-long hunger,
or the probable beating.

Nineteenth-century Ireland was visibly a very poor country, even when the famine had removed from it the poorest rural group. Accounts of travels in and visits to Dublin, the provincial cities and the scenic countryside make that plain.[1] The extent of this poverty could not be glossed over or ignored; it permeated not only factual writings about Ireland, but also her fiction—in stories, verse and songs. Concomitants of poverty, like ignorance, neglect, squalor and disease, affected all classes directly or otherwise and thus motivated the study of ways to make Ireland less deprived. The causes which people then found for Ireland's apparent inability to prosper seemed to fall into two groups: external causes, arising from the way in which the society was structured and thus requiring political will for that society to change; and internal causes originating from the inborn character of the people themselves, requiring *them* to change. On the whole, nationalists held the first view, unionists and conservatives the second.

One of the stereotypical qualities with which the Irish were frequently said to be endowed was cheerful insouciance. It was thought that hardship and deprivation meant little to them, did not depress them, for instance, because they did not feel it. They were not accustomed to anything better, also they were lighthearted and unimaginative. A typical expression of this belief occurs in an anonymous *Spectator* review of May Laffan's best-known story, "Flitters, Tatters and the Counsellor," in which the reviewer notes "the immense joyousness and naivete of the book" and further remarks, "[O]ne feels that it was quite conceivable how Flitters and her companions were always happy, although they never knew how they would get their next meal or where they would find refuge at night."[2]

In reality, as the story makes clear, the three waifs were not at all invariably happy, and were frequently suffering from hunger, cold, and then exhaustion caused by their attempts to find food. The impression made on the reviewer owed something to his own preconceived idea of how poor children felt—he assumed they just did not feel as keenly as he did, and he believed their cheerfulness to be genuine where others might suspect a cover-up. For him to take a different view might put the obligation on him to do something for the children. It was easier, therefore, to think they did not really suffer—it meant they did not need help.

The subject of the review, a "sketch" or short story (rather long, by standards of today, at about eleven thousand words), was first brought out as a little book on its own by Hodges Figgis, Dublin, in 1879 and, later in the same year, by publishers in London, Edinburgh and Aberdeen. It was subsequently reprinted by Macmillan in 1881 in one volume with three other "sketches." These consisted of "Baubie Clarke" (London & Edinburgh: Blackwood, 1880), "The Game Hen" (Dublin: Gill, 1880), and "Weeds" (1881). Apart from "Weeds," the other stories had already been published as small paperbacks, possibly with an eye to the Christmas market.

It may be asked what, apart from their author, these stories have in common. As analysis will show, the four stories actually form a progression, with a unifying theme of poverty and deprivation. The subject group gradually alters from deprived children to equally deprived adults, the scene from an urban to a rural setting, and the atmosphere from resigned acceptance of deprivation to striving against it. In the final story, "Weeds," children appear as peripheral characters only, but in the three other stories they are much more in evidence and in the first two they play central roles.

Stories with children as the central characters became, to judge from the great numbers that were published, immensely popular in Victorian times and not only with child readers. Adults too were moved to admiration and to tears by the emotional death scenes of Charles Dickens's Little Nell and Paul Dombey, or Harriet Beecher Stowe's Evangeline St. Clair. Stories about the sufferings of children generally emphasised their innocence and charm, often to an unreal degree. It is difficult to avoid the impression that in Protestant countries at least, such histories replaced the florid legends of saints in popular Catholic fiction of the time. Some stories about poor children were frank religious tracts, intended to carry a clear and specific moral message home to the reader, and usually quick to point out the consequences of disobedience to authority. Greater weight, on the whole, was attached to conduct than to its motivation, and the administration of justice generally took a retributive form.

It must not be forgotten also that there were other child-centred stories with an appeal to the darker side of the human psyche, stories which, describing in detail the physical punishment of children, verged on what would now be recognised as sadism and pornography. But apart from these extremes, accounts of deprived children helped to awaken public compassion for them and support for the voluntary and statutory services which gradually throughout the nineteenth century undertook responsibility for children's welfare, and in which Laffan was to show a practical interest and involvement in her later years.

Joseph Robins[3] comments on the change of emphasis from needs of adults to needs of children in European social provision of the last quarter of the nineteenth century, and the manner in which fiction writing of the time reflects this change. He suggests that a reduction, evident by the 1850s and probably due to such practical factors as better drainage, in the formerly very high child mortality rates worked to change the attitude of resigned acceptance towards child suffering and early death. A people now aware of the possibility of avoiding *some* premature deaths found they could allow themselves to become more emotionally involved with their children, and to enjoy them more. It is important of course to note the other influences contributing to this change of attitude, such as the spread of popular education and the greater availability of information about the value of childhood experience in relation to adult life.[4] During the nineteenth century, in war-stricken Europe and post-Civil War America many children were wandering homeless and separated from their families. In Ireland particularly, the social upheavals caused in turn by famine and emigration, typhus and cholera epidemics, left numbers of children on the streets, in workhouses, and even in prisons.[5]

Nineteenth-century Ireland was developing a growing but somewhat insecure Catholic middle class, with a buried consciousness of the realities of terrible and haunting deprivation. One way to deal with hidden fear and anxiety is to turn them into popular art, and there was certainly a lively fashion for stories, songs and poems about needy children—for what might be called the whole range of waif-literature, from Hans Christian Andersen's "The Little Match Girl" to music hall songs such as "Won't You Buy My Pretty Flowers," or "On Mother Kelly's Doorstep." Laffan appears to have had a special interest in this genre for, in addition to writing the three stories already mentioned, she translated a novel about child street musicians from the French of Hector Malot, as already mentioned. Her version was published anonymously by Richard Bentley in London in 1886, its original title of *Sans Famille* being rendered as *No Relations*.

No reviews of this translation have yet come to light, but the other stories in the Laffan-Macmillan collection were very favourably received. Referring to "Flitters," Frances Hays, writing in *Women of the Day*,[6] referred to May Laffan as "The Irish Charles Dickens." Another anonymous reviewer in the *Scotsman* praised "a rare combination of realism, humour and genuine pathos. . . . [S]o high a faculty for the dramatic treatment of this peculiar class of subjects has not been revealed in any other writer since Dickens."[7]

This is very fulsome praise, but can the comparison with Dickens be justified? Dickens made explicit some of his aims when he wrote about poverty; he wrote to awaken public concern, and to support specific social reform, for instance the setting up and financing of a specialist hospital for children.[8] His vignettes of street-children illumine lengthy novels. Laffan's "sketches" are self-contained, not parts of anything else, nor do they appear intended directly to influence social policy or to teach moral lessons as many of her contemporaries aspired to do.[9] However, taking into account its somewhat dramatic ending, Laffan's "Flitters" is marked by an absence of sentimentality and a wry, dry humour far removed from Dickens—comparison with whom seems to rest at least in part on a resemblance in the subject rather than in the treatment. Flitters herself, for example, is no Dickens heroine:

> Of the genus street-arab Flitters is a fair type. Barefooted, of course, though were it not for the pink lining that shows now and again between her toes one might doubt that fact—bareheaded too, with a tangled tufted matted shock of hair that has never known other comb save that ten-toothed one provided by Nature, and which indeed Flitters uses with a frequency of terrible suggestiveness.

> The face consists mainly of eyes and mouth; this last-named feature is enormously wide . . . furnished with a set of white, even teeth, which glistened when Flitters vouchsafed a smile, and gleamed like tusks when she was enraged, which was often, for Flitters had a short temper and a very independent disposition . . . with her tawny skin and dark eyes one might have taken her for a foreigner, were it not for the intense nationalism of the short nose and retreating chin and the mellifluousness of the Townsend Street brogue that issued from between the white teeth.[10]

Flitters is not a romantic gypsy, though she looks like one. She is an abandoned child living on the Dublin streets, then a part of the world's richest and most powerful kingdom. The term "street arab," which was first applied to children like her by the social reformer, Lord Shaftsbury, implies a different culture and according to the prejudices of the time, a different and inferior racial background.[11] But her creator makes it clear that Flitters, or Eliza Byrne to give her real name, is actually Irish, not anything else, and her style of life is not hers by choice. Her mother died, and her father deserted her to go to America. Street-singing for a hungry living may be very well in summer; but winter is a different matter, and the glimpses Flitters has of another way of life when she goes to see Mrs. Kelly, her godmother and "the only one who called her by her own name,"[12] impress her deeply. Her friend's act of trust in allowing Flitters to nurse her new-born baby marks the high spot of the girl's existence, suggesting also that Laffan was well aware of deprivation as not being material only. The emotional temperature of the story is much lower than, for example, in the Dickens narrative of the life and death of Jo, the crossing-sweeper in *Bleak House*, but this more controlled manner probably reflects a growing inhibition about showing feelings in the later Victorian period in which "Flitters" was written.

The story covers two summer days in the life of a group of street-children, a girl of eleven (Flitters), a lame boy of nine (The Counsellor), and a six-year-old boy (Tatters). Homeless and destitute, they manage to scrape a living through their own sharp wits and the charity of equally poor women in a Dublin slum known as Commons Lane. Their philosophy is voiced by the Counsellor, "'Sure, won't anyone give ye a bit if ye want it; and so long as you've got a bit to ait [sic] what do you care?'"[13]

The Counsellor, otherwise known as Hoppy, is described thus:

> He might have been ninety, for the Weltkunst his wrinkled, pock-marked countenance portrayed. . . . [He was] one of those people who seem all-sufficient in themselves, and for whom one feels instinctively, and at the first glance, that no one could or ought to be responsible. He had on a man's coat, one tail of which had been removed—by force, plainly, for a good piece of the back had gone with it, giving him an odd look of a sparrow which a cat has clawed a pawful of feathers out of.[14]

Hoppy is the organising genius of the group in which Flitters is the performer and chief earner, while the role of dependant member is played by Tatters,

. . . [who was] about six years old, small and infantine of look, but with a world of guile in his far-apart blue eyes. . . . He had an interesting, sweet little face; his little black nose was prettily formed; a red cherry of a mouth showed in the surrounding dirt , and gave vent to the oaths and curses of which his speech was mainly composed, in an agreeable little treble pipe.[15]

"Flitters, Tatters & the Counsellor" describes a children's world, albeit a harsh one, in which adults appear occasionally and usually when things have gone wrong. The spotlight is very much on the three children—their code of behaviour, their interaction, their individual characters. Following a string of entertaining incidents, the climax of the story is reached when Flitters stops to watch a street fight between two drunken draymen. She recognises one of them as her godmother's husband, Hugh Kelly, and promptly joins in the fight to help him. Not recognising her, Hugh knocks Flitters down and she is trampled underfoot, rescued by the police and taken to hospital unconscious and seriously injured. Both combatants are arrested, and when Flitters recovers consciousness they are brought before her so that she can identify, under oath, the one who hit her. The dying Flitters realises that if she names Hugh it will have terrible consequences for his wife and family. Accordingly, she denies that either man hit her, and dies in a heroic manner with the perjured testimony on her lips.

John Ruskin, the celebrated art and literary critic, commended the story "Flitters" highly, but in a fashion which underlines some differences between Victorian and present-day perceptions. He thought the death of Flitters totally appropriate, his idea being that life could hold nothing for such girls anyway. Ruskin had, since the death of his early sweetheart Rose La Touche, an obsessive interest in tales about adolescent girls.[16] He had also read and approved another Laffan story, "Baubie Clarke." What seemed to matter most to him was that the incidents related should be closely based, as in "Baubie Clarke," on actual occurences. He had been disappointed to learn from Laffan that the death of Flitters was made up:

> The study of those three children, given by Miss Laffan, is, in the deepest sense, more true as well as more pathetic than that of Baubie Clarke—for Miss Laffan knows and sees the children of her own country thoroughly, but she has no clear perceptions of the Scotch. Also, the main facts concerning Tatters and Flitters and their legal adviser are all true—bitterly and brightly true; but the beautiful and heroic death was—I could find it in my heart to say, unhappily—*not* the young girl's. Flitters, when last I heard of her, was still living her life of song, such song as was possible to her. The death, so faithfully and beautifully told, was actually

that of an old man, an outcast like herself. I have no doubt Flitters could, and would, have died so, had it become her duty, and the entire harmony of the story is perfect; but it is not so sound, for my purpose here, as the pure and straightforward truth of Baubie Clarke.[17]

It is interesting, and perhaps significant, to note from the above that Ruskin apparently did not like the way in which writers of fiction use their material, changing and moulding it in the service of their art, rather than leaving it plain and without creative additions. He seems to have had a literal notion of the nature of truth, and a consequent preference to see it unadorned, and these qualities must be unusual to find in the successful writer of a celebrated fairy tale.[18] Perhaps Ruskin's attitude arose from his evangelical upbringing, for as his contemporary Trollope was to discover, Dissenters belonging to the strict Calvinist tradition tended to view all fiction with suspicion.[19]

Ruskin went on to offer a critique of "Baubie Clarke," the second of the sketches to be published. Baubie is a twelve-year-old Edinburgh street-child described as "a stunted, slim creature, that might have been any age from nine to fourteen."[20] She is a street singer like Flitters, and the mainstay of a family consisting of a violent alcoholic mother and a father of low intelligence. Both parents go simultaneously to jail, the mother for causing a fight, the father for disobeying an official warning not to let Baubie sing in the streets. Yet Baubie enjoys her singing, which furnishes her with an artiste's role in life:

> To be commended for knitting and sewing was no distinction worth talking about. What was it when compared with standing where the full glare of the blazing windows of some public house fell upon the Rob Roy tartan, with an admiring audience gathered round and bawbees and commendations flying thick? She never thought . . . of the cold, the day-long hunger, or the probable beating.[21]

The story concerns Baubie's successful escape from a children's home in order to rejoin her father when he leaves the prison. Baubie is intelligent and resourceful, for though illiterate she contrives a way to calculate the day on which her father is to be discharged; and she is mature enough to be ready to assume again her difficult role as his guide and minder. Baubie, replacing the drab institutional clothes with her original red tartan dress, absconds from the children's home early in the morning of the right day, makes her way to the gaol gate, and in the final scene of the story is shown leading her father along the road to Glasgow, where relatives live who can help them start a new life, beyond the reach of the violent and terrifying Mrs. Clarke.

Evocative, convincing and carefully written as it is, "Baubie Clarke" misses some of the vigour of "Flitters." What it does, though, is illustrate both its writer's grasp of the laws relating to the protection of vagrant children (laws which at that time operated in Scotland and England but not Ireland, and which were aimed at preventing parents from exploiting children for money) and the limitations of institutional care available at that time.

Baubie, taken by the welfare officer from the Sherriff's Court to a home for girls, is scrupulously washed and tidied: "Miss Mackenzie surveyed her with great satisfaction, the brown wincey and the coarse apron seemed to her the neophyte's robe betokening Baubie's conversion from arab nomadism to respectability, and from a vagabond trade to decorous industry."[22] However, no attempt whatever is made on the part of the welfare worker or the staff to allow for the feelings of a child suddenly separated from her father and her familiar life. The marks of beating observed on her thin body are questioned, but when Baubie is reluctant to talk about her home life this is accepted as final, and matters are allowed to rest so. The child's needs are seen wholly in terms of food, shelter, clean clothes and useful occupation. It is, of course, far simpler to provide these than to supply understanding and affection, and it must be remembered that the Society for the Prevention of Cruelty to Children (SPCC) was not then in existence to question the right of a parent to ill-treat a child. Baubie, in the children's home, is to be given training in the skills and subservience required of domestic servants, for that is what the home destines all the children to be. Baubie, a strong character, does not care to see herself in this light: "Artist-like, she remembered only her triumphs; she could earn two shillings by her brace of songs, and for a minute, as she revelled in this proud consciousness, her face lost its demure watchful expression, and the old independent confident bearing reappeared."[23]

Laffan here shows a degree of sympathy with people who do not fit the welfare system of her time, of which the Scottish provision was a relatively positive example. She shows understanding of the need for Baubie to keep her self-respect and her identity as an entertainer intact, for they are all she has. One of the reviewers of "Baubie Clarke" in the *Aberdeen Free Press* commented on the serious thoughts which this glimpse into the lowest stratum of society is fitted to call up. And along with this an uneasy questioning whether we have yet hit upon the most judicious mode of civilising such young barbarians, even after they are caught, cleansed, clothed, fed and set on the highway to acquire a useful education.[24]

This attitude which Laffan evidently shared with this reviewer was most unusual for that time, if one can go by the number of waif stories which avoid exploring the feelings of destitute children at all, except to describe miraculous changes wrought in them by study of the Bible. Perhaps sensing Laffan's indirect criticism of the system, Ruskin, disagreeing with the *Aberdeen Free Press*, the *Aberdeen Journal* and the *Scotsman* of January 1881, said he thought that she had not got "Baubie Clarke" quite right—maybe it was not true? Or not true enough? Laffan, in a letter quoted by Ruskin in his article, strongly protested:

> "It all happened in Edinburgh, exactly as I relate: I went into every place in which this child was, in order to describe them and her, and I took great pains to give the dialect exactly. I remembered how disappointed you were to learn that Flitters' death was not true;—this story is quite true, from first to last."[25]

"The Game Hen," third of the Laffan stories about poverty, is the most complex and melodramatic, recalling as it does the slum episodes in Victor Hugo's *Les Miserables* [26] or indeed, as a reviewer in the Dublin *Warder and Weekly Mail* suggested with disapproval, the work of Zola himself.[27] The scene is again Commons Lane on the south side of the Liffey, where an open sewer runs between a double row of wretched cabins. At the far end of the lane is a neglected field, at the street end a brothel. The sinister Mrs. Carmody lives in a cabin in the field, collects rents for the hovels, and bullies all the tenants except the gasfitter's wife Mrs. Dowling, who alone has the confidence to stand up to her.

The complicated social life of Commons Lane is not idealised or made deliberately entertaining. It is shown to be just as formal in its way as social structures elsewhere in Irish nineteenth-century society. At the top of the class structure are Mrs. Carmody and her partner Paudheen. They have a monopoly on power, since they collect the rents of the other inhabitants, and they also have relative wealth—owning, as well as a horse and cart, two of the cabins, which "were both let, as Mrs. Carmody preferred the sensation of being landlord to other people."[28]

The Carmodys set the social standards and are feared by their neighbours, with the exception of the outspoken Mrs. Dowling. The Dowlings have a large family, but no debts, and will be leaving Commons Lane when they have outgrown its attractions. A couple named Brady, and the Connollys, an elderly pair of fruit-hawkers, are residents much further down the scale. The Bradys are moreover childless, which is held to tell against them. Right at the scale's lowest point are the three women in the brothel at the top of the lane, and of these, only "Peggy" is named in the story. "Peggy" tries to make friends with a newcomer to the lane, Honor Walsh, a young countrywoman like herself. Honor's husband being in prison, she picks rags to keep herself and her two children—Petie, a strange little boy, probably autistic, who never speaks except to echo others; and a four-month-old baby girl who is not her husband's child and is never given a name. Honor Walsh seeks to distract attention from her own misdemeanours by treating "Peggy" with special contempt—a strategy which completely fails to deceive anyone. Laffan explains that "Peggy's" way of life has not hardened her:

> She was a country girl, as we know, barely more than twenty, though there was
> little to tell of youth or the country either in her haggard white face. She had a
> gentle subdued manner and a sweet voice. . . . [E]ven her dread of the fierce, con-
> temptuous looks of Mrs. Walsh did not restrain her from showing kindness to
> those two desolate little creatures. . . . [T]he others either knew what she was or
> aped unconsciously their parent's manner to her. Petie's mental infirmity and
> the baby's youth forbade this, so she had them in a way all to herself.[29]

"Peggy" realises that Honor excites anger in the others, but does not understand why. The reason is that, unlike "Peggy," Honor is not at all prepared to accept the lowly place she has been given in the social structure of Commons Lane, and she resists attempts to make her conform:

> The determined and cruel way in which these women closed up their ranks
> against [Honor] afforded a curious contrast to their attitude towards the black
> sheep of the place. . . . [T]hey were disapproved, certainly, . . . nevertheless their
> position was an easier one. . . . [T]he line of demarcation was in their instance
> laid down and acknowledged by both sides as tangible and real, whereas in the
> other it was only in process of creation."[30]

Defensive and reserved, Honor discourages intimacy, the more so because she has actually identified "Peggy" as Mary, the missing sister of her lover William Kennedy. Honor wants to hide from her lover but also from her betrayed husband who is due out of prison shortly, and of whom she is mortally afraid. She has come to Dublin in order to lose her past and begin again.

But she finds it impossible to do this in Commons Lane. Her reserve acts as a challenge to the other residents; they taunt her, and victimise her when they find out from a travelling huckster[31] about her past; and Honor, nicknamed the "Game Hen"[32] for her aggression, literally fights back. Mrs. Carmody reveals Honor's history to her employers, and they dismiss her. Honor's growing anger and desperation lead her to drink heavily and neglect her two children, leaving them to the care of "Peggy." Finally, she attacks Mrs. Carmody, beats her up and is arrested. An hour later, William Kennedy turns up, seeking Honor to tell her that her husband is dead, and to offer to marry her. Mrs. Dowling tells him about the arrest, referring him to "Peggy" as the present carer of the children. William tries to get Honor released; then finding he is too late and she is in prison, he returns to interview "Peggy." Petie, not understanding where his mother is, has fallen asleep waiting for her by the archway into the lane. He is awakened by overhearing the dialogue between "Peggy" and her brother:

> "We thought to hear of you every day. . . . [W]e all thought you had gone out to America, to Margaret, without telling us, in a freak. Oh My God, but I've been punished this day! And to find you here, you of all!"

> He had thrown himself against the railing, standing always between her and the door of the house they had left.

> "There, I have the money with me; I meant to—I was late, one half-hour late, an' she's in prison. I'll take you now this minute to the Liverpool boat on the North Wall. She goes at eight, av you'll only say the word, an' leave this place of perdition for ever."

> She had hidden her face in her shawl, and a long, half-choked sob was the only sign she made of having heard him.

> "Mary, raise yourself, for God's sake I implore you! Go."

> The muffled sobs came faster and thicker. She had thrown one arm round the spikes of the railings and rested her head upon it, and the tossed brown curls were hanging in disorder about her face. . . .

> "O God, O God! How can I go?"

> "Go!" echoed Petie, whose dull ear the half scream had reached, startling him . . .

.

The clear strange note of the child's voice fell on the two without as if it came from above.

"Did you—did you hear that?" the girl gasped. . . .

With one simultaneous impulse they took each others' hands and passed from before the archway and down the street, and then towards the river, eastwards, the red morning sun kissing Peggy's face as she turned towards it, and gilding her brown head as with a glory.[33]

As melodramatic as the ending of the story of "Peggy" is, it illustrates the use of emigration, in fiction as in life, as a way of removing marginal people—the abandoned mistress in "Weeds" is also sent to America when her lover marries, and this solution seems, according to George Moore, to have been usual at the time.[34] Laffan evidently had no inhibition about offering the "fallen" "Peggy" a way to change her life, whereas some contemporary English novelists saw death, preferably heroic death, as the only way a woman could atone for sexual deviance.[35]

Found shortly afterwards by the Dowlings, Petie is taken to the police and then, as a vagrant, committed to the newly-founded industrial school at Artane. On arrival, he meets two other boys from Commons Lane—Paul and Peter Cassidy—who turn out to be Tatters and the Counsellor. (In default of any records about them, the managers of the school have assumed the two to be brothers.) They are shown as changed members of society. Peter (the Counsellor) is now an industrious shoemaker's apprentice; Paul (or Tatters) is cheerfully hoeing cabbages, a job given to him in acknowledgement of his liking for an open-air life. Clearly they are rehabilitated, in Laffan's estimation, but clearly also, Petie is never going to be able to reach their level.

Honor's unnamed baby daughter is adopted by the Dowlings and brought up with their own children, perhaps as restitution for the rejection of her mother. Therefore the unfortunate Honor may be said to have lost everyone close to her. Only Honor's infant girl excites compassion enough to make her inclusion in a family possible. This is demonstrated in a scene where Mrs. Dowling intervenes to prevent "Peggy" encouraging Petie to take the infant with him on a begging expedition:

"Girl, no one that knows anything 'ud spake ov such a thing; the polis even wud'nt allow it." The lofty, distant manner with which Mrs. Dowling conveyed this piece of information to Peggy was in its way inimitable. . . . "Deed then," she said, addressing the baby, "but yer time enough into hardship, God help ye, an' not be put to cadgin' this early time o' yer life."[36]

Honor Walsh's own pride, aloofness and self-respect led to her undoing—had she been more concerned to "fit in," to please the public opinion of the Lane, her tragic history would not have evolved as it did. With Cosmo Saltasche and Helena Ferrard she is yet another of Laffan's marginalised characters.

Between them these three stories show us a range of children with differing circumstances and needs. Flitters and Baubie are both streetwise, illiterate adolescent girls in vulnerable situations. Left to themselves their futures would certainly come to include petty crime and prostitution. Middle-class young women tried to teach girls like these the elements of literacy, in a project run in the Liberties by Fr. Charles P. Meehan of the *Nation,* and referred to both in "Flitters" and in *Christy Carew*.[37] Once literate, the girls would have a chance of getting work. Thus, the "ragged schools" of English cities had counterparts in Irish cities, organized by members of religious congregations or voluntary lay groups. Laffan remarks that at the period when she is writing, education is not yet compulsory in Ireland, and she shows us Mrs. Kelly trying without success to persuade her goddaughter Flitters to go to the literacy classes.

Tatters, whose real name no one including himself knows, offers an example of the workings of nineteenth-century infant care. He was born in the maternity ward of a workhouse, the usual refuge of unsupported pregnant women. Infants born in workhouses were frequently left there. Their deathrate within the institution was shockingly high, approaching 95%. So they were usually, at the time of which Laffan wrote, fostered out until deemed old enough to survive back in the workhouse. Apparently, when the money paid by the Dublin corporation for his foster care ran out, Tatters was not returned to the workhouse as he should have been—he was just abandoned.[38] At six or seven he is an accomplished thief, drinks beer, smokes and has a gambling habit. He would also be too little to cope with street life if it were not for Flitters, who supports all three children by her singing. Hoppy the Counsellor, intelligent, literate and angry, has a deformed foot for which he has received no treatment and which debars him from most work available to an unskilled person. He was reared by a grandmother, and so is possibly a genuine orphan, his street career being a consequence of the grandmother's death. A charity boarding school would, if adequately funded and managed, help such a child to an independent and satisfying life.[39] Unfortunately such institutions tended to start well, but then lost impetus, as only industrial schools received government support. Lastly, Petie Walsh, who has both an intellectual and a communication disorder, lacking the skills of other children, will probably not survive long on the streets unless he gets help. In accordance with the thinking of the time, this is most likely to take the form of restrictive care in an institution.

The needs of the five children are actually resolved in various ways. Flitters, as has been seen, meets a death described by Ruskin (representing one school of thought) as heroic. She is nursed, while dying, in what seems to be Jervis Street Hospital, where she experiences for the first time a measure of good care from the Irish Sisters of Charity. Laffan felt in two minds about nursing nuns, grudgingly recognising their skills, but seeming almost annoyed at their detachment, though partly aware of the need for it: The nun "was well used to these scenes; and tender and gentle as her voice sounded, the ring was that of the kindness of experience rather than that of sympathy. The form remained, though by constant habit the force behind was somewhat spent."[40]

Something of the extent of practical help dispensed in convents of the time is demonstrated when Tatters, assumed to be Flitters's brother, is given a meal and clothes by the nuns when he visits her in the hospital. The Reverend Mother, in response to Flitters's dying request, promises both boys will be provided for, by arranging their admission to Artane Industrial School. From the detail of her description of Artane in action, Laffan must have seen it herself, and though in later life extremely critical of Catholic institutions she seems to have approved of this one. Here she describes Petie's first sight of his future home:

> Petie glanced round him timidly. Two great fields lay on either side of the roadway, planted with potatoes in long even drills; the strong growing smell of them filled the air. There were trees everywhere, and all around the white house a blaze of flowers. . . . [T]he glass doors of the entrance flew open. . . . [T]hey entered together a large hall painted a clean, cool, green colour. In this hall was standing... an old priest — tall and thin, and with a kind, wrinkled face. "Good morning, sergeant, good morning," he replied in a pleasant voice; "only one this time, eh?"...
>
> They had walked round the house, and came to a great building situated at its back. A door opened, letting out an extraordinary sound, a kind of low murmur, like that of swarming bees, and mingled with it and rising above it the rapid click clack of sewing machines. A long hall lay before them with two rows of benches,

the inner one higher than the other, along the wall, and on these benches sat about a hundred small boys, all of them under ten, some of them not yet six years old. Each had on a clean white blouse and a pair of red slippers.

Everybody was working; some tiny creatures had crochet needles in their hands, some were knitting, and others stitching. More advanced ones were tending the sewing machines, which they worked with a gravity and steadiness that was wonderful. The boards of the floor were scoured white, the paint was fresh and clean, and through the tall, open windows came sweet-smelling country air. . . . [T]hey went on to a low wooden building that ran round three sides of a playground. This building was composed of workshops—tailor's, carpenter's, joiner's, painter's—boys were learning trades in all parts of it as they passed through....[41]

Artane was at that time (1870s) newly opened and consequently smaller than it afterwards became. The majority of boys Laffan described seeing there were street children, who would not all have been seriously delinquent or have presented great management problems to the inexperienced staff, as did the intake of later years. It is possible therefore that the favourable impression made—not only of Artane's external appearance, but of the individual way the boys were cared for—was not entirely mistaken. The value of a remote country location to boys reared in city streets might be questioned now, but to the Victorians it was almost an article of faith, as evidenced by the fact that almost all children's institutions built in that period were situated in the country or by the sea, as far as possible from the city air which was thought to generate disease.

There are some obvious inaccuracies in Laffan's account of Artane. For example, she refers to the staff as priests, but they were actually monks—Christian Brothers. They were strict about refusing to take boys with obvious intellectual disabilities or communication difficulties, so Petie would not have been eligible. She was mistaken also in her belief that Artane industrial training was accepted as part of apprenticeship—unfortunately it was not, at least in the twentieth century, as trades unions were not prepared to agree to that. This had implications when boys leaving the institution tried to get employment.[42] In the short term, the boys learnt industrial and craft skills because these were essential to the economic working of the whole system, a real "total institution," which could not function unless self-sufficient in clothing, food and maintenance.[43] Laffan seems to have internalised the idea, expressed by Harriet Martineau[44] and those who shared her views, that continual manual activity of some kind was necessary to occupy the poor, even poor children, lest they give way to delinquency and to idleness, which was considered to be a sin for people in their station in life. But it evidently did not occur to Laffan to ask about other aspects of institutional life—for instance education, discipline, and sanctions or punishments.

It was then fashionable for people interested as Laffan undoubtedly was in the welfare of children to go to see the new institutions for themselves. There are records of notables like Lady Wilde, with her children, visiting the reformatory at Glencree in the 1860s. But Laffan's brief impressionistic account in "The Game Hen" is, so far as known, the earliest written description of Artane, which with its eventual 1,000 pupils was the largest of the Irish institutions for children.[45]

The abusive behaviour found out to have occurred at Artane in the twentieth century does not seem to have been a feature of the nineteenth. This may be due at least partly to the smaller numbers of child inmates then, and the greater public interest in them. It may also have to do with the changing nature, over time, of the client group. The street children for whom Artane was originally founded were homeless and without parental involvement, and any offences they had committed came under the general heading of vagrancy. Gradually there were fewer of these children to be admitted, and more who came into institutional care either with existing behavioural disorders, or damage already acquired within dysfunctional families. These children would need help which the institution could not supply; and, lacking it, they would be difficult to control and exceptionally vulnerable to abuse.[46]

Baubie Clarke, the Scottish street-girl, found her own encounter with institutional care disheartening. Her Rob Roy tartan dress was taken away, her curls were cut off, and, worst of all, she was not allowed to sing the Jacobite[47] songs which were her stock-in-trade, or indeed to sing anything else. Small wonder if the prospect of living with her aunt in Glasgow held out a more interesting future. Her creator shows us that the lure of a vagrant life was, for some children, very strong indeed. Laffan also implies that a somewhat rigid outlook inspired the Scottish system of welfare.

Irish child care of the time (the 1870s) was starting at least to be organized and staffed by people of the same religion and culture as the children.[48] The religious institutions were not without critics. One comment often made, and probably valid, was that convent-based residential institutions did not do enough to prepare girls to cope with the outside world.[49] It was also true that late-nineteenth-century Irish society made rather more and better provision for children at risk of becoming criminals than for disabled children; this reflected a poor understanding of disability, as much as any intention to make a value judgement. In Ireland, as else-where in Europe, services for children were moving away from an exclusively institutional model, but doing so very slowly.

On 10 July 1881 Laffan wrote to her publisher George Macmillan to tell him that her new "sketch" was almost ready for submission. This was good news—the sketch being needed as soon as possible to add to the three others for publication in book form. But first it was to appear in *Macmillan's Magazine,* of which George Grove was editor. As has already been mentioned, he initially was not happy about "Weeds," because in his view it seemed to condone if not to support the use of violence to achieve political ends. George Macmillan, although appealed to by Laffan, supported his editor's decision, and she reluctantly had to revise her story to suit them. Unfortunately, we only have the amended version. We can, though, make some attempt to work out a theory as to why the revision had to be made, and what form it took, and for that it is necessary to refer briefly to the historical background of the story.

"Weeds" is set in a period commonly referred to as the first phase of the Land War (1879–1884). Ireland is shown attempting to move away from a situation where almost all the agricultural land, sole wealth of a poor country, is owned by members of the colonial elite and rented by them to the native Irish, in most cases without the security of a lease and without obligation even, as would be the case in England, to supply houses for tenants or to finance improvement of the land. Irish representation in the English parliament has brought about some changes, but not enough to satisfy what is gradually becoming a demand for devolved government—for "Home Rule." The Land League, instituted by Michael Davitt in Mayo in 1879, and expanded by Charles Stewart Parnell, aims ultimately at peasant proprietorship, empowering Irish people to control their own resources. This prospect has grave implications for an England accustomed to using Ireland as a food-store, and as a source of men and horses for the wars of the nineteenth century. So, by 1881, at the time when "Weeds" is being written, the Irish National Land League has been declared an illegal organization and its heads imprisoned. While they are in custody, there is a marked increase in crimes of agrarian violence in Ireland. Landlords and their agents are shot, people who cooperate with the authorities are threatened, property is destroyed by fire, and farm animals are mutilated. Fearing a full-scale revolt, the colonial government floods the country with soldiers and uses them to enforce the law, for example, at evictions. Extra local taxes are levied on the already poor to pay for the military presence.[50] Anyone who publishes anything, in fact or fiction, which appears sympathetic to the Land League, finds themselves in serious trouble.

The main message Laffan delivered to her public in "Weeds" was that when people driven to desperation by injustice commit unlawful acts, their provocation should be taken into account and the guilt shared with those whose indifference or negligence contributed to the injustice in the first place. She must have had difficulty in conveying this idea to her publishers, whose letters to her elicited a somewhat defensive protest: "The alterations you suggest shall be made though it is against my principles. . . . Still, in this case you are right undoubtedly and I had better not appear as the apologist of crime. . . . I shall do all I can with the sketch to tone down the bad pre-eminences."[51]

Unfortunately copies of the letters from Grove and Macmillan to which Laffan refers either were never made or were destroyed and are not now to be found in the Macmillan letter-books. Also missing from the archive at Reading University are her letters to George Macmillan on the subject of the Land League, to which he refers very discreetly in later correspondence: "I'm glad you stop before the 'No Rent' cry. We are tremendous admirers of the Irish as you know, especially of the author of Flitters, Tatters and the Counsellor and other brilliant productions. I sincerely hope you will not be lodged at the public expense—harder than in Montagu Place![52] But your letters are rather dangerous?"[53]

Shortly before publication of the Laffan stories, including "Weeds," the Ladies' Land League,[54] a branch of the National League organized by Parnell's sister Anna, and which had not been suppressed, became active in the matter of tenants on the Kingston estate in Co. Cork. A monster meeting was held locally on 5 December 1880, and a Rent Strike involving 400 tenants took place, which was to last until April 1882. In spite of publisher's censorship, which would have removed all Laffan's references to the Land League, "Weeds" in its amended version comes across as openly sympathetic to the urgency of the need for radical change to provide security for tenants. Gladstone's Land Act (1881), though it excluded leaseholders, was to grant some of the others fair rent, free sale, and fixity of tenure.[55]

Laffan's three earlier "sketches" had dealt with the urban poor, and with vagrancy and petty crime. "Weeds," written later, was different, being a detailed and realistic account of the murder of an unpopular land agent and the circumstances leading up to this. In fact, some of the adults in the story are in almost the helpless position of the poor children earlier described. Almost, but not quite. They are more keenly aware that the system which oppresses them is unjust, and they know that they can take steps to alter it, at least temporarily. One of these steps is the use of violence.

The story begins on a market day in early August in "Galteetown" (probably Mitchelstown, Co. Cork). Countrywomen discuss the latest news: Lawder, agent to the local absentee landlord, has just married again after a three-year period as a widower, during which time he joined the Church of Ireland. He also seduced his housekeeper Mary Clifford, a local girl, on promise of marriage. The bride he brought home last Friday (an unlucky day anyway) was not, however, his mistress, but a girl from the Protestant middle-class set he has joined, a girl who brought him a dowry of four thousand pounds—an unimaginable sum to the local women, who predict bad luck to the couple.

Later, two tenants' wives start their journey back home up the mountains—the prosperous one Maryanne Roche giving Mary Heffernan, the poorer one, a lift on her ass-cart. Mary's attempt to propitiate the bank manager with chickens (to renew their loan) having failed, she laments their probable eviction. When their son comes home from England, he may insist on going to America, and what will they do then? As it is, after three generations on the mountain, they have very little:

> The flickering light of the turf showed the interior in all its poverty. An old dresser, in the boards of which there were great cracks, held half a dozen plates and three jugs, only one of which was not past its work—a few cups, all of different colours and shapes, hung from nails and a black teapot, with a broken nose, occupied one corner of a shelf, where it had long enjoyed a holiday. The churn was laid away in a corner. It was close on a year since the cow had been sold, and there was no pig.[56]

The daughters in America have been ill and cannot send any money, the son in England has lost his job. The only purchases Mary could make in Galteetown were a sack of maize meal and a bit of tobacco for her ailing husband.

The better-off Roches, tenants of a bigger farm lower down the mountain, are shown living not very differently from the Heffernans: "There was the same clay floor, the turf burning on the hearthstone—everything was much the same, but there seemed to be more of it . . . the same smell of turfsmoke, of featherbed, of hens and in this instance of sour milk also."[57]

Nothing is mended or planned; and in the fields poppies and ragwort flourish, but the weeds of the title are also human weeds. The children, out of school, enjoy themselves and have few duties. Sprawling hedges and great ditches take up land that could be used to grow food, for Tom Roche is a lazy farmer:

> Nothing could be more thriftless or untidy than his method of farming; a gap was stopped with a bush, a cartwheel or a plough, just as his father and grandfather had done before him. He steadfastly ignored all improvements and hated novelties. . . . [H]e never saw the hideous squalor of his own daily life. The habits of centuries are not so easily rooted out, especially when interest and national prejudice combine to preserve them.[58]

But the main reason behind the preservation does not escape Laffan:

> Lawder had been agent for seven years, and had with impunity raised rents here and there, wherever an improving tenant had built a couple more rooms to his house, that his growing-up daughters might be separated from their brothers and from the farm servants; or if he observed that they were taking good crops off the land, though it might have been bog when the tenant got it. . . . [T]here was no law to help them.[59]

As night falls, Tom Roche and other local men gather in the back room of the Cross Roads pub to plan Lawder's killing. An Enfield rifle is produced, admired, and lovingly handled. There are at least two spies present, so although a nominal assassin—the absent James Heffernan—is picked by lot, the "inner circle" knows the real perpetrator is going to be someone else—Charles, brother of the discarded Mary Clifford: "Lawder must be stopped by someone, and Clifford was the right man to do it."[60]

Clifford does accomplish the assassination of the agent, shooting him from cover, as the latter smokes a cigar on the steps of his house. The killing takes place almost within sight of the new Mrs. Lawder and her little stepson. Clifford then fords a wide river—the Suir—and, handing the rifle to Heffernan to dispose of, escapes for several miles across country and takes refuge in a Catholic chapel, where worshippers provide Heffernan and himself with alibis. Laffan adds that "the reward of five hundred pounds [is] added to the accumulation of blood-money in Dublin Castle."[61] This implies that the crime remains unsolved. It also suggests that few were prepared to inform against those who broke the law, even seriously. Local farmers like Tom Roche might not be prepared to carry out agrarian crimes themselves, but neither are they prepared to refuse to help someone bent on revenge for a personal injury.

"Weeds" does not lack interest today. It is vividly told, and the tension, the sense of being present, being near to what is actually going on, is well maintained. But it is interesting as well because it illustrates Laffan's methods. She seems to have pillaged more than one true account to make one fiction, and she refers to her main source thus: "This story is perfectly true and the scene town and place are all fresh in the recollection of the Tipperary people. It makes it all the harder to manage."[62]

Laffan here seems to be alluding to one in particular of several similar accounts, the murder in 1857 of John Ellis, agent to John Trant of Dovea, Loughmore, North Tipperary. The Cormack brothers, employees of Trant, were accused of shooting Ellis through a hedge as he was driven home at night from the local railway station. Evidence against the Cormacks rested entirely on the testimony of two unreliable young men, plus the presumption of a strong revenge motive, because Ellis, a noted seducer of servant girls, had made sexual advances to both the Cormack sisters. The case was tried by Judge William Keogh, whose unpopularity with Tipperary people was due to his perceived political treachery in 1852, and also to his close past association with the speculator John Sadlier, the failure of whose schemes a year previously had ruined a number of small investors in the Tipperary Joint Stock Bank.[63]

It was not usual practice at that time to convict on the main evidence of "improvers," that is, accomplices of the accused, but for reasons which still remain unclear, on this occasion it was permitted to happen. Turning Queen's Evidence to convict former friends was financially worthwhile, for the least one could hope to get would be a free passage to one of the colonies, with a suitable emigrant's outfit included. Such rewards must have been very tempting to poor young men especially if they already had reason to be unpopular at home. As givers of evidence, the two informers concerned were not convincing, and one could question why they were believed so readily, apparently without much attempt to investigate their accounts. One possibility is that as a landlord Trant wielded enough power to control events. The motive for this crime, as Trant reasoned, could not possibly be agrarian—that was not to be thought of, as he thought he was a good landlord. It must be therefore a case of personal revenge on Ellis, a middle-aged Scotsman unpopular in the district. John Gore Jones R.M.,[64] the local investigating magistrate, shared Trant's opinion. He also went so far as to imprison illegally one Ann Brophy, a twelve-year-old servant girl, for two months, apparently because some evidence she gave was not explicit enough to use against the Cormacks, and he felt—mistakenly as it happened—that a prison sentence might stimulate her memory.

A petition to the authorities, signed by local clergy and laity of all classes and denominations failed. William and Daniel Cormack were duly tried, condemned, and publicly executed in Tipperary in April 1858 outside Nenagh jail, both protesting their innocence to the last. On four occasions in the summer of 1858 the case was raised in the House of Commons by The O'Donoghue, M.P. asking for an enquiry on the grounds that the evidence offered had been unsound and the whole was a miscarriage of justice. This was denied, and The O'Donoghue suggested that the authorities were concerned more to get a conviction, than to distinguish between the guilty and the innocent.

Fifty years later (1910), the Cormacks were exhumed from the prison yard and their remains, expensively coffined, placed ceremoniously in a vault in Loughmore graveyard, with an inscription engraved by Joseph K. Bracken, a Fenian and a connection of the Laffan family, denouncing comprehensively Judge Keogh, the jury, the Viceroy and "the Ascendancy caste."[65] The size of the funeral cortege—over 10,000—indicated the strength of remembrance of the Tipperary people, and the symbolic importance to them of the Cormack brothers, in whose innocence most believed. This story would have been well-known in Munster, but one can speculate how much weight it would carry with London. One might wonder also what comprehension there would be of the importance of the elaborate funeral, which in its time was obviously a gesture of political defiance.

A recent work by Tipperary historian Nancy Murphy leaves the question of the Cormack's involvement open, yet effectively removes their assumed motive for murder and challenges the value of the evidence for the prosecution. Anecdotal evidence offered also by Nancy Murphy suggests that Keogh himself thought the brothers were mistakenly convicted; and local sources have identified an evicted local man who speedily emigrated to America as the real perpetrator.[66] As the "home place" of the Laffan family was in the parish of Loughmore, the scene of the crime, May Laffan would have been well informed by relatives about *their* view of the Cormack case. The opposite view would have come from her mother's first cousin, Gerald Fitzgibbon (II) QC, who was involved (on the Government side) in a case brought by Ann Brophy's parents to get compensation for the imprisonment of their daughter.

This incident may have stressed to Laffan the manner in which wishful thinking can influence the course of an investigation, when people find only what they want to find. Thus the murder motive in "Weeds," assumed to be agrarian, also includes personal revenge—the exact reverse of the Cormack case. An additional significant piece of background scene-setting in "Weeds" is the use of the Suir river to facilitate the escape of Clifford. The Suir, of course, does not go anywhere near Mitchelstown, but it runs very near Loughmore, in North Tipperary.

The second of the accounts which furnished Laffan with usable material is probably the best known, as it involved the Fenian John Sarsefield Casey, remembered in Cork by his pseudonym of the "Galtee Boy." It certainly provided the physical background to "Weeds." The scene was the huge Kingston estate which included mountain areas in North Cork, South Tipperary, and Limerick—areas which Laffan knew well. This estate fell into debt during a period (1820–1833) when the Third Earl of Kingston, known as "Big George," became mentally ill and before incarceration spent upwards of £400,000 (several million in today's sterling) on building the largest private house in the United Kingdom. Previous to this, in the words of Laurence M. Geary, "His vast estate was modelly run, and his tenants suffered no oppression but his."[67]

Big George's heir was unable to recoup the debt. The widow of a cousin eventually inherited, and, again in the words of Laurence M. Geary, "Lady Kingston was placed in a very inflexible financial position, and was totally dependant on the goodwill of her tenants."[68]

Eventually, 50,000 Galtee acres had to be sold under the Encumbered Estates Act. Some tenants had leases, but much of the Galtee mountain land was occupied by tenants-at-will and was of poor quality. Of this land, some became the property of Nathaniel Buckley, an English MP, some went to speculators, and some remained with Lady Kingston. Buckley, an absentee, employed an agent, Patten Smith Bridge. The mountain land, bog and heather and scree, was so poor that rents had always been nominal, as almost anything occupiers managed to do to the soil would improve it. In the late 1870s came a series of wet summers, and soon the subsistence farmers were in debt. In addition many who had leases had to pay Poor Law rates to support workhouses, and fees to transfer land to sons. It was at this point that they were threatened with relatively large rent increases, not only by

Bridge, but also by Lady Kingston herself, whose relations with these tenants consequently deteriorated.[69]

Patton Smith Bridge was particularly harsh in his treatment of the Galtee tenants, and in 1876 made clear to them that all rents would be raised, some 25%. An evicted tenant tried to shoot Bridge and failed but escaped capture and went to America. A second attempt on the agent's life a year later resulted in the death of the driver of his vehicle. Bridge, who now wore body armour, escaped. Another evicted tenant was promptly convicted and executed for this crime.[70]

John Sarsefield Casey, back in his native Mitchelstown after five years penal exile in Australia, wrote two letters, one appeared in the *Cork Examiner* and the other in the *Freeman's Journal,* to bring the Galtee tenants' situation to public notice. Patton Smith Bridge speedily brought an action against him for "criminal information," that is, incitement to violence. A complicated and lengthy court case ensued which eventually petered out, as the jury could not agree; but not before the public all over Ireland and England was made aware, by reports of the evidence for the defence, of the excruciating poverty and hardship endured by the Galtee tenants and the injustice of their treatment, commented on even by the judge who presided at the preliminary hearing. Laffan would have read the articles commissioned by the *Freeman's Journal* and written by William O'Brien MP, in which he gave an eye-witness account of his visits to the Galtee tenants at Christmas time.[71] She must also have read legal reports, widely available because they were printed in book form to raise funds for Casey's defense.[72] This extract from the affadavit of a tenant, Thomas Kearney, is typical of many:

> "My farm is situated on the side of the Galtymore mountain, more than half-way up. When my father took the holding more than fifty years ago it was a barren waste, all heath and stones; he and his family, including myself, reclaimed it, carrying manure and lime to do so on their and our backs up the mountain; the land is miserably poor; I cannot grow sufficient potatoes for food—such as I do grow, are bad in quality . . . for nine months in every year we have to live on indian meal."[73]

None of the Galtee tenants complained about the hardship of their lives, but only about having no security of tenure, and no legal redress against their landlord or his agent.

This is the factual background to Laffan's story, and she uses its material, for example, in the plaint made by her character Mary Heffernan:

"Look at us served with the process to quit come Michaelmas. And it was my boy's grandfather built the house over our heads—dere above on Sheena Rinkey (Skeagheenarinnce) and carried de lime up dat mountain on his back dere too. Forty years I am sleeping in dat house now, and I never can sleep in any other house. No! I will die! And dere is my son James comin' home next week, can get no work in England—an' we all to be put out."[74]

All tenants eventually paid their rents and were reinstated, but relations between Lady Kingston and themselves apparently remained fraught.

Traces of the haunting sense of frustration and insecurity which was to enter so powerfully into Laffan's later work as it did into much Irish fiction of the last quarter of the nineteenth century can already be perceived, but along with them a growing conviction of the inevitability of major social change. There are changes in the way the tenants perceive themselves, and they are growing less deferential to their masters. For instance, Lady Galteemore (possibly Lady Kingston) visits tenants to instruct them in what she sees as the duties of their state in life. She comments adversely on the wearing of bonnets by tenants' wives, seeing this custom as inappropriate to their lowly status. (The wearing of bonnets on formal occasions was a middle-class convention.) Maryanne Roche, a representative tenant's wife, resenting the unannounced visits of her landlady, resolves that *her* daughters, when they come home from convent boarding-school, shall wear their bonnets every day. She also punishes severely one of her sons who "mitched" from school. She is in her own way demonstrating what she thinks about the social system, as well as her belief in education as the path to social advancement. Her husband may be a careless farmer, but the money the gentry would like to see spent on the land he rents from them is not being wasted—it is going to educate his family.

Other tenants are shown to resent openly the way that Lawder the agent and others like him fulminate against people who, living in debt and poverty, still manage to give "fortunes" to their marriageable daughters. Laffan comments on this custom in *Miss Ferrard*, explaining that it fulfils the traditional Irish practice that gave girls in a family equal shares with their brothers.[75] Criticism from Lawder, a man of the people who has prospered, is resented even more than from "the gentry" because Lawder is actually Irish and originally Catholic—"one of our own."[76] He has reneged against his background in an unacceptable way. Consequently Clifford, his assassin, is supported and protected by people who are thus indicating rejection of Lawder.

Another tenant, Connor, demonstrates his feelings also, which would not have been unique. He is illiterate, and his landlady prefers tenants like him who are unable to read or write because, according to Laffan, they are less motivated to demand their rights:

> Lady Galteemore had a sort of regard for him as a tenant who had a due sense of his own humble station, and held rightminded ideas. She met him one day, and after some conversation, asked him if he could read. Connor replied,"No, my Lady, I cannot; I cannot, indeed; what use would reading be to me?"[77]

In fact Connor is ashamed of his inability to read, and angrily envious of the local Fenian organiser, the Irish-American journalist Cassidy, who not only reads but writes and actually gets paid for doing so. Lady Galteemore, here representing the whole landowning class, is simply unable to pick up the feeling behind Connor's rationalization, any more than she can understand why he, in common with her other tenants, should silently resent her visits so much.

In these four stories, written at the start of Laffan's brief writing career, a wide spectrum of Irish social history discloses itself. The urban stories about children emphasise how little community provision was being made for them. Flitters dies a sacrificial death, and for Baubie as for the three boys the opportunity to improve their circumstances seems to be, though limited in nature, at any rate a bettering of their original circumstances. These stories stress the vulnerability of children, but also their capacity to live for the day, a quality which Laffan seems at once to admire and deplore. Extrapolating from a remark of the Counsellor (in "Flitters"), she seems to associate resilience in adversity with an over-optimistic and presumptuous belief in the operations of Divine Providence, expressed by the Counsellor but encouraged, as she sees it, by the Catholic faith:

> "What do you care as long as you have a bit to eat? and if you haven't it, won't anyone give it to you? The history of the nation and the people is summed up in that sentence. The charity of the poor to the poor is boundless as the charity of God. Hence thrift is unknown and industry nullified. Poverty is the great and almost only qualification for heaven; therefore the poorer the better. Comfort, respectability, luxury, are for Protestants, Presbyterians and such heretics, who are welcome to them, for is it not God's will that they should have them in this world, it being an article of faith that in the next they can have nothing?"[78]

The surface implication is that Catholics were encouraged to reason in this way, which was not true then any more than it is now. But unless she is being ironic, the somewhat ranting paragraph above does not "fit" with Laffan's approving description of the industrious children of Artane. That she is not quite whole-hearted in all her strictures either is shown by her sympathy with the Baubie Clarkes of the world, the people who do not fit in with the provision the rest of us make for them. She writes, not so much to excite our pity, as to challenge us, and point out that building of mutual trust and respect is a necessary start to giving anybody effective help.

Her comments apply in equal measure to the poor tenants in "Weeds." They are vulnerable because if unable to pay extortionate rents they have no peaceful recourse but emigration or a pauper's existence in the work-house. Increasingly, the resort of some is to stay and fight their circum-stances, not always in the most effective way. Laffan's sympathies are certainly with the people who have to carry lime and manure up the mountain on their backs to improve their tiny fields, and however she may conventionally deplore their involvement with illegal organizations, she is also stating very clearly that what they think they have to do in order to survive is to make themselves feared. In reality, the short-term benefit from Lawder's murder to the characters in her story is negligible, for Laffan also explains that the projected rent increases will go ahead, unaffected by Lawder's death. She does not mention the activities of the Ladies' Land League during the actual Galtee rent strike—or at least, not in the pub-lished version of "Weeds" which is all we have.[79] It is certain that if she had referred to it, her publishers would not have let it pass, any more than they would be likely to do at the present day, if one of their novelists wrote in support of contemporary terrorist activities.

It is possible also that the somewhat half-hearted description of the Roche family's laid-back lifestyle is an attempt on the part of Laffan to ful-fil the stereotype of the lazy Irish in order to mollify Macmillans.

The reality that the people were succeeding in creating a menacing im-age is shown in the transcript of pre-trial proceedings in the "Galtee Boy" case. The judges presiding decided the case should go to trial, not because they thought Bridge was in the right, "but because they thought Casey had the power to cause another attempt on Bridge's life, and this they could not allow to happen."[80] This is an extraordinary reason, implying that the in-fluence of one young man, an ex-political prisoner, could send out a mes-sage to accomplish the death of another, a message which the colonial government of the country would find difficulty in dealing with.

The dilemmas of people slowly emerging from the shadows into a sense of their own political power are demonstrated in "Weeds," reflecting the actual situation of that time; the choices, the hesitations. The Galtee farmers, in the "Whiteboy"[81] tradition, are shown as readily having recourse to physical violence, but only by default. Offered a choice, the implication is, they would not choose that route. The Irish-American Fenian Cassidy preaches straight socialism, using jargon and pretentious language, but we are told "the young fellows listened to him as if he spoke with the tongue of an angel."[82] They admire him, because he does not drink whisky and lives by "writing for the papers," a calling greatly esteemed but not yet accessible to most of them. Maryanne Roche, the tenant farmer's wife, still superstitiously puts a spark from the fire in the churn before making her butter, but she also tries to prepare her children for a future she wants to be different from the past. There is a sense of transition, of people travelling between old and new worlds. Also there is the hope that the street-children, child survivors of post-famine emigration, are not going to be left behind, that they, too, may be able to turn their lives around. It can certainly be said of these four stories, that each one ends on a note of hope.

CHAPTER 7

A Political Allegory of Fenian Ireland?

Time might bring about a wonder, the wheel might turn for them at last.

In the course of a letter to George Grove, editor of *Macmillan's Magazine*, about her short story "Weeds," May Laffan referred to other work which she had in hand: "I am busy with a new story of the same class of Irish—but of a different sort & showing different & better feelings."[1] It seems certain that the new story referred to was *Ismay's Children,* the last of her full-length novels, and the only one set in Co. Cork. It also seems to be identical with the novel that, in 1882, Laffan told George Macmillan she was having serialised under the title *Beyond the Back Gates.*[2] Unfortunately she did not say which of the scores of literary magazines of the time had accepted it, but nonetheless *Macmillan's* expressed interest in future publishing rights, and in fact did publish *Ismay's Children* in 1887.

Laffan's previous books had all been different, not only from the generality of contemporary novels and stories set in Ireland, but different from each other. As we have seen in earlier chapters, *Hogan MP* was a satire; *The Honourable Miss Ferrard,* a Cinderella story; *Christy Carew,* a novel of manners with tragic overtones. The "sketches" or short stories were about different forms of poverty and deprivation—they had a social problem content, as also had the children's novel which Laffan translated from the French under the title *No Relations.* The novella *A Singer's Story,* written and published last so far as we know, was an example of a moral tale for the young.[3] Laffan evidently liked to experiment and preferred not to cover the same ground twice.

As might be expected, *Ismay's Children* does not closely resemble any of her other novels. It is the only one to have been serialised, and this had some bearing on its shape, accounting for the somewhat episodic form, as well as for the interpolation of anecdotes which, though well written and amusing in themselves, did nothing to advance the plot. The classic three-volume novel format, long as it usually was, apparently did need stretching to be long enough for a serial. As regards the story's theme, Laffan seems to have intended to put before English readers some aspects of the complex relations between their two countries, showing the causes of hurt and conflict, and hinting at how they might be resolved. The form she chose to do this was that of the political and social allegory, or "description of one state of things under the image of another."[4]

Allegorical images had of course been transmitted in story and verse form in Ireland long before then. Several examples must have come to the mind of the novelist, indicating possible ways to go. She had read Spenser's *The Fairie Queen*, from which she quotes, and probably she had also read Swift's *A Tale of a Tub*, or even Thomas Moore's *Captain Rock* or *An Irish Gentleman in Search of a Religion*[5]—all of which could be said to be allegories. Though critical of English rule, Laffan was a unionist. She would have found more to agree with in the sentiments of Lady Morgan or Maria Edgeworth than in those of Thomas Moore, because the world-view of each of these women writers was somewhat closer to what we know of her own. The plot of *Ismay's Children* in particular draws extensively on ideas and forms in the best-known of Lady Morgan's post-Union novels, *The Wild Irish Girl* (1806).

This celebrated *bildungsroman* charts the discovery of Ireland, a country hitherto unknown to him, by Horatio Mortimer, an Englishman exiled to his father's estate in Connaught. That estate was seized in Cromwellian times from a noble Irish family, now reduced to poverty and consisting only of the musically talented Glorvina O'Melville and her ailing widowed father, the Prince of Inismore. Horatio's experiences teach him to respect the identity and culture of Ireland; and he also learns to love Glorvina, who overcomes her dread of his people, long hereditary enemies to hers. With the betrothal of Horatio and Glorvina, the allegory demonstrates an ideal resolution to English-Irish conflict by "marriage" between the two countries. It is seen as a perfect solution because Horatio (England) has the material resources which Glorvina (Ireland) lacks, but needs to be able to develop her talents and shine in society. A certain amount of stereotyping was felt necessary, to emphasise the message. The English were credited with a natural gift for ruling others, coupled with practical skills and common sense—though it cannot be said that the impulsive Horatio Mortimer displays much of either. The Irish were described as charming and full of aesthetic sensibility, but incompetent in practical affairs and needing, indeed welcoming, a strong hand to direct their volatile natures.

In one sense, this marriage of opposites had already taken place with the passing of the Act of Union in 1801, but Catholic Emancipation, which would ensure Catholic representation in Parliament, was seen as also necessary before Ireland could begin to have actual parity with England.[6] Sydney Owenson, Lady Morgan, Anglo-Irish by birth, was politically an Irish Whig who actively supported Catholic Emancipation (although she seems to have distrusted Daniel O'Connell personally), and this novel was a part of her contribution to the cause.[7]

The Ireland in which the story was set was one in which the 1798 Rising had been a recent event. The brutal, reprisal-driven measures taken to put the insurrection down were presented to the English public as necessary because the Irish would not respond to anything else.[8] It seems that *The Wild Irish Girl* was an attempt to modify the unattractive stereotype of the people of Ireland which prevailed at that time. English cartoonists of the period, for example, showed Ireland as a wilderness peopled by primitive beings—ragged, ignorant, and speaking only a debased form of English.[9] Glorvina, the Prince, and their Gaelic entourage were convincingly different and made an instant appeal to amateurs of archaeology, history, and romantic folklore. Glorvina's clothes, hairstyle and jewelry were copied by fashionable Regency ladies, and to some extent by Lady Morgan herself.[10] Her Irish characters—alleged to be drawn from life, while less realistic in this novel than in the later novel *O'Donnel: An Irish Tale* (1807)—were shown as unremittingly noble and virtuous as well as "brave, hospitable, liberal and ingenious."[11] They were equal but different and therefore clearly worth emancipating, if only to encourage them to be loyal to their English rulers, who were already threatened by events in nearby France and could well do without more trouble in Ireland.

It has been suggested that Lady Morgan replaced one Irish stereotype with another. This theory is borne out by the frequency with which such descriptive phrases as the following occur: "Their naturally impetuous characters render them alive to every enterprise, and open to the impositions of the artful or ambitious," or elsewhere "The ancient Irish, like the modern, had more *soul*, more genius, than worldly prudence or cautious calculating forethought."[12] This praise conveys an element of condescension, rather than genuine respect for difference.

It was obvious to Lady Morgan's readers that when it came to legend, myth and tradition, the writer had drawn on a large store of information to which her own half-Irish background and upbringing and her father's knowledge of the Irish language gave her access. She did not have to search far away for interesting material for her stories; it was all near to hand. *The Wild Irish Girl* was a commercial success, but also in literary terms it was extremely influential—giving rise to many imitations and variations on questions of identity, and introducing the theme of intermarriage, literal or otherwise, as a resolution to political and racial conflict.[13]

Ismay's Children may be counted among these derivations. Laffan made no attempt to equal the full achievement of Lady Morgan, but concentrated rather on adapting the basic plot and value system of *The Wild Irish Girl* to her own needs. She followed the original plot quite closely, although with some differences. Writing in the 1880s, she set her novel some years back, in the time (1865–1866) when direct action by the Fenian organization was shown to fail, as the 1798 Rising had also failed. Laffan, too, chose to write about a beautiful young girl, disinherited by mischance, whose status and future were uncertain, and whose powerless elderly guardians lived in the past. Into her obscure life came a handsome young man who was instantly attracted to her, seeing her as different to all the other girls he knew. He was also drawn, though somewhat ambivalently, to her Irish setting and the lure of a society contrasting with the one he has already experienced. The heroine, portrayed in the style of Jean-Jacques Rousseau as an unspoilt but well-read child of nature,[14] loved her hero for himself, never suspecting him to be wealthy and the heir to an English title.[15] When he suddenly had to leave her for a time, she feared that he had gone for good, and only then began to realise how much she cared for him.

At this point the two plots diverge, for Laffan, unlike Lady Morgan, did not have a mission to popularise the Irish. In the Laffan variation, the heroine's brother joined the Irish Republican Brotherhood (IRB), and through his agency the threat of contemporary violence, absent from Lady Morgan's story, became evident in this one. Though *Ismay's Children* is nominally set in 1865–1866, its political ambiance is more like that of almost twenty years later. During the 1860s, legislation affecting Irish land use and ownership was dealt with by a Parliament in which landlord interests predominated. By the 1880s, the scene had altered; a higher proportion of Irish MPs were at least nominal Home Rulers, and there were also fewer landlords among them and more radical ideas regarding the ownership of land. Gladstone's Church Act (1870) disestablished the Church of Ireland, thereby removing its privileged status and in a way, the unique status of its members also. This event was welcomed by some Dissenters and by those who wanted to rationalise the way in which the Church of Ireland organized itself. The Church of Ireland population of Ireland was about twelve percent of the whole but not all Protestants gave allegiance to the state church, and some felt that it was unrealistic to continue to maintain a presence in the more remote areas of Ireland, employing clergy to minister to very small numbers.

The majority of the Protestant Ascendancy, however, took it as a betrayal on the part of England, and in fact, it seems to have been experienced as a great psychological blow to them.[16] Much of the social and emotional support which they had was delivered through their parish churches. Reorganization of parishes led to closure of isolated churches and amalgamation of their congregations, making regular church attendance in many areas more difficult and in some cases impossible. This encouraged people who could do so to move from rural areas to large towns, and those unable to move felt vulnerable.[17] Moreover, in 1870 and 1881 Gladstone brought in legislation which protected the rights of certain tenant groups.[18] It became clear to landowners that some form of peasant proprietorship, which might ruin them financially, was likely to evolve and probably to be followed at length by self-government, in which the majority community would share and even hold the balance of power. Experiences of the landlords, absentees and others, depicted in *Ismay's Children* recall not so much the 1860s as the 1880s, with agrarian violence taking on a personal dimension with the settling of old scores, which does not seem to have been the case to any great extent in the late 1860s.[19]

Laffan is concerned to show her English readers some of the causes for political unrest in Ireland, and not surprisingly, given what we know of her interests, when it comes to political incompetence at a local and national level she blames lack of education in the Irish middle classes and makes the assumption that Catholic education is always inferior to that available in Protestant schools.

Her variant of *The Wild Irish Girl* story is complicated as well, by a separation of the role of alien lover from that of returned absentee landlord—in the Laffan version, they are two different people. Chichele Ansdale, the hero of *Ismay's Children*, has no land in Ireland, and the absentee character, Tighe O'Malley, is connected by marriage to the hero and by blood ties to the heroine, Marion Mauleverer. This unusual situation suggests a wish to demonstrate the theory that there is no difference *really* between the peoples of Ireland and England, other than that brewed up by malcontents to further their own ends. The two countries are from the one eggshell, so to speak, and separate Irish identity as such does not exist. Separation of roles, though, has further implications for the heroine, because in *The Wild Irish Girl* she did not merely receive English bounty, but had a reciprocal role in persuading her tenants and the local people to transfer their allegiance, or rather to extend it, with their trust, to her new spouse. There is no question of such action as this being necessary in *Ismay's Children*, where the estate apparently remains with the absentee who inherited it by default, and the hero and heroine plan, not to stay and rehabilitate the land and its people, but to leave Ireland forever as soon as possible.

The introduction of Fenianism to Laffan's story was evidently meant as a warning of what she thought would happen if the ideal union, the marriage, between wealthy male England and impoverished female Ireland did *not* take place. Instead of the fruits of symbolic marriage in the form of peace, prosperity, reform of agrarian abuses and expansion of education, there would then be violence, insurrection, and anarchy.[20] The quasi-socialist programme which the IRB was understood to have would, it was feared, deprive nobility and gentry of their land in order to redistribute it, sack their houses and finally murder them.[21] There would be a terrible war, which Britain would of course win, but not without inflicting severe coercive measures on Ireland. It was impossible anyhow for Ireland ever to attempt self-government, her people not being mature enough to undertake it—in fact, they are shown as truly illustrative of the "good but weak" Irish stereotype presented in *The Wild Irish Girl*.

This view reflects the opinions of the Irish Whigs, or Liberals—a political group to which Lady Sydney Morgan certainly and Laffan probably belonged. While acknowledging the need for reforms in Ireland, Whigs believed closer Irish ties with England were needed for Parliament to agree to sanction these reforms. Common ground between both peoples and countries was consequently stressed—prefiguring the "Union of Hearts" theme later initiated by Gladstone and English Liberals.[22] Most of these latter saw Ireland's future to be always within the United Kingdom and the Empire, and never as an independent European state.

Contemporary Conservative and unionist thinking naturally went somewhat further. Representative Conservatives such as Laffan's granduncle Gerald Fitzgibbon wanted a continuous, peaceful and stable society, and felt Ireland jeopardised this by making unreasonable demands on Parliament, and on England's financial resources.[23] They did not perceive Ireland to have an identity of its own; and the following passages serve to illustrate this particular mind-set. They are taken from "Little Dorinn: A Fenian Story," a "Fenian novel" serialised in a Canadian journal in 1873, and the writer came from an Ascendancy family in Co. Wicklow:

> [T]he real world of the past slips away from their grasp, leaving them weak, ignorant and impoverished; and it is much to be feared that generations must pass away before they cease to rebel against the dominion of fact, and keep pace with the growing enlightenment of other nations. . . . Now Ireland has really nothing to complain of, or if there is still anything that could reasonably be considered a grievance, the means of redress are as open to Irish Catholics as to English Protestants. There is in truth nothing now to justify a revolution. . . .[24]

This story relates the gradual awakening of a simple-minded Fenian recruit as to the real nature of the organization and its leaders. This theme is also used in *Ismay's Children* to rather more realistic effect, though Laffan's knowledge of the workings and organization of the IRB appears dubious, probably because few authentic and detailed accounts of the movement were available to her at that time.[25] Where she did at least partly succeed was in her attempts at analysing the motives of recruits to Fenianism. This approach was then unusual, and won her book a favourable review in the London *Athenaeum*:

> [This novel is] marked to a singular extent by a combination of qualities rare in female writers—strength, breadth of humour, and impartiality. . . . The author is at least as much at home in delineating the characters and conversations of "the quality" as she is in reproducing the racy idiom of the North Riding of Cork. . . . [T]his liberal use of local colour may, perhaps, discourage the Sassanach reader, but no one who is anxious to fathom the enigma of the Irish character will be deterred by such considerations from the careful study of what we have no hesitation in pronouncing to be the most valuable and dispassionate contribution towards the solution of that problem which has been put forth in this generation in the domain of fiction.[26]

At least part of the problem as seen from England was the ready recourse allegedly had by all Irish people to physical violence. Avoiding the question of whether violence can ever legitimately be used to achieve political ends (a highly relevant topic at the time of the book's publication in

1887), the plot of *Ismay's Children* managed to include discussion of a number of contemporary—and contentious—social issues within its framework.[27] The plot itself is arguably the most complex of those Laffan used.

The story of *Ismay's Children* begins with a preamble set in the 1860s, but refers back to a period almost twenty years earlier, when Captain Godfrey Mauleverer, an impoverished officer, eloped with Ismay D'Arcy, an orphaned Catholic. Following a secret marriage, the couple lived in Jersey where Mauleverer's regiment was stationed. They had three children, Marion, Godfrey and Gertrude. Ismay died young, and her aunt Juliet D'Arcy came from Ireland to care for the children. Some years after, Captain Mauleverer inherited Barrettstown Castle and its estate in Co. Cork.[28] Before he could claim it he died suddenly, and, the assumption being made that he was without a legitimate male heir, his first cousin Tighe O'Malley inherited instead.

The novel then re-opens at the point when, some weeks after Captain Mauleverer's death, Juliet and the three orphans arrive at Barrettstown to press their claim. They fail, because a stroke brought on by Tighe's angry reception of the group causes Juliet to forget details essential to prove the children's legitimacy. Father Paul Conroy, Juliet's cousin and local parish priest, negotiates with Tighe to permit the orphans to live with their aunt in the neglected Mill House, opposite the back gate of the demesne.[29] There, Father Paul supports them financially by supplementing Juliet's tiny income with his, and he effectively shares the parental responsibilities. The children are regarded as rightful heirs to Barrettstown by most of the local people, but are despised by the gentry who see them as Captain Mauleverer's bastards. Father Paul, and Juliet who is by now confined to a wheelchair, try to temper the harshness of life for them, but by the time the children are in their teens they are all, in various ways, starting to resist their guardians' authority. Aunt Juliet and Father Paul—she obsessed with "tracing" family history, he weighed down by conservative religious tradition—both elderly and in Juliet's case partly paralysed, stand for the Ireland of the past and the contemporary Catholic Church as Laffan perceived them to be: "'Juliet D'Arcy and her relative were in much the same plight. The present was too unsatisfactory, the future uncertain, if not hopeless. So they also took refuge in the past. There, there was life and active romance, perhaps glory. Who knew? Time might bring about a wonder—the wheel might turn for them at last.'"[30]

In keeping with the allegorical form, these two characters, the parent-figure and the priest, are almost stereotypes, reminding one of the Prince and his family chaplain in *The Wild Irish Girl*. This resemblance could of course have been deliberate on Laffan's part. But how may we explain the way in which the emphasis given to Juliet's disability prefigures the theme of paralysis and the sense of personal inadequacy pervading James Joyce's *Dubliners*? Likewise, mention of fortune's turning wheel brings to mind the scene in a Cork hotel with Stephen and his father in *A Portrait of the Artist as a Young Man,* when the latter sings a popular ballad ending with an invocation—not actually quoted in *Portrait*—to the wheel of fortune.[31] It seems probable that Laffan intended to call attention to a reckless and blind disregard of painful reality in Irish elders, but with less of the conscious art available to her that Joyce was able to use with his characters. It is possible also that she picked up, without being fully aware of it, the stale spirit of the Victorian-Edwardian age in Ireland, coming into the closing decades of British rule and described so brilliantly by Joyce as well as by George Moore.

It is at this stage that Laffan introduces into her book the radical element which she uses to support her views on the need for land and education reform. (It is possibly these aspects of her book also that the *Athenaeum* reviewer was thinking of when he commended her political insights). Laffan saw educational and political reform as closely linked—Ireland was unlikely to achieve the second until she had the first. Examples given in the previous Laffan books are mainly taken up with the education of girls, but here Laffan concentrates on the situation of the Mauleverer boy.

Godfrey Mauleverer attended a nearby diocesan college, where he imbibed little else but nationalist ideals.[32] He now angrily rejects a career as a customs officer or a bank official, nor does he want to study medicine at the Catholic University, which is the best Father Paul can offer. When Godfrey refuses this offer, the implication is that he sees it as "second-best," and that the "first-best," Trinity College, Dublin, is put beyond his reach by the prejudices of Catholic bishops against that institution.[33] Financial cost is never mentioned, but would have been a major factor—as fees were higher in Trinity than in the alternative colleges, and Catholics were not eligible for Trinity scholarships or exhibitions in the 1860s. Resentful and frustrated, fifteen-year-old Godfrey joins a Fenian circle. His sisters and the servant Kitty Macken conceal his activities, less for security reasons than for fear of upsetting Juliet, from whom they have been warned to keep all agitating news.

Godfrey represents what Laffan perceives as the headstrong and self-destructive element in the Irish character, an element which she chooses to see in terms of response to poor, that is, Catholic education—leading to unreal expectation and consequent frustrated ambition. She underlines what she feels about this in her description of a local Fenian leader or "Head Center," a returned American emigrant referred to as the Commodore:

> He had been born and educated in Ireland, the second the greater misfortune if possible of the two, at a time when Catholic education, at first proscribed by the state, was gradually falling into the unskilled hands of the Catholics themselves. [He was] fit for nothing, too uneducated to be a clerk, unfit to be a tradesman, not strong enough to dig . . . ignorant and wrongheaded to a degree difficult to comprehend. . . . [H]e was unpractical and unreasonable, his habits of thought, which were perfectly childish, had been formed on a wrong system.[34]

Laffan does not say what system would have been "right" for him, but she contrasts him, as she does Godfrey Mauleverer, with the book's romantic hero Chichele Ansdale, a far more polished product of English public school and university. With her occasional, and typical, inconsistency she then goes on to say that the Commodore, orphaned son of an evicted tenant, emigrated alone to America in his teens and was later commissioned as an officer in the Northern army during the Civil War—factors which are creditable to him rather than otherwise. She also mentions that Chichele is the only son of an extremely wealthy family; so he has obviously had advantages denied to most other men.

Godfrey Mauleverer is presented as *naïf*, undiscriminating, and easily led. It is suggested that his Fenian involvement comes about solely through lack of a more constructive outlet for his energies. But it is also implied that he has anyway a tendency to self-dramatise: "How would it be if these representatives of a foreign tyranny were dragging him off to the constabulary barracks with them? He rather liked the idea."[35]

Godfrey has no idea of what might really be in store for him if he were captured, nor has Father Paul, who knows about the Fenian membership but does not take it seriously, until Captain Lethbridge of the police tells him that Godfrey's present activities rate a twenty-year prison sentence. The boy's immaturity and romantic nature lead him to embrace Fenian recruitment until it becomes his sole occupation:

Any traveller meeting Godfrey on some wild mountain path or lonely road might have fancied himself for the moment in the wilds of Corsica or Calabria. There was nothing native in the beautiful swarthy face with dark melancholy eyes that looked from below the broad-brimmed hat, or the slender shapely figure of the boy.[36]

To what extent did Laffan really intend *Ismay's Children* to be a Fenian novel? There were already a number of contemporary novels with Fenian settings, written with varying degrees of competence and authenticity, for the subject was certainly exciting.[37] Today we can compare this fiction with the autobiographical accounts by actual members of the IRB of events leading up to their abortive rising, the rising itself, and its aftermath.[38] However, in many cases these accounts were not published until years after the writers' deaths, and Laffan could not have had access to more than one or two of them before she wrote *Ismay's Children*. Her description of Godfrey's rapid promotion to a post of responsibility in the IRB sounds too unlikely to have any factual basis, remembering that he is supposed to be less than sixteen, and comes from a family with no tradition of political activism. Though vivid and amusing, her accounts of the meetings, the drinking, the drilling and the oath-taking, and the ways in which the organization designated by non-members as "Fenian" took decisions, do not tally with accounts given by actual members.[39] To give one instance, Fenian oath-taking does not seem to have been the almost public group ceremony Laffan describes, but something far more secretive and discreet. This is not to say, of course, that all her statements are untrue, only that positive evidence for their accuracy is lacking. In some ways, her descriptions call the 1700s to mind; they seem like the activities of Whiteboys rather than Fenians.[40] It appears that in this novel Laffan is trying to offer a detached and ironic view of the Fenians, as a counter-weight to novels which give the reader a wholly romantic and partisan picture. She is even, at times, inclined to mock aspects of the drilling and military training which take place, choosing to see these secret activities as a sort of fantasy game holding a mysterious appeal for some men.

While Godfrey believes his activities to be secret, they are known to the local chief of police. No action is taken, since his father's cousin Tighe O'Malley has forbidden it, and Tighe, as a magistrate, apparently has power to tell the police what to do. An absentee for seven years, he recently came back for reasons of economy to Barrettstown Castle with his wife, Lady Blanche. Accompanying them are Blanche's English cousin Ida

Courthope, her husband Jack, a Liberal Member of Parliament, and Ida's younger brother Chichele Ansdale. The three last named are new to Ireland. They are not impressed by their host:

> Tighe rarely spoke seriously to a woman . . . a fine presence, large dark eyes, and a reputation for fastness made him, according to report, quite irresistible. He was perpetually in love with someone, and liked his wife best of all: extravagant in some things, in others parsimonious; fond of display and effect, no one could call him consistent. . . .[41]

Tighe has an overriding need to stand well with people, which leads him to present situations not as they are, but as he would like them to be. He has little moral courage, and finds unreal excuses for dealing unjustly with his tenants. These never know what he is going to do or when, so they cannot trust what he says and are the more afraid of him. They prefer his agent, the severe and straightforward Captain Marchmont, who tries, insofar as Tighe will let him, to treat them fairly—a similar situation to the one described in Maria Edgeworth's novel *The Absentee*.[42] His guests are uneasy at the way Tighe treats the Mauleverers, whom he always represents as refusing his help, when the truth is that he offered it with conditions they could not accept. He offers to finance them if they will go back to Jersey and stay there, and he offers to pay for Godfrey's further education if the latter will convert to the Church of Ireland. The Courthopes are intrigued because Father Paul is never invited to the house to meet them. Tighe says the priest is so uncouth that he would simply not know how to behave in the presence of gentry, but again, the real reason is somewhat different. Tighe fears the outspoken Father Paul might unwittingly reveal the lies Tighe has been telling the Courthopes about his good relations with his tenants. Chichele Ansdale, exploring the countryside, meets Marion Mauleverer and is instantly drawn to her: "What a curious, striking-looking creature! Foreign, surely—who and what can she be? And so beautiful!"[43]

He follows up his vision by rescuing Marion from the consequences of a dangerous prank. She is furious and humiliated—but attracted also: "She stole a look at her companion. He was very tall, she thought. She had never seen anyone like him before—so curiously dressed—and what a face! It reminded her of a picture of Napoleon as a young lieutenant—his were just such straight features, only with colour and life."[44]

Chichele's resemblence to a conquerer, but one acceptable to Irish sentiments, suggests both a link with the historic past and success in love. The two lovers soon meet again in the Mill House garden, which is clearly a microcosm of Ireland:

> There was something characteristic of its owners about this semi-desert. Preoccupied as Chichele was he became aware in some measure of this. It was charming; it was pitiful. The wrong of it forced itself on his English conscience, but the sweet wildness and unusualness took him captive. It was all so Irish, so foreign, so attractive therefore. He forgot his promise to meet his people on the Limerick road, he forgot everything but the spell that held him. . . .[45]

When it comes to meeting the neighbours, he is less sure of how he feels:

> He had that almost religious horror of every rank of society below his own which it seems to be the duty of the well-bred Englishman or woman to entertain and express. . . . "They are all as civil and friendly as if we had known each other all our lives, Sassanach and all though I am. But what on earth has she to do with these people?"[46]

Fearing a plot to ensnare her brother, Ida Courthope arranges by deception to have him recalled unexpectedly to England. (She believes Catholics to be linked in a conspiracy to seduce and convert rich Protestants, though Lady Blanche, Tighe's wife, tries to convince her otherwise.) Ida and her literal-minded husband Jack provide comic relief in the story, unable as they are to relate their new experiences to any of their existing fixed ideas; but they are also part of the allegory as representatives of upper middle-class English opinion:

> [Jack] was thinking how glad he was that his property lay in the South of England and not in the South of Ireland, and he thought of Tighe's queer ways, his handing out money to the beggars—even their goodwill he found it necessary to purchase—his assumption of an Irish brogue when speaking to his tenants or dependants. In his way, O'Malley appeared quite as much afraid of them as they were of him. Extraordinary country, extraordinary people, and abominable system! [47]

Yet, the fears which O'Malley expresses are justified to some extent. A poor harvest leads to greater hardship and discontent, but it is made worse by Tighe's insistence that local police and military be reinforced at local people's expense.[48] Tighe, a gambler always short of money, borrows from Peter Quin the local moneylender, giving in exchange the promise of a coveted lease due for renewal. Quin, to make sure of his prize, informs against the current holder of the lease, the Fenian Luke Ahearne. Ahearne's family farm is successfully searched for arms, a Fenian meeting is raided, Luke and the leaders are arrested, and the others, including a disillusioned Godfrey, allowed to escape: "The movement into which he had thrown himself with all the energies of his wild and undisciplined nature was crumbling into dissolution. . . . [T]he paltriness and ignorant folly of every-thing seemed revealed to him in all their squalid nakedness, and at once revolted and oppressed him."[49]

It is implied as well that the Courthopes, by first sending Chichele away, and then leaving the scene themselves, have shown a wish to escape in-volvement, which causes Tighe's selfish and unjust actions to worsen, once he is left to himself. Godfrey discovers a plot to kill Tighe, breaks his Fenian oath to tell the latter, then, realising the danger to himself, asks Juliet for money to leave the country. She agrees, but the shock of the disclosure jolts her memory enough for her to recall and write down the lost details of the place and time of the Mauleverer marriage. Shortly afterwards Juliet dies suddenly, but Father Paul receives and understands the message she left.

While all this is happening Marion is made aware by Honor Quin, the moneylender's spiteful daughter, of the social stigma of her supposed ille-gitimacy. Marion begins to fear Chichele will reject her when he knows, and she writes to him begging him not to see her again. Then, attempting to distract her troubled mind by exploring a beautiful and lonely lake, she suddenly experiences an overwhelming insight which almost magically restores her hope:

> It was another, and a different voice, that filled Marion's ears . . . that made her let go her oar and press both hands over her eyes. It was that for one instant Chichele's face rose before her, unbidden, unsought, that for once she saw him as his real self. For, by dint of trying to build up a picture of his image in her own mind, she had confused and almost destroyed her memory of him, so much so that sometimes she felt herself in doubt that she could recognise him if she were to meet him. . . .[50]

Laffan's ability to describe her heroine alone with herself can also be made to serve the allegorical form. Absence may make a heart fonder; it can also help an individual to reflect more clearly on what is actually hap-pening; and perhaps it is implied that Marion/Ireland needs to be given space to do this. Marion realises that Chichele's sudden departure, the rea-son for which she does not know as he was unable to see her before going, does not mean he does not love her. Caught between the wish to believe his declaration and fear of the future arising from her own unhappy circumstances, her unconscious self makes its decision and comes down on the side of hope.

Chichele does come back, to find friends and neighbours "waking" Aunt Juliet and comforting her grandnieces. Father Paul is in Scotland seeking the proofs of the Mauleverer marriage. But when he returns, carrying evidence of Godfrey's legitimate right to the Barrettstown estate, Father Paul learns that the boy's body has just been found washed up on the riverbank below the town, apparently drowned but with a head wound. No explanation of his death is forthcoming. An exacerbation to the sisters' grief is Tighe's insistence that Godfrey's wake must take place at Barrettstown Castle, which in life no Mauleverer was ever allowed to enter. Tighe begins to show compunction and a somewhat belated desire to make amends for the way he treated his kindred. It becomes evident as well that both O'Malleys want to claim Ismay's orphaned children as their own.

Father Paul accompanies Lady Blanche and Chichele to the Mill House, and leaves them in the sitting-room while he fetches Marion and Gertrude, who have just returned from Juliet's funeral. As he tries to comfort them, he begins to anticipate the pain that the loss of the children will give him. Yet he has to resolve the situation, and he tells them that the Castle, where Godfrey is being "waked," is where they really belong now.

> He opened the door and led them both in. . . . Gertrude held fast to Father Paul, her flushed excited face upturned to Lady Blanche. Chichele had taken and was holding both Marion's hands. Her white sad face proved more appealing to her new friend, for she stooped forward suddenly and kissed her.
>
> "Little girl," she said then to Gertrude, "will you be my daughter?"
>
> Gertrude made a half step forward, still not relaxing her hold of Father Paul.
>
> Lady Blanche laid her white hands on the child's head, and drew her gently towards herself until the tangled beautiful hair was resting on her breast.
>
> "Gertrude," she said again, "will you not? Will you take me instead of your poor aunt—instead of poor Godfrey?"
>
> But a quick sob shook her as the answer came. "Not Godfrey! Oh, Godfrey, poor Godfrey!"[51]

The book ends thus, abruptly, with one at least of Ismay's children not prepared to forget the recent past.

Where other writers of allegorical stories liked to end on a positive note, Laffan seemed even to take pains to avoid doing this. Did she really see it as an ideal resolution that Tighe and Blanche should take over responsibility for the two bereaved girls? Apparently, yes. Lady Blanche, it is stated, will prepare them for their obvious destinies. Marion is to marry Chichele and be a rich noblewoman, the beautiful Gertrude is to make an equally brilliant marriage, and both are to be presented at Court. No choice about it seems offered them or Father Paul either, although one might have expected this to be the case, as he is their *de facto* guardian. Is Laffan really trying to say that contemporary (that is, Victorian) social prestige and convention must come before everything else? And how does this combine with the need to remember an idealistic brother who died a mysterious and violent death?

A further development of the political allegory appears on offer at the conclusion of the novel, when Godfrey's death has removed the violent and forceful element from the scene. Tighe and Blanche O'Malley represent the Protestant Ascendancy in the south and north of Ireland respectively.[52] Their personal relationship may be close, but they are dissatisfied and insecure because they have no one to inherit from them—in a sense, they have no future. They want to adopt Marion and Gertrude, children from the fruitful but irregular "mixed" marriage of Tighe's cousin. Marion passively accepts from the O'Malleys a destiny which will prepare her to share the life of Chichele, Blanche's wealthy relative and a member of the English governing class. Marion can therefore be seen as reflecting the desire of Irish Unionists to stay part of the imperial system.

But Gertrude sees the offer of adoption as an attempt to deny the events of the past. She is not prepared to agree to that, and she can be seen as personifying aspirations towards political independence and a separate national identity for Ireland. Accordingly, she appears to reject what the O'Malleys can offer. Her future is uncertain, but it is implied that she may remain with Father Paul. If Tighe and Blanche O'Malley stand for Anglo-Ireland, then according to the allegory they are given a part in the future scheme of things, but only if they agree to share their advantages with Irish poor relations. Ironically, it is made clear that in doing so they would only be restoring to people what was taken away from them in the first place. One may suspect that Laffan after all did not really have faith in the possibility of that perfect union of England with Ireland. There are too many questions left when the story finishes. These questions are not answered explicitly for us, but instead a series of themes is indicated as important to the writer, in fact, as indirect answers.

The first pervasive theme, affecting all three Mauleverers and their guardians, is that of the effects upon them of uncertainty about who and what they are. Questions of identity haunt other Anglo-Irish novels in different forms: for example Lady Morgan's *O'Donnel: An Irish Tale (1814)* and Maria Edgeworth's *The Absentee* (1812), in each of which the real identity of the main female character is concealed for much of the story. Indeed, the heroine Grace Nugent in *The Absentee* is at one stage thought to be illegitimate, which if true would apparently disqualify her from heroine status. The situation of an orphan, already hard enough, was always much worse if there was any suspicion regarding legitimacy of birth. Illegitimate children had no legal claim on the goodwill and finances of their father's family, as the identity of that father could seldom be proved. Their existence was curiously shadowy in many respects; they seemed to have had no place in the social order; and their being, their very existence itself, was seen as tainted, arising as it did from the unregulated and hence illicit sexual passions of their parents. The assumption was that as the parents had been, so the child would be, and a narrowly puritan ethic held "sins of the flesh" to be more serious than other sins, needing more than one generation to expiate.

Nineteenth-century novels dealing with the difficulties faced by people born outside wedlock are many. Obvious examples include Charles Dickens's *Oliver Twist* (1837) and *Bleak House* (1853), Wilkie Collins's *No Name* (1862), Anthony Trollope's *Doctor Thorne* (1858), and William O'Brien's *When We Were Boys* (1890). A heavy sense of inferiority compounded by lack of social acceptance often characterises the fictional illegitimate, and humiliation is frequently their lot, as Dickens illustrates in *Bleak House:* "Your mother, Esther, is your disgrace, and you were hers. The time will come—and soon enough—when you will understand this better and will feel it too, as no one save a woman can."[53] There were few able to summon up the spirit and humour of Trollope's Mary Thorne:

> "If I humble myself very low; if I kneel through the whole evening in a corner; if I put my neck down and let all your cousins trample on it, and then your aunt, would that not make atonement? I would not object to wearing sackcloth, either, and I'd eat a little ashes,—or at any rate, I'd try."[54]

Marion, Godfrey and Gertrude Mauleverer each react to their situation differently. Marion appears extremely sensitive and vulnerable to depression; Godfrey is sullen and withdrawn sometimes, at other times reckless.

Twelve-year-old Gertrude alone lives in the present, and she appears assertive and confident.

In cases where the parents' marital situation was not at all clear, this
added a measure of insecurity to life for people like the Mauleverers. Living
as they already did on the uneasy ground between two cultures, Anglo-Irish Protestant and Irish Catholic, the important question for them
was not only whether a marriage had ever taken place between their parents, but what form it had taken. If their parents had had a Catholic marriage only, then Ismay's children were illegitimate.[55] On the other hand, a
marriage by affirmation—a "Scotch Marriage"—such as Captain
Mauleverer and Ismay were actually found to have had, *was* recognised as
valid for a Protestant, if witnesses could be produced to prove it took place.
As marriage certificates were not always issued, the personal testimony of
these witnesses was vital and obviously depended on knowing who they
were and where they could be found. Juliet D'Arcy, after her illness, forgot
the name of the Scottish village where Ismay was married and so was
unable to seek proof to legitimise Ismay's children.

In view of the alleged lack of charity displayed by Irish Victorians to children born outside wedlock, the attitudes of the local people to the
Mauleverers are very positive. They are seen as last descendants of a family
once Catholic and Irish, now represented officially by the Protestant Tighe
O'Malley. As they are gentry and "old stock" the actual circumstances of
their birth are evidently not seen as too important. Peasants and townspeople give them the formal title Miss or Mr. and do not expect to be on the
same footing. For instance, Marion calls school friends by their Christian
names, while they call her Miss Mauleverer. People who want to be insulting in a discreet way, however, like Honor Quin, the moneylender's daughter, drop the final syllable and say "Maulever." This practice of
abbreviating a doubtful surname also occurs in Somerville and Ross's
novel *The Big House at Inver*.[56]

However poor and obscure they may be, their heroic family background, including service in countries at war with England, ensures that
the Mauleverers are generally respected. When help or advice is needed, local people go more readily to Juliet or Marion for it than to either of the
O'Malleys, a circumstance which Lady Blanche O'Malley notices and
resents.

The source from which Laffan drew her knowlege of marital irregularity
is not difficult to guess—her legal relatives the Fitzgibbons would have

known cases similar to that of the Mauleverers. Their contemporary, Judge William O'Connor Morris, lists several instances in nineteenth-century Ireland where unscrupulous members of the Ascendancy used knowledge of the vagaries of the marriage laws to accomplish seduction.[57] Probably the most famous of these was the Yelverton case of 1861 (discussed in chapter five), which aroused so much indignation that it brought about a repeal of the law regarding mixed marriage in 1870.[58]

Such cases underlined forcefully the low expectations which the Ascendancy still held in regard to the Irish Catholic population during the mid-nineteenth century. Catholics, as has been said, whatever their background were second-class citizens with few actual rights. From the accounts available it seems that this despised majority saw the Yelverton case as an example of sexual exploitation. The victim, though English, was a Catholic and symbolised their own vulnerable position in a culture where they were perceived as so unequal that any cross-creed relationship carried with it an abnormally great risk of betrayal and final rejection. This case achieved the publicity it did because for the first time, the victim, an articulate, intelligent woman, fought back. In view of Laffan's low opinion of Catholic education, it is interesting to note that this woman was educated at a convent school in France.[59]

Another theme concerns the legitimacy or otherwise of physical violence. In the sense in which *Ismay's Children* is interpreted as allegory, the Mauleverers, representing the Irish people, are at last found to be legitimate heirs to the land, whereas at first they were assumed to be nothing of the kind. But the death of Godfrey, apparently by violence, deprives them of their rights all over again, because the Barrettstown Castle estate appears to be entailed in the male line, meaning that a female could not inherit it. The second loss of possession, therefore, is shown as an indirect consequence of Fenian violence.

Allegorical interpretation of the novel's last chapters suggests a number of points about violence which Laffan evidently wanted to make. The first is that violence is better avoided than confronted, and must be so avoided not only by exercising legal justice, but by encouraging the practice of self-control and logical thinking in the victims of injustice. Educated in the exercise of these qualities, they will mature, become better citizens, and then cease to follow advocates of physical force; in other words, they will make an intellectual rather than an emotional response.

Laffan gives a specific explanation also for the ambivalent attitude shown in Ireland and elsewhere towards violent leadership. She thinks it arises from a humble, misplaced admiration on the part of inarticulate men for anyone who possesses the "gift of the gab." She mentions, only to disagree with, the widely held belief that verbal fluency is commoner in Ireland than elsewhere; she sees most Irishmen as inarticulate.

On her next theme, the need to reform land legislation, Laffan supports various measures to prevent summary eviction. The measures were the ones popular at the time when she actually wrote, rather than at the period nearly twenty years earlier which she was writing about. "Free Sale" and the use of the "Ulster Custom," she thought, would promote good husbandry; farmers would look after their tenancies better if there was financial gain in doing so. "Fixity of Tenure" would give security to farm families. "Fair Rent" she was less sure about, for how should it be defined?

Laffan believed that the Scots practice of farmers' daughters going out to be hired as servants to earn their own marriage portions was a good one. It would mean that any spare capital not needed to meet the rent could be put back into modernizing the farm, which should be, she considered, left intact to the eldest son in accordance with English practice. Then there would be less shortage of money. The Irish tradition that all of a farmer's children, girls as well as boys, must have a share in the family resources was, Laffan thought, outdated.

About eviction, however, she had no doubts, and she believed it should not happen. All her most deprived characters in this novel are shown to have been at some time evicted—the Devoy family, the Fenian "Head Centre," widowed Helen Talbot whose farm Tighe took to complete his park, even "Lord Cork," leader of the town beggars. The tragic sub-plot of Luke Ahearne and his family is used to illustrate the reality of dependence on such as Tighe, who is not at all a dependable person. The Ahearnes go within a few months from relative affluence—hosting a big party to celebrate the "settling" of their three children in life—to abject poverty and the ruin of all their hopes. Their landlord, Tighe O'Malley, who ruins them to please a moneylender, is depicted as, in some sense, an eighteenth-century figure, and here indeed he speaks like a character from Maria Edgeworth's novel *Ennui:*[60]

> "I don't believe in education for the lower orders of Irish . . . the great secret of managing them is to let them alone. . . . They can't have a Catholic University . . . and after all you see it is their religion, and in fact [the priests] suit their people all

the better for not being too well educated . . . never meddle . . . respect their little prejudices and customs. . . . . Oh! the muskets, that is an old story. They get them periodically, bury them magpie fashion, and then forget where they are. They are just like children."[61]

Tighe's remarks are regularly reported to the outside world by his house servants but typically, he remains unaware of this. Amusing and grotesque as this totally self-absorbed character may be, he holds great power over others, denies responsibility for them and remains a devastating picture of one kind of Anglo-Irishman, a sort of 1860s Barry Lyndon.[62]

Another theme, but related to identity factors, is that of stereotyping. Laffan generally tried to avoid it in her novels; however, in this allegorical novel she stereotypes freely. The most obvious example of a stereotyped scene happens early on in *Ismay's Children,* when Father Paul invites Chichele to dine at his house. The Mauleverers and some young friends join the party, the old people withdraw, and the young ones first listen enraptured to their guest's piano playing. Then, inspired by it, they take up the carpet, dance wildly until exhausted, and end the evening by climbing out of the window and over the garden wall to chase each other around the fountain in Tighe's demesne woods. At first a spectator of this spontaneous and for the time unconventional behaviour, Chichele is drawn into it and enjoys it even while he wonders why. He is shown as more sophisticated and inhibited than his love, as befits an Englishman. The other young people are shown as volatile, highspirited, living for the moment, and interested in enjoying life—all characteristics traditionally attributed to the Irish. The English characters depict at times a typical English unease with strangers and people not of their own sort—people who are different. The Courthopes manage their unease by going away, but Chichele seeks to confront his by uniting with Marion in marriage—by literally embracing her and her alien identity. He takes a positive line; but not as regards Ireland the place, only as regards the person of Anglo-Irish, exotic-looking Marion.

Chichele is the epitome of the admirable, educated young Englishman, sympathetic yet reserved, whereas Marion is shown as the more daring and adventurous of the two. It is implied that they will complement and support each other; but somewhere other than in Ireland, where the atmosphere of violence sickens the hero: "I'll take you away with me, clear out of this—to the other side of the world if you like—you shall choose. We shall be married by Father Conroy. We will take Godfrey and Gertrude and go away for ever."[63]

Perhaps Laffan wanted to call attention here to the belief, sometimes seen as typical of the English, that there is an obvious practical solution to every problem. In this case, a "mixed" marriage conducted by a Catholic priest would not be a solution, it would simply, in the 1860s, have been an invalid ceremony as far as Chichele was concerned.[64] It is interesting to see here attempts being made by Laffan, somewhat ahead of her time, to explore the manner in which the Irish were perceived by the upper-class English, personified by Chichele Ansdale. The stereotype of the Irish "other" was usually negative. Writing about Irish identity, Declan Kiberd reminds us that colonists tend to project onto subject peoples what they actually fear to be *their own* shortcomings.[65] Partly this is done to deflect criticism from themselves, partly to justify the methods they have been using to rule others.

Much reference has already been made to Laffan's obsession with educational questions. In *Ismay's Children,* where it forms yet another theme, there is for the first time some real acknowledgement of the difficulties faced in devising *any* appropriate system of education, given Ireland's unusual circumstances. Accounts of the Irish education scene in the 1860s emphasise the differing perspectives of those concerned to change it, as well as the dependant and mendicant position in which Ireland generally was in regard to England. The apparent intransigence of Irish bishops at that time—their reluctance to compromise or to permit lay involvement with the management of the Catholic University, for instance—can be understood now as springing from awareness of the need to present a strong and united front, and the belief that a "hard line" on education planning would be easier to achieve without lay involvement, and more likely to bring results than a too obvious readiness to negotiate, which might seem like weakness.[66] As was evident from the failure of Gladstone's 1871 initiative, there was to be no quick answer to Ireland's education problems.[67]

There is one particular episode in *Ismay's Children,* when local worthies, dining with Father Paul Conroy, discuss education and reveal what seem to be representative contemporary views on the subject. Father Paul Conroy, a constitutional nationalist, shows little trust in the English whatever they promise to do. Macaulay the inspector of national schools is a Presbyterian sympathetic to Catholic problems and critical of the system he operates. As a Dissenter, he has experienced, as he makes plain, some discrimination also from members of the Church of Ireland. Daly, the local dispensary doctor, is a victim of the "snob" aspect of medical education. The other guest, Flynn, the local bank manager, falls asleep and does not contribute to the discussion. Chichele Ansdale, a product of what Laffan considered the ideal system—public school followed by Oxford University—is present as an observer. Tighe O'Malley, landlord, school manager and principal local employer, significantly does not bother to come, but his views are known. He has never even entered the school, and openly says he sees no point in educating people from the district. His needs are paramount, the peasants and townspeople are there to serve them, and if he wants a few skilled people, he can always import them from England or Scotland.

Father Paul is asked by Macaulay about plans for Godfrey's future. The priest starts with what he perceives to be most important, the danger of secularizing education:

> "I would rather see Godfrey dead than exposed to the danger of losing his faith, Mr. Macaulay. My grandfather was shot by the soldiers of a Protestant sovereign. My own brother is an exile for his devotion to a Catholic fatherland—an exile—an outlaw.[68] It is not for me to give in to a godless system of education devised by aliens and conquerors for the further enslavement of my country—no, sir!"

> "I am able to appreciate your feelings perfectly," answered the Presbyterian, "but this is a sad state of things, and our promising young friends are liable to suffer. Now, there are a great many Catholics in Trinity College."

> "There are. I know it—the children of the Dublin Roman Catholics, the meanest, most cringing creatures that ever disgraced their faith and country. It is those people who destroy the prospects of this country, who give the lie to our demand for liberal education in a Catholic University. . . ."

> "But don't you think, sir, that the Catholics, being confessedly backward in the matter of education, ought to grasp at any opportunity, no matter by whom presented, of improving their intellectual position in the country? They are behind, you know, and so you must get teachers. Well, where are you to get them?"

> "The Penal Laws are to blame that we have no Catholic teachers," grumbled Father Paul.

> "Well, granted, granted! How do you intend to create teachers?"

> "The Church must be obeyed," said Father Paul after a pause. "That is the first condition."

"Mind, I don't dispute your position in the least. I too am an advocate of denominational education. I only point out to you that by refusing these existing means
of education you are retarding your own cause. . . . You want a University. Yes,
and you ought to have one. But why is it with a Government grant of thirty thousand a year for Maynooth, the hierarchy did not make a Catholic university
then?"[69]

Father Paul is represented as nonplussed by those questions, and unable
to answer them. He cannot apparently even give the obvious answers, although there were some. The whole concept of formal training for school
teachers was then new and controversial. British politicians, already reluctant to sponsor denominational education for Catholics, would be even
more reluctant if they could persuade them to accept teacher-training in
secular colleges. Maynooth was an Irish seminary funded by the British
government to prevent Irish priests being trained in continental Europe. (It
was feared they would pick up revolutionary ideas there and disseminate
these in Ireland.) A "mix" of lay and clerical students was tried at
Maynooth to start with, and did not work. Macaulay, a pragmatist, is sympathetic but only up to a point. He counsels amalgamation of resources
across the board, but Father Paul is concerned about the separation of
teachers from their own religion and culture, as would be the case if they
were trained in a secular college supervised by someone less tolerant than
Macaulay.

Father Paul Conroy, the only genuinely likeable priest character in all
Laffan's fiction, is modelled on a real person. Father John Cooney, parish
priest of Bansha, in South Tipperary, in the late 1860s took Laffan's five orphaned little cousins into his house and looked after them with the help of
his housekeeper, until by slow degrees he succeeded in getting the relatives
involved—a circumstance which may have been the original inspiration
for *Ismay's Children*. Fr. Paul Conroy is shown as kind and indulgent, but
perhaps a little too kind, too self-sacrificing, quite unlike his other acquaintances, such as the local medical man, Dr. Daly, who has always something to complain about regarding his own professional standing: "The
fact is . . . if I had gone to the Queen's College or Trinity, I'd be in a very different position today. I've been passed over, over and over again, for men
who disobeyed the Church. Look at my sacrifices, all gone for nothing."[70]

The doctor, like the school inspector, probably reflects Laffan's own
views. Two of her brothers and no doubt some of her friends were medical
students at the Catholic University. Physical conditions at the Cecilia Street

Medical School (1854–1914) were extremely primitive in the 1870s, but the instruction and clinical training were good and so were the examination results.[71] The medical education offered at the Queen's Colleges was not any better, and fees there were higher. Trinity College however had some advantages over both. It offered a more prestigious qualification; it was residential, unlike the other colleges; and medical students were obliged to take a concurrent course in liberal studies. In the Catholic University this extra was optional, but it was not, apparently, available in the Queen's Colleges.[72] Some doctors were therefore more broadly educated than others—a fact which no doubt influenced interviewing boards, and led the resentful Dr. Daly to speak as he did. His reference to people disobeying the Church by attending Queen's Colleges is somewhat exaggerated; Catholics were not forbidden to attend them, they were only discouraged from doing so.[73]

Herself a nominal Catholic, Laffan seems to have adopted a view of Catholic education as inhibiting to the intellectual development. To her, education evidently meant systematic formal learning; and she seems not to have acknowledged the wider functions of schools—for instance, in socialising and training children, and supplementing or even, at times of need, replacing the part played by the child's family. Her own introduction to a Catholic convent school took place when she was thirteen and at about the time of her mother's death, which probably did not make adaptation to its system any easier.[74]

In her report to the Recess Committee May Laffan expressed the opinion that education at Catholic schools for boys was not as good as that provided by the endowed Church of Ireland schools.[75] In fact, she saw it as positively harmful:

> One day some daring spirit will strike a match in the magazine [sic] I hope so. . . . [A] rebellion among the educated would be still more acceptable to me. The most dreadful thing of all is that the boys of the Priest's schools, of the Jesuits, the Marists and the Oblates' schools, (I omit other Orders and denominations), appraise their masters precisely as do I . . . [C]ommonly known and asserted it is that in the Priest's schools boys do learn to drink. . . . [A]n ex-Father Superior of the University College, Blackrock, (who for drunkenness was deprived and sent to Australia) at the point of death confessed to a friend of his that the moral results of his school had been deplorable, and that he pitied the parents.[76]

The reference to drinking is interesting. The school Laffan refers to is the French College at Blackrock, where her three brothers were educated.

Staffed by a French order of priests, it was run on the lines of a French academy. On feast days, formal dinners were held at which the senior pupils made speeches and drank toasts with a moderate amount of wine. The purpose was, besides enjoyment, to accustom the boys to what was then a usual form of social get-together for men involved in politics or the professions—the celebratory dinner. It underlined the school's alternative mode of education following French rather than English models. Not everyone approved of this introduction to another culture.[77]

On a more mundane level, Laffan complained, with reason, that Catholic teachers of her time were usually untrained, whereas the Church of Ireland Protestants had their own teacher training college by the 1860s. Her knowledge of their endowed schools was probably derived from her father, who had attended such a school as a day-boy in Tipperary town. However, she does not appear to have known that her father's old school was in fact given unfavourable mention by an inspection team which investigated and reported on endowed schools in 1854–1858.[78]

Laffan's preferred model for the education of such as Godfrey was the English public school system, which she saw as inculcating self-esteem, self-reliance and industry—qualities apparently lacked by the Irish. It was also a recipe for success, as it was part of the education and socialization system of the ruling caste, or colonial elite. It seems unlikely that Laffan had read many of the contemporary novels about public school life, which presented a very different and less reassuring picture.[79] But some of Laffan's beliefs about education were certainly shared by prosperous middle-class Irish people of all denominations, who until the mid-twentieth century eagerly sent their children to be educated in England, hoping that English self-assurance would be acquired together with an English accent. Perhaps the saddest and oddest legacy of colonists to a native population, is the final offer of themselves as role models.[80]

The enhancement of Laffan's reputation with literary critics did not depend, in the case of *Ismay's Children,* on her educational opinions alone, but on her attempts at analysis of the reasons why men joined the Fenians. Her theory balances between the two extreme theories—the one stating that motives for joining were mainly social, the other, that they were mainly idealistic. The individual recruits she describes are from a cross-section of the Munster population, and do not come solely from the urban lower-middle class, as the Fenians were sometimes assumed to do.

Laffan does not go into great detail, either, about the general situation in Ireland during the early 1860s, but some background factors need to be taken into account. A series of bad harvests in the early part of the decade made the need for legislation to improve the situation of tenant farmers more pressing.[81] Constitutional nationalists saw this as a first priority and more urgent than achieving Home Rule, but republicans believed a more radical solution was necessary, involving political independence first, then, secondarily, reform of land legislation and a redistribution of wealth in order to halt the high level of emigration. There was a feeling that the country would "bleed to death" unless some radical action took place.[86] The British government of the time was conservative politically and opposed to any change in the status quo in Ireland, the affairs of which were seen as less urgent than other Imperial matters.[82]

It was realised that Ireland alone could never effectively oppose the richest and most powerful country in the world, but if England were involved in a war, and her opponents prepared to give Ireland aid, then there was a possibility for success. During the American Civil War (1861–65) England for economic reasons supported the Confederate side, and the friction which developed between the two countries suggested that war between America and England was a possibility.[83] It seems to have been when hopes for this were already receding, but conspicuous numbers of Irish-American ex-officers were still being dispatched to Ireland to mobilise the country by training and organising men, and money was entering Ireland also for that purpose, that the decision was taken in Britain to crush the IRB.[84]

According to Laffan's reading of the situation, the men who volunteered to join the Brotherhood all had something in common:

> Every one, save Luke Ahearne and a few others, had some complaint to make, some grievance to address. They knew of no other way but this. The magistrates were all landlords, and what was the use of complaining of your landlord to a fellow landlord. [Gentry] all sided with one another. . . .[85]

Laffan reviews the individual reasons which led Godfrey Mauleverer, Jim Cadogan and Tony Devoy to join the IRB. She singles out these three as representative of many.

Godfrey, apart from a natural desire for adventure, is motivated by the need to assert himself, to challenge the denigrating label of "bastard"given him by the local gentry. He feels his ambivalent status keenly, and wants to change it by proving himself to be a hero. This is clear even to Marchmont,

Tighe's agent, who is genuinely concerned about the threat to the boy, and intercedes with the police on his behalf: "He has one terrible grievance against society as it is. Don't, in mercy, add more to his burden! To imprison him would be to cast a ruinous stigma upon him for his whole life."[86] Godfrey is an example of the idealistic young man, ignorant of the full consequences of his actions.

Jim Cadogan is the alcoholic son of the local postmistress, a hard-working widow who made sacrifices to send him first to the diocesan college and then to the Catholic University's medical school: "The dissipation of the metropolis proved too strong for an ill-ballasted temperament, and Jim returned, a hopeless drunkard, to the little household in Barrettstown."[87] Jim, when sober, acts as half-kindly, half-cynical mentor of Godfrey, and recruits him to the IRB. His only direct reference to his abandoned profession comes when Godfrey asks him if he plans to return to Dublin:

> "I can't pass. I've given up reading—in fact, I don't mind telling you, I pledged the books. Ah! where's the good of it? where's the good of anything? Better be born with a millstone round your neck than be born a Roman Catholic, sneered at and looked down on by any member of the ascendancy, and those Trinity College boys. I used to see them at hospital in the mornings. . . . But just wait! Pack of upstarts! See if we don't pay them off."[88]

Depression and lack of self-worth are factors in his alcoholism. Jim has made several attempts to kill himself, and to injure his mother and sister when they intervened to stop him. He represents troubled people who are drawn to a radical political group because it offers direction and meaning to their lives—it offers hope.

Tony Devoy, on the other hand, represents the large group of people with unmet basic needs, in this case, for food:

> A big gaunt man with an expression of face strongly resembling that which conventionally represents famine, [he] was a typical member of the labouring class of the community. He had a wife and seven children alive out of nine that had been born to them. Seven shillings a week represented his maximum of prosperity and comfort. He could not read or write. Abjectly miserable and wretched as his lot seemed to be, it was not without some alleviations, some compensations.[89]

The "alleviations and compensations" refer to the attention and hospitality Tony earns by his story-telling gift and his ready wit. Tony and his wife have no false shame about accepting help from others when necessary. Often the help is given in kind, by Jim Cadogan or the Mauleverers. Out of his pittance Tony pays his dues regularly to the IRB and in the evenings after work attends drills and meetings, sometimes falling asleep at the latter through sheer exhaustion. He does not want to emigrate and leave his neighbours and friends, but he is being pressured by Tighe O'Malley's agent to accept the twenty pound grant offered to tenants who go to America. Tony values the education he never had, but poverty limits choices: "He had a promising boy of an age to go to school, but debarred therefrom by want of clothes. How could a child who was at that moment clad in one leg of an old corduroy trousers, fastened mysteriously and inefficiently round his neck by a bit of string, be sent to school to the nuns?"[90] Tony's political activism is the way he retains his self respect, and he dreams it will eventually help him to achieve basic human rights for his family, which he sees in terms of food, clothes and education for them.

Thus Laffan demonstrates how people at the margins of society, for whatever reason, come to seek involvement in an association which offers them an acceptable identity and a hope of the power to effect favourable change. The IRB was thought to be in a position to offer these things to people at that time. The nature of the organization, even its secrecy, gave a sense of power. It may be asked if it did confer any lasting benefit on its members. It seems to have had at least the power to keep the ideal of political independence for Ireland alive in them.

Power is a major feature in the allegorical message of this novel, which seems to insist that in order for the "marriage" of two countries to work, the stronger of the two parties to the symbolic union should be permitted to dominate the other, and in any difference, to prevail. This sounds very like a development of the teachings of Thomas Carlyle, who wanted to justify the Right of Might. For peace and prosperity to reign, the weaker party must give in, and sink their identity in the powerful other.

The confused Mauleverer identity must therefore be given up, and exchanged for something more solid and worthy. Unfortunately Laffan does not sufficiently characterise the young couple, Marion and the oddly-named Chichele, well enough to make us feel absolutely sure that their marriage is the ending which is inevitable and most appropriate, like the union of Horatio and Glorvina in *The Wild Irish Girl*. In the Laffan story, Marion has already had to lose so much—her foster-parents, her brother, and her home—that the allegory, especially towards the end, seems to become rather strained. The leaving of Tighe O'Malley in possession of an estate not rightfully his, and then placing him in charge of his cousins, is presumably intended to symbolise a gradual transfer of Ireland's resources from hands which held on to them for centuries. Somehow, in view of Tighe's financial history, this transfer seems unlikely to work. Even archaic and ingenious touches, like the chorus of beggars sitting on the town bridge, commenting shrewdly and accurately on the passers-by;[91] or the prophecy of Marion's future well-being uttered by the aspiring nun Mary Ahearne, [92] are not quite enough to convince us that the wheel of fortune is about to turn for the dispossessed at last.

ᎷᏢᏢ CONCLUSION

May Laffan's writing life, as we have seen, finished in the early 1880s, and this timing no doubt had some responsibility for the swift descent of her work into obscurity. The literary revival directed by W. B. Yeats, Lady Gregory and their associates, which also began in the 1880s, found plays and poetry more effective than the novel at spreading ideas they thought important. Few works of fiction met Yeats's exacting standards either. The fact that he approved one of Laffan's short stories enough to count it among the best of its day (1895) signifies that it impressed him, even despite himself.[1] The story, "Flitters, Tatters and the Counsellor," did not contain any hint either of national consciousness or Celtic symbolism; it was highly realistic and almost devoid of sentimentality. It was also extremely popular with a wider public than that generally addressed by Yeats.

Laffan's social comment confined itself to two main topics, class and poverty. She had had practical experience of both. Her nominal Catholic allegiance placed her firmly as a second-class citizen at a time when Ireland was administered and governed by a Protestant elite, and her voluntary work kept her informed about the extent and nature of Irish poverty. Laffan's concentration on writing about people at odds with their world quickly established another difference between herself and the majority of fiction writers. The attraction which the margins of society evidently held for her seemed to arise from a sense of kinship with people on the borderlines, as if she was aware that like them she did not quite belong. She was after all a hybrid, the offspring of two different and often conflicting religious traditions. On one side of her lay the world from which her father came, that of Norman Irish Catholic peasants living in the style of their ancestors, between the earthen floor and the straw thatch of houses tiny by standards of today, the dark interiors warmed by hearth-fires which were never suffered to go out. Even when prosperous, the inhabitants lived as if they were not, because it was safer to do so.[2]

We may imagine, perhaps wrongly, that these people never questioned their religious or political beliefs, that their piety and conservatism secured them against the storms of life. Yet we have no evidence to prove that they were essentially different from ourselves. They did not reach positions of power or esteem, but they lived through periods of history when survival itself must have been a heroic business. They educated their male children, at what sacrifice one can only imagine, and when circumstances made it possible, they educated girls also. At least two female cousins and contemporaries of Laffan achieved Royal University qualifications in the 1890s.[3]

May Laffan's mother came from a very different background to that of the Laffans. Ellen Fitzgibbon was part of a wealthy legal family making its way upward in the world of nineteenth-century Dublin. Finding their original Norman-Irish Catholic identity a handicap, the Fitzgibbons changed it as far as possible, joining in turn the Church of Ireland, the Freemasons, the Conservative party, and in at least one instance, even the landed gentry. They did not lack resources for education. Perhaps significantly, we know virtually nothing of the women in this family, but a good deal is known about the public lives of the men. They were, it seems, people with a strong and probably justified sense of their own importance in the social hierarchy, and by the middle of the nineteenth century they must have felt secure, with connections in Belfast as well as in Dublin, a summer villa at Howth and a house in Merrion Square. In all of Laffan's writing we can sense a conflict between the two world views and lifestyles presented to her. At some times, she chose to attack one side, at other times the other. Occasionally, she attacked both: "A plague 'o both your houses! They have made worms' meat of me."

It was in truth very difficult. Laffan saw Protestants as members of an intellectual elite which with all her heart she wanted to join. In this, she shared the world view of W. B. Yeats and his associates, who perceived the Ascendancy of which they saw themselves as members to be the thinking organ of contemporary Irish society. Laffan also wanted to be appreciated for the clever and original person she was. Her literary friends, mentioned in letters to her publishers, all belonged at least nominally to the Church of England. Most of them, living in London or Oxford, perhaps did not share to a great extent the class feeling about the inferiority of Catholics which truly seems to have been a characteristic of the Irish Ascendancy. When she was in England, therefore, Laffan could appreciate the Protestant side of her identity.

But in rural Ireland things were different, and when she stayed with her Tipperary relatives she had to adapt to their deeply unfashionable view of the world. No doubt she enjoyed the scenic beauty, but perhaps not the somewhat undomesticated lifestyle, which with its emphasis on drinking, card-playing and nationalist politics, its lack of high culture, must have seemed like a return to the eighteenth century. Still, she appreciated the warmth, exuberance and intimacy as well as the sense of belonging to a large extended family. She did not, in spite of her pride in being a Dubliner, see her cousins as inferior people.

We do not know what the Fitzgibbon family thought of Laffan as a writer. Some of them may well have been shocked by her books, particularly if they shared the evangelical aversion to novels. Although they may have agreed with her somewhat inaccurate strictures on Roman Catholicism, at the same time they could hardly go along with her frank and witty descriptions of themselves as a narrow-minded, snobbish and bigoted set of people. Nor would they have anticipated the value Laffan's novels could have for anyone interested in social history.

Most novels set in nineteenth-century Ireland were stories about the very poor or the landed gentry; there were few with middle-class characters and settings. Laffan's contribution to our understanding of the social history of her time is therefore important. Full of topical allusions, she gives realistic and detailed accounts of middle-class life, its political views, aspirations and customs, its social and personal relationships. We are told how characters behaved when short of money, and when they had it, what they spent it on. We learn how people travelled, how they entertained, and the vital roles played by servants in the lives of their employers. In each Laffan novel, in addition to intimate scenes, we find a series of set-pieces reminiscent of the large, crowded paintings of Frith and some of the Pre-Raphaelites, in which the detail is pitilessly accurate and the colour and force of style have not lost their impact in 130 years.

Such, for example, are the ballroom and card-party scenes in *Hogan MP*, and the description of Kingstown (now Dun Laoghaire) Pier, with afternoon strollers showing off their finery, overlooked by row upon row of well-fed clerics on the upper terraces. By way of contrast, an episode in *The Honourable Miss Ferrard* describes the wedding of a prosperous farmer's daughter in 1870s Tipperary. After a brief ceremony in a local chapel, a lengthy, almost medieval-style feast is held at home, where a hired cook officiates, treated with mixed respect and fear by her employers. A whole lamb and a side of roast beef, cooked on the spit before the open fire, are flanked by boiled turkeys and hams. There are no vegetables served but potatoes, and no salads or fruit. Drinks consist of sherry for women and whisky punch for men, and Helena Ferrard, as "gentry," is served first, with the priests. The bride, who hardly knows her new husband, sits isolated in purple satin splendour, weeping copiously because today for the first time she has to leave her home place. While she weeps, negotiation to make a match for her brother begins, and the farmyard animals, whose needs have been forgotten, get in everyone's way.

In *Christy Carew* the urban middle-class dinner-parties and musical evenings are counter-pointed by acrid political discussion. Here also, near the end of the book, appears the biggest of the set-pieces, an all-day picnic on Dalkey Island at which the real attitudes of a whole cast of characters are gradually and mercilessly exposed to the glaring light and heat of an August day. Finally, in *Ismay's Children* are two contrasting, memorable crowd scenes: Helen Talbot's death in a hovel, surrounded by the many beggars she helped in better times, and the noisy, lavish party given by the Ahearne family just at the stage when they think, mistakenly, that all is going to go right for them.

These set-pieces convey vividly to us a sense that May Laffan enjoyed writing them, and that she considered them important. Ambivalent and critical as she was, she wanted to show the public quality of the life she wrote about by emphasising that in the Ireland she knew grief and gladness were not private emotions, but were to be shared. She depicted a society in which individual wants were not considered paramount, and material insecurity was a part of daily life, yet the involvement of people with each other carried messages of hope. This society was not English; indeed, it struck her English characters as foreign to them. Certainly in her descriptions it had a quality of humanity and realism more characteristic of the life shown in novels of life in Russia or France than in contemporary English fiction. But Laffan could not fully inhabit this enticing world, since she was convinced it was also obscurantist, anti-intellectual and chaotic, offering no place to people like herself, who needed to feel secure.

Setting Laffan on the continuum from more traditional storytellers like William O'Brien[4] or Charles Kickham[5] to the technical sophistication of George Moore[6] and James Joyce,[7] one might group her with the "Somerville and Ross"[8] partnership and with Emily Lawless.[9] But unlike the three latter, May Laffan was not from the Ascendancy, nor was she a Protestant. She was unable to pretend to being so, either, but could only continue on her obstacle course between the two "wretched castes,"[10] bruising herself in turn on one or the other, neither of which, she thought, could offer her what she wanted.

Caught also between two opposing cultures, that of the colonist and of the colonised, Laffan probably felt with some truth that she belonged nowhere, to no country and no people, and that at the centre of her being was a void which remained unfilled. She seems to have hoped at first that she could at some future point make a choice of where to belong. When she met Walter Hartley, it is likely that she saw him as someone stronger than herself. He was an agnostic and thus apparently independent of both religious traditions. We do not know if her hopes were fulfilled or not, but the results of her decision to marry him seem to have been negative: an end to her writing and a gradual decline in her mental health. On first reading the *Recess Committee Notes,* and without having any factual information about Laffan's history, I could not help getting the impression that she was depressed enough to consider taking her own life. This is a measure of the anger and misery the *Recess Committee Notes* conveyed to one reader.

Laffan's four novels were set in the era just before leadership of the Irish Party at Westminster passed to Charles Stewart Parnell. His rise to power in the 1880s marked an end to the period she wrote about. From her *Recess Committee Notes,* it appears that she held the populist view that Parnell was a helpless victim of hostility on the part of the Irish Catholic Hierarchy, which brought about his political failure and death by withdrawing support from him when he was ailing and needed it most. This view no doubt contributed to Laffan's general state of depression about Ireland's future.[11] It need not, however, have inhibited her from continuing to write. Even though the political system had altered, some other things had not. The poverty and deprivation described in Laffan's short stories formed an eternal theme, everlastingly there for compassion and skill to work on. It is a great pity that, so far as we know, she was never again able even to try.

Laffan's memory and even copies of her neglected books were to survive among the very people of Tipperary, the provincial Irish, whom she had implied lacked the education to appreciate them. However incomplete her ideas on the subject of education for women were (for although she realised that women needed to expand their activities outside the home, she was not able to describe convincingly how this could be done), her novels and stories offer the reader a unique perspective of middle-class life in nineteenth-century Ireland, moving, though almost imperceptibly, towards great political and social change.

ᘒᘒᗒ Notes

Introduction

1. Robert Lee Wolff, "Preface," facsimile edition of May Laffan Hartley's *Hogan MP* (New York: Garland, 1979), iiv.

2. Anon., Review of *Ismay's Childern*, *Athenaeum*, 15 October 1887, 501.

3. R. V. Comerford, *The Fenians in Context* (Dublin: Wolfhoud Press; Atlantic Highlands, NJ: Humanities Press, 1985),165–67.

4. Ibid., 158–60.

5. Thomas W. Moody, *The Course of Irish History: Fenianism, Home Rule and the Land War* (Cork: Mercier Press, 1966), 276.

6. Roy F. Foster, *Modern Ireland: 1600–1972* (London: Penguin, 1989), 422–23.

7. Emmet Larkin, *The Consolidation of the Roman Catholic Church in Ireland, 1860–1870* (Dublin: Gill & Macmillan, 1987) and *The Roman Catholic Church and the Home Rule Movement in Ireland, 1870–1874* (Chapel Hill: University of North Carolina Press, 1990). May Laffan, *Islay's Children* (London: Macmillan, 1887), 296, 427–28.

8. *Ismay's Children*, 296.

9. David Thornley, *Isaac Butt and Home Rule* (London: MacGibbon & Kee, 1964), 162–63, 165.

10. Gerald Fitzgibbon, *Ireland in 1868* (London: Longmans, Green, Reader & Dyer, 1868), 198, 225–55. William O'Connor Morris, *Memories and Thoughts of a Life* (London: George Allen, 1895) 315, 320–21.

11. Anon., Review of *The Honourable Miss Ferrard*in, *Saturday Review*, 23 September 1877.

12. Frances Hays, "Women of the Day" (London: Chatto & Windus, 1895).

13. Richard Hayes, "Manuscript Sources for the History of Irish Civilization," in Volume 3, "Persons," re. May Laffan (Mrs. Walter Noel Hartley), *Recess Committee Notes,* N 5364, Cambridge University Library, MSA DD 6553.

14. Standish Hayes O'Grady (1832–1915) was born at Castleconnell, County Limerick, into an Anglo-Irish family. He became a noted Gaelic scholar and translator, and was a cousin of the historical novelist and cultural activist Standish James O'Grady.

15. Donal A. Murphy, *Blazing Tar Barrels and Standing Orders* (Tyone, Co. Tipperary: Relay Books, 1999.) An account of the changeover to democratic local government in North Tipperary. Ellice Pilkington, Horace Plunkett and George Russell, *The United Irishwomen: Their Place, Work and Ideals* (Dublin: Maunsel & Co. Ltd., 1911). The "manifesto" of a voluntary organization which aimed to improve the lives of disadvantaged women,

by working with them on an individual befriending basis. Horace Plunkett, *Ireland in the New Century 1904* (London: John Murray, 1905).

16. Francis Phillips, "Obituary and Appreciation of Dr. Thomas Laffan," *The Tipperary Star,* 1918.

17. Kevin Whelan, "An Underground Gentry? Catholic Middlemen in Eighteenth Century Ireland," in *Irish Popular Culture 1650-1850.* J. S. Donnelly and Kerby A. Miller, eds. (Dublin: Irish Academic Press, 1998), 118–64.

18. Personal Communication from Tom Donovan, Corcamore, Clarina, County Limerick. Donovan, a local historian and member of the Historical Society (Glynn, Co. Limerick), generously provided me useful materials and information in my research.

19. J. Y. B. "Sir Walter Noel Hartley (1846–1913)," *Obituary Notices of Fellows Deceased, The Royal Society, London.*

Chapter 1: Origins and Early Years

1. Oliver MacDonagh, *States of Mind: A Study of Anglo-Irish Conflict 1780–1980* (London: Allen & Unwin, 1983), 3. Regarding "prudential conversions."

2. Personal communication from Tom Donovan, member of the Glin Historical Society, Corcamore, Clarina, County Limerick. Regarding burning of pre-1850 estate records, and topography of Ballyhoulihan.

3. William Shaw Mason, "Parish of Kilfergus in the Diocese and County of Limerick," in *A Statistical Account or Parochial Survey of Ireland* (Dublin: Graisberry and Campbell, 1816), 301, para. XI.

4. Gibbon Fitzgibbon, letter to John Fitzgibbon, 24 March 1946, in the possession of Tom Donovan.

5. William Sha Mason, 301, para. x.

6. *Home Thoughts From Abroad: The Australian Letters of Thomas F. Culhane,* Thomas J. Byrne, Tom Donovan, and Bernard Stack, eds. (Glin, County Limerick: Glin Historical Society, 1998), 56.

7. Ibid., 56. Tom Donovan's translation:

Deich bpunt is taistiún ón Ridire bhfiúntach

Agus dá pinginn ruadh ó Bhrídín neamhiontach

Cúig giní óir ó Dónal na Féile

Ní ón ngaoith ná ón ngreín a thóg sé na tréithre

Dhá phúnt is coróin ó Chathal de Brún

Ach, dada ní bfuaireas ó Sheanín Giobún!"

8. Ibid., 189.

9. May Laffan, "Weeds," *Macmillan's Magazine,* 44 (September 1881), 314.

10. Ruth McKenzie (Canadian writer researching James Fitzgibbon), letter to John Fitzgibbon, 27 June 1973, in the possession of Tom Donovan.

11. Anon., "James Fitzgibbon," *Dictionary of National Biography* (London: Smith, Elder, 1880).

12. "Application for Marriage Licence on behalf of Thomas Fitzgibbon and Eleanor Mackay Cunningham," Public Record Office, Joyce House, 88–11 Lombard Street East, Dublin 2.

13. Gibbon Fitzgibbon's Family Tree, original in possession of Tom Donovan.

14. Alexander Thom. *Irish Almanac and Official Directory* (A. Thom, Printer/Publisher. 87 & 88 Middle Abbey Street, Dublin, 1835).

15. Gibbon Fitzgibbon's Family Tree.

16. Ibid.

17. Anon., Obituary of Gerald Fitzgibbon (I), *Irish Law Times*, 7 October 1882, 494.

18. J. G. Swift McNeil, *What I Have Seen and Heard* (London: Arrowsmith, 1925), 132–33.

19. W. J. McCormack, *Sheridan Le Fanu and Victorian Ireland* (Oxford: Clarendon, 1980), 13.

20. "Gerald Fitzgibbon" (I) in *Dictionary of National Biography* (London: Smith, Elder, 1890), 155. The letters "Q.C." stand for Queen's Counsel, and after a British lawyer's name they denote that he or she is a senior barrister appointed as a legal advisor to the Crown. (If the reigning monarch is a King, the designation is King's Counsel). A Q.C. has certain privileges including that of wearing a silk legal gown in court, hence to accept nomination as a Q.C. is to "take silk." Should a Q.C. wish to become involved in an action taken *against* the Crown, he/she must get formal permission to do this. This situation had relevance to Ireland for example in political trials when lawyers were briefed to defend individuals accused of treason.

21. Second Leader, *Irish Times*, 28 September 1882. An evaluation of Gerald Fitzgibbon (I)'s legal and political career. The *Irish Times* "Second Leader" was and is a short, untitled anonymous piece about a significant happening—in this case, Fitzgibbon's death. The Second Leader is placed directly beneath the official editorial, or First Leader, which usually deals with major current issues. The tone of the September 28 piece suggests that the writer saw Fitzgibbon as an interesting historical figure but mainly of importance as the father of the current Lord Justice of Appeal, Gerald Fitzgibbon (I).

22. F. Eldrington Ball, *The Judges in Ireland: 1221–1921* (London: J. Murray, 1926), 372–73.

23. R. F. Foster, *Lord Randolph Churchill: A Political Life* (Oxford: Clarendon, 1981), 41.

24. Sir Charles A. Cameron, C. B. *History of the Royal College of Surgeons in Ireland* (Dublin: Fannin, 1916), 523–24.

25. Patrick Corish, *The Irish Catholic Experience: A Historical Survey* (Dublin: Gill & Macmillan, 1985), 221. The introduction of this book is dated 1984. There is a first reprint, 1986.

26. Edward MacLysaght, *The Surnames of Ireland* (Dublin: Irish Academic, 1999), 187. The Huguenots were French Protestants expelled from France in 1685 at the revocation of the Edict of Nantes which originally granted them religious tolerance. Over 10,000 emigrated to Ireland where some joined the army of William of Orange, and others helped in the foundation of the linen and banking industries. Compared to most immigrants they were well-off, most having skilled trades and some even having titles of nobility. French-speaking and strictly Calvinist, they maintained their separate identity and modes of worship until the early nineteenth century, but eventually were absorbed into the Church of Ireland. As people who had undergone persecution for their faith they were greatly respected even by those who did not share their beliefs, and to be able to claim descent from a Huguenot family was a source of pride, as Laffan implies in *The Honorable Miss Ferrard.*

27. Walter Skehan, "Index to Priests Ministering in the Cashel/Emly Diocese 1600–1970," in James O'Shea's, *Priest, Politics and Society in Post-Famine Ireland: A Study of Co. Tipperary 1850–1891* (Dublin: Wolfhound, 1983), 326–57.

28. Michael Dwyer Laffan (1864–1958), *The Orphans,* c. 1943. An unpublished account of his early life.

29. May Laffan Hartley, *Recess Committee Notes* (unpublished 1895), 15. Held by Syndics of Cambridge University Library.

30. *The Irish Catholic Experience,* 220–21. A persistent remainder of penal legislation of 1746 (19 Geo.II c.13.) laid down that a marriage ceremony where one or both parties was Protestant was void in law unless performed by a minister of the Church of Ireland. This statute was not repealed until 1870. Effectively it meant that a "mixed" marriage must take place in the local Church of Ireland parish church. Catholic marriages of that time were not generally celebrated in a church, but in the bride's family home or in the priest's house; and they were not accompanied by Mass.

31. *British Biographical Index,* David Bank and Anthony Esposito, eds. (London: K. G. Saur, 1885), under Hartley, no. 336.

32. "Gerald Fitzgibbon" (II) in *Dictionary of National Biography* (London: Smith, Elder, 1890), 30. He is described as: "Eldest of the three children, two sons and a daughter" of Gerald Fitzgibbon (I). No details of the daughter are given.

33. Mona Hearn, *Below Stairs: Domestic Service Remembered in Dublin and Beyond, 1880–1922* (Dublin: Lilliput, 1993), 8, 77.

34. Personal communications from Michael Joseph Laffan (1909–2002).

35. Hazel P. Smyth, *The Town of the Road: The Story of Booterstown* (Bray: Pale, 1994), 90–95.

36. *Thom's Irish Almanac and Official Directory* (Dublin: Alexander Thom, Printer & Publisher, 1862). Re: entries of Laffan family, for 1861–1551, for 1862–1515. These page numbers refer to the index of surnames of ratepayers. *Thom's* provides a record of Dublin ratepayers, but although the index is accurate the "street pages" are not, because when people moved often the "street pages" did not always keep up with their new address.

37. Death announcement of Sarah Ellen Fitzgibbon Laffan, *Irish Times,* 29 October 1862. Memorial inscription on family grave in Glasnevin Cemetery.

38. May Laffan, *Hogan MP* (London: Macmillan & Co., 1881), 58.

39. List of pupils attending Blackrock College in 1862, supplied by Rev. Fr. Sean P. Farragher CSSP. With the achievement of Catholic Emancipation in 1829, a need for higher education for the Irish middle-class became more obvious. Trinity College, Dublin, the only university in Ireland was unable to fulfill that need even if the will to do so had been present. English legislation of 1845 set up and financed "Queen's Colleges" in Belfast, Cork and Galway ostensibly for all students, and these were constituted as the "Queen's University." But, to satisfy English Protestant opinion, which resisted denominational education and wanted to avoid controversy, these colleges were without faculties of Theology, Philosophy or History.

The Irish Catholic Church, fearing the spread of religious indifferentism, discouraged Catholics from attending the new colleges, where lowered entry requirements had already attracted criticism.

In 1854 the Irish Bishops, with Papal encouragement, founded the Catholic University in Dublin with Cardinal Newman as Rector. Financed by church-door collections, with no charter or state funding, it struggled to survive but its Medical School attended in the 1870s by Laffan's brothers William and James, became highly successful and achieved independent recognition for its qualifications

Newman resigned in 1858, and the Catholic University went through a period of decline until reconstituted by the Jesuits in 1883 under the name of University College with the non-teaching Royal University validating its degrees. Both the College and the Royal University were later included with the Queen's Colleges in the National University of Ireland (1909). Famous students of University College include James Joyce (from 1895), later Padraig Pearse and Eamon De Valera.

40. Sean P. Farragher, *Pere Jules Leman* (Dublin: Paraclete, 1988).

41. Record of entry of the Laffan girls to St. Catherine's convent school, Sion Hill, Supplied by Sister Dominique Horgan, OP, Archivist. Catherine Laffan's date of birth is unknown but can be deduced from her known year of entry to St. Catherine's (1871). She would then have been twelve or thirteen years old.

42. Mary Carbery, *The Farm by Lough Gur: The Story of Mary Fogarty* (Dublin: Mercier, 1937), 94–106. Sister Ursula Clarke, *The Ursulines in Cork* (Cork, 1996), 98–105. Sister Mercedes Lillis, *Two Hundred Years A'Growing* (Roscrea, 1987). Katherine Tynan, *Twenty-five Years Reminiscences* (London, 1913).

43. Tony Fahy, "Nuns in the Catholic Church in Ireland in the Nineteenth Century" in *Girls Don't Do Honours: Irish Women in Education in the Nineteenth and Twentieth Centuries,* Mary Cullen, ed. (Dublin: Women's Education Bureau, 1987), 23.

44. Personal communication from Sister Theophane O'Dwyer, OP, Local Archivist, Sion Hill Convent, Blackrock.

45. Pat Jalland, *Women, Marriage and Politics 1860–1914* (Oxford: Clarendon, 1988), 7–17.

46. John Nicholas Murphy, *Terra Incognita, or the Convents of the United Kingdom* (London: Longmans, Green, 1873), 167, 620.

47. Eibhlin Breathnach, *"Charting New Waters: Women's Experience in Higher education 1879-1908,"* in *Girls Don't Do Honours,* 55–78.

48. Ibid., 55–78.

49. *Hogan MP,* 128–30.

50. "Programme of 1876 Prizegiving at St.Catherine's Convent, Sion Hill, Blackrock, County Dublin," courtesy of Sister Theophane O'Dwyer, OP. Sister Mercedes Lillis, *Two Hundred Years A'Growing* (M. Lillis, Roscrea, Co Tipperary: J. F. Walsh, 1987), 77–80.

51. May Laffan, "Convent Boarding-Schools for Young Ladies," *Frazer's Magazine,* June 1874, 778–86.

52. Anon., *The Ursuline Manual, or, A Collection of Prayers, Spiritual Exercises, Interspersed with the Various Instructions Necessary for Forming Youth to the Practice of Solid Piety* (New York: Edward Dunigan, 1840).

53. "Convent Boarding-Schools for Young Ladies," 784.

54. Ibid., 783.

55. Ibid., 786.

56. Anne V. O'Connor, "The Revolution in Girls' Secondary Education in Ireland 1860–1910," in *Girls Don't Do Honours: Irish Women in Education in the Nineteenth and Twentieth Centuries,* ed. Mary Cullen (Dublin: Women's Education Bureau, 1987), 37.

57. Ibid., 45–48.

58. "Terra Incognita," 390–91.

59. George Moore, *A Drama in Muslin,* Belfast Edition (London: Vizetelly & Co., 1886), 77.

60. May Laffan, letter to G.A. Macmillan, undated letter written apparently between November and December 1881. Macmillan Archive, Reading University, no number. Mrs. Pattison (née Emilia Strong) was the wife of Mark Pattison, Rector of Lincoln College, Oxford. Well-known intellectuals, they were both friends of May Laffan. See chapter two.

61. Census of Ireland Form A, dated 31 March 1901. No. 414, signed by W. N. Hartley.

62. Lawrence MacBride, *The Greening of Dublin Castle* (Washington D.C.: Catholic University of America, 1991), 25, 27, 37.

63. *The Irish Catholic Experience*, 217.

64. Clare C. Murphy, "North Tipperary in the Year of the Fenian Rising," *Tipperary Historical Journal* (1995).

65. Captain W. T. Lynam, "Mick M'Quaid," *The Shamrock* (Dublin). It first appeared in this magazine, running from 5 October 1872 to 27 September 1873. This was one of a light-hearted series written around the same comic character.

66. Michael J. McCarthy, *Gallowglass, or Life in the Land of the Priests* (London: Simpkin, Marshall, Hamilton, Kent & Co., 1904). This was a satiric novel with a strong anti-Catholic slant.

67. Raymond Chapman, *Faith & Revolt* (London: Weidenfeld and Nicolson, 1970), 21, regarding "electionism." George Sigerson, *Modern Ireland* (London: Longmans, Green, Reader, and Dyer, 1869), regarding Protestant sense of superiority to Catholics.

68. *Terra Incognita*, 371–74.

69. S. J. Connolly, ed., *Oxford Companion to Irish History* (Oxford: Oxford University, 1998), 552.

70. Thomas J. Morrissey, *Towards a National University: William Delaney, S.J.: An Era of Initiative in Irish Education* (Dublin: Atlantic Highlands, 1983), 33.

71. Pope Pius IX : Encyclical to Italian Bishops, 10 August 1863. An example of contemporary Catholic teaching on salvation: "We and you know that those who lie under invincible ignorance as regards our most holy religion, and who, diligently observing the natural law and its precepts, which are engraven by God on the hearts of all, and are prepared to obey God, and lead a good and upright life, are able, by the operation of divine light and grace, to obtain eternal life."

72. *Faith and Revolt*, 12,13.

73. Gerald Fitzgibbon (I), *Ireland in 1868*, 2nd ed. (London: Longmans, Green, Reader, and Dyer 1868), 138–41, 201–207.

74. Thomas Carlyle, *Reminiscences of my Irish Journey* (London: S. Low, Marston, Searle, & Rivington, 1882). James Anthony Froude, *The English in Ireland in the Eighteenth Century* (London: Longmans, Green and Co., 1872). William Makepeace Thackeray, *The Irish Sketchbook* (London: Smith & Elder, 1845).

75. Edward R. Norman, *Anti-Catholicism in Victorian England* (London: Allen and Unwin, 1968); see Introduction, Section 5, "Ritualism," 105–21. Tractarianism, also known as the "Oxford Movement," began in the 1830s with the publication of a series of articles ("Tracts for the Times") emphasizing the Church of England's neglected Catholic heritage and seeking to recover this. The celebrated writer and preacher John Henry Newman(1801–1890), led the reform and, with a number of his supporters, eventually joined the Roman Catholic Church (1845). Most Tractarians, however, remained within the Church of England.

Tractarian clergy aroused considerable hostility in England when they rejected the title "Protestant," identified themselves as priests rather than ministers and introduced a Roman Catholic style liturgy in which plainchant, incense, elaborate vestments and ceremonial were used. At first mainly a clerical revolution, the movement came to affect most areas of Victorian life, including art, literature and politics. The Church of England (or Anglican church) formed a division into "High" and "Low" which it has retained in a modified form until the present day. One positive effect of the Tractarian movement was the development of greater tolerance between Anglicans and Catholics; this was noticeable by the end of the nineteenth century.

The Church of Ireland much less influenced by Tractarianism, remained generally "Low Church" in ethos, and maintained a strong Protestant identity.

76. Ibid., Introduction, Section 3, "Papal Aggression," 52–79.

77. Margaret M. Maison, *Search your soul, Eustace: A Survey of the Religious Novel in the Victorian Age* (London: Sheed and Ward, 1961). Regarding widespread misunderstanding of Catholic belief and practice.

78. Elizabeth Bowen, introduction to *Uncle Silas*, by Sheridan Le Fanu (London: Cresset, 1947), 8.

79. Bram Stoker, *Dracula* (London: Penguin Popular Clasics, 1994), 436–40.

80. *Ireland in 1868*, 23.

81. Ibid., 123–27. Regarding "Tenant Right" to receive recompense for improvements.

82. Ibid., 191. Regarding lack of Protestant interest in Irish language.

83. Ibid., 100–107. Regarding Charter Schools and their result. Kenneth Milne, *The Irish Charter Schools 1730–1830* (Dublin: Four Courts, 1997), 12.

84. Ibid., 81, 85, 252. Regarding deficiencies of Charter Schools.

85. R. F. Foster, *Paddy and Mr. Punch: Connections in Irish and English History* (London: A. Lane, 1993), 313 n.64; 322 n.6.

86. May Laffan, *The Honourable Miss Ferrard* (London: Richard Bentley, 1877), 266.

87. *Paddy and Mr. Punch*, 188. Illustration of contemporary cartoon with Britannia and Hibernia shown as two sisters.

88. Recess Committee Notes, 6.

89. E. P. Mitchell, *Dictionary of American Biography* (New York, 1923), II: 539–40.

90. Frank M. O'Brien, *The Story of the New York Sun: 1833–1928* (New York: D. Appleton and Co., 1928), 196–98. Account of W. M. Laffan's successful career as a journalist/editor.

91. Davis Coakley, *The Irish School of Medicine* (Dublin: Town House, 1988), 65–72. Regarding the importance of the Pathological Society. "Chronic Medical"—This colloquialism of the period describes a medical student who is taking an unusually long time to get through his examinations. The medical course was long anyway and it was felt that

students were not always motivated to qualify, because life as a perpetual student was much easier than being a doctor. . . ."

92. May Laffan, letter to G. A. Macmillan, 28 July 1881. Reading Archive, No. 202/91. "I hope it will be all right with Lippincott, I am also writing to my brother in New York to look after the matter."

93. *A Drama in Muslin*, Belfast edition (Vizetelly,1886; Belfast: Appletree, 1992), 161. Regarding rowdy Fancy-Dress Ball for Charity attended by heroine.

94. May Laffan, *Christy Carew* (London: R. Bentley, 1878), 91–108.

95. Peter Costello and John Wyse Jackson, *John Stanislaus Joyce: The Voluminous Life and Genius of James Joyce's Father* (London: Fourth Estate, 1997), 107.

96. *Hogan MP*, 114–17.

97. *Christy Carew*, 37–49.

98. *Twenty-five Years Reminiscences*, chapter 4. Regarding moral guidance versus social conventions in the 1870s.

99. *The Honorable Miss Ferrard*, 279–80.

100. Patricia Phillips, "The Queen's Institute, Dublin 1861–1881," in *Prometheus' Fire*, Norman Macmillan, ed. (Kilkenny: Tyndall Publications, 2002). An overview of technical and vocational education for Irish women in the nineteenth century.

101. *Christy Carew*, 310–11.

102. Examples of widely different supporters of "Home Government": John Hamilton, *Sixty Years experience as an Irish Landlord* (London: Digby, Long, and Co., 1884), 429. J. G. MacCarthy, *A Plea for the Home Government of Ireland* (Dublin: A. M. Sullivan, 1872), 9. George Pellew, *In Castle and Cabin* (New York: Putnam 1889), 36.

103. Malcolm Browne, *The Politics of Irish Literature: From Thomas Davis to W. B. Yeats* (London: Allen and Unwin, 1972), 294. William O'Connor Morris, *Memories and Thoughts of a Life* (London: G. Allen, 1895), 275.

Chapter 2: Adult Life and Works

1. May Laffan, *Hogan MP* (London: Macmillan & Co., 1876), 52.

2. James. H. Murphy, *Catholic Fiction and Social Reality, 1873–1922* (Westporth, CT: Greenwood Press, 1997), chapter 13.

3. Anne Coleman, "Far From Silent: Nineteenth Century Irish Women Writers," in *Gender Perspectives in Nineteenth Century Ireland: Public and Private Spheres,* eds. Margaret Kelleher and James H. Murphy (Dublin: Irish Academic Press, 1997).

4. W. J. McCormack, *Sheridan Le Fanu and Victorian Ireland* (Oxford: Clarendon Press, 1980), 264–66.

5. John Sutherland, *Stanford Companion to Victorian Fiction* (Stanford: Stanford University Press, 1989), 320–21. W. J. McCormack, 254–55.

6.   Philip L. Marcus, *Yeats and the Beginnings of the Irish Renaissance* (Syracuse: Syracuse University Press, 1957), 285–87.

7.   Carmel Quinlan, *Genteel Revolutionaries: Anna and Thomas Haslam and the Irish Women's Movement* (Cork: Cork University Press, 2000), 122.

8.   Anon., Review of *Hogan MP* in *Dublin University Magazine,* August 1876.

9.   Ibid.

10.   Mrs. J. Hazlett, Librarian/Archivist at Alexandra College, Dublin. Re: attendance of May Laffan and sister Catherine Laffan at Alexandra in 1870s.

11.   May Laffan, *Christy Carew* (London: Macmillan & Co., 1878), 8.

12.   Frank M. O'Brien, *The Story of the New York Sun* (New York: D. Appleton, 1928), photograph facing page 198.

13.   Personal communications from J. Laffan Kelleher and M. J. Laffan.

14.   *British Biographical Index*, David Bank and Anthony Esposito, eds. (London: K. G. Saur, 1885), under Hartley, no. 336.

15.   May Laffan, letter to G. A. Macmillan, December 1881, Reading University Macmillan Archive.

16.   Anon., "Miss Laffan," in *The Cabinet of Irish Literature: Selections from the Works of the Chief Poets, Orators, and Prose Writers of Ireland, with Biographical Sketches and Literary Notices* (London: Blackie & Son, 1883).

17.   Sara Jeanette Duncan, *A Voyage of Consolation: being in the nature of a sequel to the experiences of "An American girl in London"* (London: D. Appleton, 1898).

18.   The Reading University Macmillan Archive consists of eleven unnumbered letters addressed by May Laffan to members of Macmillan, Publishers. Correspondence from Macmillan with less well-known nineteenth-century writers was apparently distributed among various British universities in the recent past.

19.   The Macmillan Archive in the British Library contains the firm's letterbooks with numbered and date-stamped copies of all the outgoing correspondence.

20.   *The Stanford Companion to Victorian Fiction*, 400.

21.   Ibid., William Black (1841–1898), 64–65.

22.   Ibid., Annie Keary (1825–1879), 345.

23.   G. A. Macmillan, Letter to May Laffan, 7 January 1881. No. 1082. British Library.

24.   May Laffan, Letter to G. A. Macmillan, 9 January 1881. Macmillan Archive, Reading University.

25.   G. A. Macmillan, Letter to May Laffan, April 1881. No. 277. British Library.

26.   Michael Sadleir, *Things Past* (London: Constable, 1944), 84–93.

27.   V. H. H. Green, *Oxford Common Room: Mark Pattison* (London: Edward Arnold, 1957), 310, 315. *The Stanford Companion to Victorian Fiction*, under Dilke, 187. Anon.,

"Emilia Francis(sic) Pattison Dilke" in *The Feminist Companion to Literature in English: Women Writers from the Middle Ages to the Present*, eds. V. Blain, P. Clements, and J. Grundy (New Haven: Yale University Press, 1990), under Dilke, 394.

28. Roy Jenkins, *Sir Charles Dilke: A Victorian Tragedy* (London: Collins, 1958).

29. Ibid., 112–13.

30. *The Stanford Companion to Victorian Fiction*, 187.

31. *Oxford Common Room*, 315.

32. *The Stanford Companion to Victorian Fiction*, under Francillon, 232.

33. May Laffan, Letter to George Grove, editor of Macmillan's Magazine, 8 September 1881. Macmillan Archive, Reading University.

34. R. F. Foster, *Modern Ireland, 1600–1972* (London: Allen Lane, 1988), 413. Regarding the Richmond Commission: "Though the '3 Fs' (Fair Rent, Fixity of Tenure, Free Sale) might confer tranquillity. . . . they would be irrelevant to marginal tenants in the west; for such, the majority recommendations of the Richmond Commission (investment & economic education) would make more sense." "Professor Baldwin" has not yet been identified.

35. Arthur Young (1741–1820), an English expert on agriculture, wrote about social and economic conditions in France and Ireland. He spent a period as agent to the Kingston estate of Mitchelstown, Co Cork, but his frank criticisms of the way in which the country was governed, the land managed and the tenants treated angered landlords and led to his return to England. His readable if diffuse account of Ireland was very popular, especially with nationalists, as a reference book.

36. "J. J. Tyler (1851–1901)."

37. Frederick Macmillan, Letter to May Laffan 10 May (no year). No. 510, British Library.

38. May Laffan, Letter to George Grove, 8 September 1881. Reading Archive.

39. W. E. Houghton, ed., Introduction, *The Wellesley Index to Victorian Periodicals, 1824–1900* (Toronto and London: University of Toronto Press, 1966).

40. G. A. Macmillan, Letter to May Laffan, 22 October 1881. No. 48, British Library.

41. No *Athenaeum* review expressing these sentiments has yet come to light.

42. May Laffan, Letter to George Grove, 5 August (no year). Reading Archive.

43. Dorothy Tennant (Lady Dorothy Stanley) was a well-known illustrator who made a study of domestic subjects and children in particular. Her birth date is unknown. In 1890 she married the African explorer H. H. Stanley. She died in 1926. (Curators at Tate Gallery, London.)

44. *The Stanford Companion*, 22. Robert Welch, "William Allingham" in *The Oxford Companion to Irish Literature* (Oxford: Oxford University Press, 1996), 11–12.

45. May Laffan, Letter to George Macmillan, Wednesday (Probably 14 December 1881). Reading Archive.

46. George Macmillan, Letter to May Laffan, 3 March 1882. No. 1146, British Library.

47. Anon., "Novels of the Week: Ismay's Children" in *The Athenaeum*, 15 October 1887.

48. Margaret Kelleher, ed., "Women's Fiction 1845–1900," in *The Field Day Anthology* (Cork: Cork University Press, 2003), V: 926–27.

49. D. O'Raghellaigh, "Three Centuries of Irish Chemists," *Cork Historical and Archeological Society Journal*, 46 (1941), 453.

50. J. Y. B. "Sir Walter Noel Hartley (1846–1913)" in *Obituary Notices of Fellows Deceased*, The Royal Society, London.

51. Walter Noel Hartley, (WNH), Letter to Professor Haddon, RCSI Letterbook 1890. No. 114. Archive Department, National University of Ireland, Dublin.

52. Patrick Corish, *The Irish Catholic Experience* (Dublin: Gill AND MacMillan, 1984), 220.

53. Ibid., 221. The Marriage Causes & Marriage Law Amendment Act, 1870, which became law in the following year, legalised mixed marriages before a Catholic priest.

54. Personal communication from James Laffan Kelleher (1894–1956).

55. "Thomas Hartley," in *Allegemeines Lexicon der Bildenden Kunstler* (Leipzig: E. A. Seemann, 1923), 74.

56. A. C. Holland, *Introduction to the Royal College of Science in Ireland.* Archive Department, National University of Ireland, Dublin.

57. W. N. H., *Letter No. 89 to unknown addressee and Report No. 154 to Dean & Council, 1890, RSCI Letterbook* 1889–1892. Archive Department, National University of Ireland, Dublin.

58. May Laffan Hartley, *Letters to Dr. William Walsh, Archbishop of Dublin*, 1884–1885 (Dublin Diocesan Archives: Walsh Papers) Nos. 350/8(1+2), 57/1,357/J, 350/2–4.

59. Anne V. O'Connor, "The Revolution in Girls' Secondary Education in Ireland 1860–1910," in *Girls Don't Do Honours: Irish Women in Education in 19th and 20th Centuries*, Mary Cullen ed. (Dublin: Women's Education Bureau, 1987), 45–50.

60. Personal Communication from James Laffan Kelleher.

61. Census of Ireland Form A, dated 31 March 1901. No. 414.

62. Richard Hayes, "Manuscript Sources for the History of Irish Civilization," vol. 3. See "Persons," re May Laffan (Mrs. Walter Noel Hartley), *Recess Committee Notes*, N 5364, Cambridge University Library, MSA DD 6553.

63. Ibid.

64. Greta Jones, "Catholicism, Nationalism and Science," in *The Irish Review* (Winter/Spring 1997), eds. Kevin Barry, Tom Dunne, Edna Longley and Brian Walker, 47–61.

65. Personal Communication from Karen Anderton, ISPCC (4 April 1997),confirming May Laffan Hartley's membership and regular attendance at meetings of committees to raise funds and review cases. More detailed records of proceedings were not kept.

66. Count and Countess Plunkett were Catholics, as their use of a Papal title indicates. They were parents of Joseph Mary Plunkett, poet and revolutionary, executed in Dublin in 1916.

67. May Laffan Hartley, *Recess Committee Notes 1895*.

68. May Laffan Hartley, Letter to Michael Dwyer Laffan, 2 February 1904. In personal possession of Helena Kelleher Kahn.

69. Robert W. De Forest, ed., "Obituary" in *New York Sun,* 20 November *1909.* Michael J. Laffan, "Dublin Student to Millionaire" in *Irish Weekly Independant,* 29 May 1950.

70. Personal Communication from Michael J. Laffan.

71. Personal Communication from the Librarian, The Mercer Library, College of Surgeons, Dublin. James Laffan went on the British Medical Register in 1882 and remained on it until 1913.

72. Ibid. James Laffan went to Australia and worked there from 1890.

73. Ibid. Charles Morier was on the British Medical Register in Australia from 1883 to 1900 when he went to London with his wife Catherine (Casy) née Laffan and appears to have remained there until 1929.

74. May Laffan Hartley, Letter to Michael Dwyer Laffan, 13 October 1907. In personal possession of Helena Kelleher Kahn.

75. Personal communication from James Laffan Kelleher.

76. Copy of page from Bloomfield Retreat which records May Laffan Hartley's admission.

77. Joseph Robbins, *Fools and Mad: A History of the Insane in Ireland* (Dublin: Institute of Public Administration, 1986).

78. Information Leaflet on Bloomfield Retreat, and personal communication from Richard Fitzsimmons, Hospital Secretary, Bloomfield.

79. Death announcement of Sir Walter Noel Hartley, *Irish Times,* 12 September 1913.

80. Copy of entry SA052928 in British Army War Records of Officer's Deaths.

81. Personal Communication from Michael J. Laffan, who recalled that Michael Fitzgibbon Laffan died in America in 1915 and James Laffan died in India in the same year.

82. Entry copied from *National Archives, Year 1916.* Folio 473, p. 281. Re: Hartley. 15 August. Administration of estate of Mary Hartley late of 10 Elgin Road, Dublin, Widow,

who died on 23rd of June 1916, granted to Catherine D. Morier, married woman. Effects 206-5-8. Re-sworn £265-14-10.

83. May Laffan in *Irish Literature*, Justin McCarthy, ed. (New York: Bigelow, Smith & Co.; New York: Johnson Reprint Corp., 1970), 1557–71. A short biographical note is followed by an extract from the "election" chapter of *Hogan MP* and one from "Flitters."

Chapter 3: Class and Politics in *Hogan MP*

1. Anon. review of *Hogan MP*, *Spectator*, 12 August 1876.

2. May Laffan, *Hogan MP* (London: Macmillan, 1881), 324–25.

3. Max Weber, *The Protestant Ethic and the Spirit of Capitalism*, Talcott Parsons, trans. (London: Routledge, 1997), 264–265. This controversial and classic sociological text was expanded from an article in a German journal of sociology in 1904. Weber's thesis concerned the social and political effects of religious belief systems. He suggested that societies where a Calvinist or Puritan form of Protestantism flourished were more likely than others to embrace capitalism, because they thought its productive commercial activity to be essential to please God.

4. Cora Kaplan, "White, Black, and Green: Racialising Irishness in Victorian England," in *Victoria's England*, ed. Peter Gray (Dublin: Four Courts, 2004), 51–68. David N. Livingstone, Darwin's Forgotten Thought (Edinburgh: Scottish Academic, 1987), 60.

5. *Hogan MP*, 424.

6. For example: the novels of William Carleton, Maria Edgeworth, Emily Lawless, Charles Lever, Samuel Lover, George Moore, Lady Morgan (Sydney Owenson), Anthony Trollope, Katherine Tynan, "Somerville and Ross" (Edith Somerville and Violet Martin).

7. Lady Morgan (Sydney Owenson), *The Wild Irish Girl* (1806) and *O'Donnel* (1814). Also see Sean Connolly, "Ag Deanaim 'Commanding': Elite Responses to Popular Culture," in *Irish Popular Culture, 1650–1850*, James S. Donnelly, Jr. and Kerby A. Miller, eds. (Dublin: Irish Academic Press, 1998), 8.

8. For example: Rosa Mulholland (Lady Gilbert), whose novels consciously "gentrified" the Irish, for instance in *The Birds of Killeevy* (1883) and *The Girls of Banshee Castle* (1890). See James H. Murphy, *Catholic Fiction and Social Reality in Ireland, 1873–1922* (Dublin: University College Dublin Press, 1997), 55.

9. Thomas J. Morrissey, *Towards a National University: William Delaney S. J. 1835–1924* (Dublin: Wolfhound Press, 1983), 182.

10. Lawrence W. McBride, *The Greening of Dublin Castle: The Transformation of Bureaucratic and Judicial Personnel in Ireland 1892–1922* (Washington, DC: Catholic University Press, 1991), 58, 106.

11. David Thomson, *England in the Nineteenth Century 1815–1914* (Baltimore: Penguin, 1950), 107–110.

12. Margaret M. Maison, *Search Your Soul, Eustace: Victorian Religious Novels* (London: Sheed and Ward, 1961).

13. Murphy, *Catholic Fiction*, 32, 33. Note comments on conflict between English Victorian and Irish Catholic values.

14. David N. Livingstone, *Darwin's Forgotten Defenders*, 75.

15. George Moore, *Esther Waters* (London: Walter Scott Publishing, 1894). A sympathetic account of the struggle of an illiterate single mother to keep her child. Also, Rosa Mulholland, in *Nanno* (1899), wrote of the dilemma of a single mother courted by a man who wants to marry her and does not know about her child. Mulholland's earlier books were written for children and adolescents ("moral tales") and did not provoke controversy, but her later books introduced political and social issues and were less acceptable to the market. An example of one such book was *Gianetta: A Girl's Story of Herself* (1889), which contained a realistic description of an actual large-scale Irish eviction, and drew unfavourable comment from the English public.

16. Joseph Hone, *The Life of George Moore* (London: V. Gollancz, 1936), 94. Quotation from undated letter from Moore to Emile Zola.

17. Raymond Chapman, *Faith and Revolt: Studies in the Literary Influence of the Oxford Movement* (London: Weidenfeld and Nicolson, 1970), 12, 13. Paranoia about subversive Catholic influences in the Church of England.

18. Wilkie Collins, *Armadale* (1866). Unique "sensation novel" with a black journalist as hero—a rare example of a Victorian novel that did not conform to the conventions of the time.

19. *Hogan MP*, 176–77.

20. Ibid., 92.

21. James Joyce, "Two Gallants" *Dubliners* (1914).

22. George Moore, *A Drama in Muslin* (1887; Belfast: Appletree Press, 1992), 59–60.

23. *Louche*, adj. French. From Latin, Luscus (squinting), figuratively: suspicious, shady. *Concise Oxford Dictionary*, compiled by Abel and Marguerite Chevally and G. W. F. R. Goodridge (Oxford: Clarendon, 1970), 493.

24. Victoria Glendinning, in *Trollope* (London: Pimlico, 1993), quotes the following as examples: Baron Grant, alias Gottheimer, would-be developer of Leicester Square, London, and George Hudson, the "Railway King," 224–25, 443. Also see James Dabney McCabe, Jr. "James Fisk" in *Lights and Shadows of New York Life; or, the Sights and Sensations of the Great City* (1872; New York: Deutsch, 1971), 555. Fisk (1834–1872) rose from pedlar to financier, attempted to destroy the New York Stock Market on "Black Friday," and was shot dead by a former friend.

25. Robert Lee Wolff, Introduction, *Flitters, Tatters & the Counsellor* (New York: Garland, 1979), vii.

26. James O'Shea, *Prince of Swindlers: John Sadleir MP 1813–1856* (Dublin: Geography Publications, 1999).

27. M. Hynes, "Sadleir: MP & Banker," *My Clonmel Scrapbook*, James White, ed. (Waterford: E. Downey, 1917), 228–39.

28. John B. O'Brien, "Sadleir's Bank," *Journal of the Cork Historical & Archaeological Society*, No. 235 (1977), 32–38. Also see James O'Shea, *Prince of Swindlers*, 422, 439.

29. *Hogan MP*, 306–307. See Robert M. Baird, "Comte, Auguste," *Microsoft Encarta Encyclopedia* (Microsoft Corporation, 1993–1995).

30. *Hogan MP*, 185.

31. Jean Dominique Ingres (1780–1867). French artist and draughtsman, who excelled at portraits of women.

32. Adrian Frazier, *George Moore (1852–1933)* (New Haven: Yale University Press 2000), quotation from undated letter from Henry James to George Moore, c. 1884, 170.

33. *Infra dig.* Abbreviation of Latin *infra dignitatem,* meaning beneath one's dignity.

34. *Hogan MP*, 311

35. Ibid., 67.

36. Ibid., 148.

37. Donald Harman Akenson, *The Church of Ireland: Ecclesiastical Reform and Revolution 1800–1885* (New Haven: Yale University Press, 1971), 215. Also see Lawrence McBride, *The Greening of Dublin Castle*, 37; Patrick Maume, *The Long Gestation: Irish Nationalist Life 1891–1918* (Dublin: University College Dublin Press,1999), 60, 61.

38. Glendinning, *Trollope*, 50, 51. Trollope attended both Harrow and Winchester schools.

39. *A Drama in Muslin*, 77.

40. Land ownership in Ireland. During the second half of the nineteenth century, hard-won changes in the law altered the relationship of landlord to tenant. Movements to secure Tenant Right gradually developed into the realization that "peasant proprietorship" provided a more realistic and long-lasting solution to questions of who actually should own and work the land. This aim was not finally achieved until the twentieth century, but there is no doubt that nationalist landlords such as George Henry Moore, father of the writer, knew long before Tenant Right that when it came it would effectively spell the end of landlords' social domination, especially in the case of those whose sole income was derived from their tenants. See Andrew J. Kettle and Laurence J. Kettle, *Materials for Victory: Memoirs of Andrew J. Kettle* (Dublin: C. J. Fallon, 1958), 108–132.

41. Frazier, *George Moore*; Tony Gray, *A Peculiar Man: A Life of George Moore* (London: Sinclair-Stevenson, 1996). Joseph Hone, *The Life of George Moore*. Leanne Lane, "The Moores of Moore Hall." Unpublished Thesis. University College Cork, 1992.

42. Land War. The name given by the people to a movement of agrarian protest in Ireland which began in 1879 with the foundation of the Land League. Originally a non-violent campaign against unfair rents and conditions of land tenure, it gradually de-

veloped violent fringe activities, for example, assasinating landlords and their agents, maiming cattle and burning houses. During the 1880's the crime rate rose, the Irish civil authorities were seriously challenged, and increased numbers of British troops were dispatched to Ireland.

43. *Hogan MP*, 167.

44. Ibid., 52. The reference is to the poet Schiller.

45. Ibid., 52.

46. Murphy, *Catholic Fiction*, 29.

47. Examples of contemporary Irish memoirs: Davis Coakley, *Oscar Wilde: The Importance of Being Irish* (Dublin: Townhouse, 1994); Lady Ferguson, *Sir Samuel Ferguson in the Ireland of his Day* (London: W. Blackwood, 1890); Maude Gonne MacBride, *A Servant of the Queen* (London: V. Gollancz, 1938); John Hamilton, *Sixty Years Experience as an Irish Landlord* (London: Digby, Long, & Co., 1884); Elizabeth Mary Margaret Bourke Plunkett Fingall and Pamela Hinkson, *Seventy Years Young: Memoirs of Elizabeth, Countess of Fingall, told to Pamela Hinkson* (London: Collins, 1937). Examples of contemporary Irish fiction: George A. Birmingham, *The Bad Times* (1908); Charles J. Kickham, *Knocknagow* (1870); John Francis Maguire, *The Next Generation* (1871); George Moore, *A Drama in Muslin* (1887); W. E. Norris, *The Fight for the Crown* (1898); William O'Brien, *When We Were Boys* (1890).

48. *A Drama in Muslin*, 125.

49. *Hogan MP*, 56.

50. Ibid., 31.

51. Ibid., 302–303.

52. Ibid., 146.

53. E. R. Norman, *Anti-Catholicism in Victorian England: Historical Problems, Studies, and Documents* (London: Allen and Unwin, 1968). Appended is a copy of the following anonymous article: "The Blight of Popery," *The Bulwark or Reformation Journal* (Edinburgh 1851), i, 41–43.

54. Thomas Robert Malthus (1766–1834). English economist and demographer, developed the theory that the world's population must overrun its food supply if means were not taken to keep the birthrate down. He suggested discouraging marriage, encouraging the practice of celibacy, penalising those with large families, and building factory-type institutions to house people whom he thought unfitted to have children at all. He based his theory on statistical evidence which is today considered to be inaccurate. Malthus's ideas were highly influential, affecting nineteenth-century welfare legislation especially in relation to Ireland.

55. Harriet Martineau (1802–1876) came from a French Calvinist background. In spite of severe health problems including deafness she became a pioneer English sociologist and earned her living as a writer on economic themes. Her works included several novels, and "moral tales" for young people to support the Utilitarian and materialistic

philosophy in which she believed. These writings included an "Irish tale" in which she suggests that the Irish are poor because they are not industrious enough, spending too much energy telling imaginary stories. They need to be made to work hard. She had not, in fact, visited Ireland. Charles Dickens attacked Martineau and her co-theorists in his novel of industrial life, *Hard Times for These Times* (1854).

56. Joseph Robins, *Fools and Mad: A History of the Insane in Ireland* (Dublin: Institute of Public Administration, 1986), 125–26. Robins describes the fear aroused by people who behave differently to the ruling caste in a situation where the ruling caste is a distinct minority.

57. Anon. "Miss Laffan" in *The Cabinet of Irish Literature, selections from the works of the chief poets, orators, and prose writers of Ireland, Vol. IV* (Dublin: Blackie and Sons, 1880), 296–300. There were several editions of this popular anthology, some of which were published in America. The original edition was issued in 1880, but Katherine Tynan edited a revised one in 1905. See note on Charles A. Reade in *The Oxford Companion to Irish Literature*, Robert A. Welch, ed. (Oxford: Oxford University Press, 1996), 491.

58. William Carleton (1794–1869) an Irish-speaking peasant from Tyrone, became a locally celebrated writer. (Laffan may have been flattered at being compared to him.) Like her, he wrote satiric fiction, and like her maternal relatives he was a convert to the Established Church. His stories were set almost all in the countryside of south Ulster, from which he came.

59. Annie Keary (1825–1879), English daughter of an Irish clergyman, based her popular novel *Castle Daly* (1875) on his stories but, apparently, never visited Ireland.

60. Robert Lee Wolff, Introduction to *Hogan MP* (New York: Garland, 1979).

61. *Hogan MP*, 81.

62. The "Fenian priest" would have been Fr. Patrick Lavelle (1825–1886), subject of Gerard Moran's biography *A Radical Priest in Mayo* (Dublin: Four Courts Press, 1994).

63. "Young Ireland" was the name given to a group of middle-class intellectuals, Catholic and Protestant, associated with The Nation newspaper, and seeking to promote a non-sectarian Irish identity. An offshoot of Daniel O'Connell's Repeal Association, they withdrew from it in 1846 because unwilling to renounce the use of physical force. Following the example of similar movements in Germany and France at the time, Young Ireland hoped for a social revolution, but their attempted armed rising failed, not surprisingly in view of the Famine. Their real success had been gained earlier, when they succeeded in awakening national pride and self esteem through patriotic songs, poems and legends.

64. *Hogan MP*, 82

65. Ibid., 83

66. Arthur Young, *A Tour in Ireland, 1776–1779* (Shannon: Irish University Press, 1970). Young, an agriculturist, compared Ireland with England and France, of which he had already written critical accounts.

67. *Hogan MP*, 86

68. John Coolahan, *Irish Education: Its History and Structure* (Dublin: Institute for Public Administration, 1981), 3–55. Concerns the history of development of National School system.

69. *Hogan MP*, 87.

70. "St. Stephen's" is a synonym for the House of Commons.

71. *Hogan MP*, 88

72. Morrissey, *Towards a National University*, 33. Refusal of Liberals to aid denominational education.

73. Ibid., 41, 42.

74. David Thornley, *Isaac Butt and Home Rule* (London: MacGibbon and Kee, 1964), 139.

75. May Laffan, Cambridge University Library: Ms Add.6553: Memorandum on Education in Ireland, c.1895, by May Laffan. N 5364 P 5494, Manuscript Sources For the History of Irish Civilization. Vol. 3 "Persons" L-O, ed. By Richard J. Hayes LL.D Director of the National Library (of Ireland).

76. *Hogan MP*, 262.

77. Ibid., 246–47.

78. "Tenant Right." The name given generally to the aims of the Irish Tenant League in the 1850s and the Land League which succeeded it from 1879 on. The aims included: fair rent for tenancies; free sale, that is a departing tenant's right to dispose of his interest, including improvements he had carried out to the property; and fixity of tenure giving security against eviction for arbitrary reasons.

79. Charles Lever, *Lord Kilgobbin* (1872). A novel describing an Ascendancy family in decline.

80. William Carleton, *Valentine McClutchy, the Irish Agent* (1845). A novel satirizing the hypocrisy and greed of an absentee landlord's agent.

81. Pat Daly was an Irish-born emigrant to the United States, probably as a child. He returned to Ireland in the 1860s to help organize cells of the Irish Republican Brotherhood (Fenians). This activity would not have been against American law, but was proscribed in Ireland and Britain, and Pat was one of those Fenians who believed it worthwhile to support constitutional politics and consequently, was keeping a low, non-violent profile.

82. *Hogan MP*, 237.

83. Thornley, *Isaac Butt and Home Rule*, 209.

84. *Hogan MP*, 267.

85. Ibid., 231.

86. Ibid., 272, 73.

87. Ibid., 264.

88. James O'Shea, *Priest, Politics and Society in Post-Famine Ireland* (Dublin: Wolfhound Press, 1983), 46.

89. *Hogan MP*, 277.

90. Anon., "Clonmel Assizes, 1830," J. White ed. *My Clonmel Scrapbook* (Waterford: Downey, 1907). Description of Archdeacon Laffan.

91. *Hogan MP*, 261.

92. Thornley, *Isaac Butt and Home Rule*, 125, 139–41.

93. Kettle, *Material for Victory*, 108–132. F. S. L. Lyons, *Ireland Since the Famine* (London: Collins/Fontana, 1973), 154–56.

94. O'Shea, *Priest, Politics and Society in Post-Famine Ireland*, 197, 325–60.

95. Michael Davitt (1846–1905), nationalist and labour leader, he founded the Land League (1879–1882) and advocated nationalization of land. John Dillon, (1851–1927), son of John Blake Dillon, a Young Ireland leader. He was an MP and an influential politician. William O'Brien (1852–1928), MP, nationalist, journalist and novelist, at first a chief supporter of Parnell, broke with him in 1891.

96. *Eau d'opoponax* is an expensive scent derived from a variety of mimosa.

97. *A Drama in Muslin*, 55,56.

98. Ibid., 99.

99. James McConnell, "The Irish Parliamentary Party in Victorian and Edwardian London" in *Victoria's Ireland*, Peter Gray, ed. (Dublin: Four Courts, 2004), 37–50. Patrick Maume, *The Long Gestation: Irish Nationalist Life, 1891–1918* (Dublin: Gill and Macmillan, 1999), 36. See also Captain WIlliam Lynam, *Mick M'Quaid MP*, serialised in *The Shamrock*, 5 October 1872–27 September 1873. McCarthy, *Gallowglass, or Life in the Land of the Priests* (London 1904). These two novels give comic descriptions of the life of an MP.

100. Thornley, *Isaac Butt and Home Rule*, 215, 239.

101. Ibid., 174, 194–95. Theodore Hoppen, *Elections, Politics and Society in Ireland (1832–1885)* (Oxford: Oxford University Press, 1984), 119. Frank Hugh O'Donnell, *A History of the Irish Parliamentary Party* (London: Longmans, Green, 1910), 274; O'Shea, *Priest, Politics and Society in Post-Famine Ireland*, 197–98.

102. R. F. Foster, *Modern Ireland, 1600–1972* (London: Allen Lane, 1988), 395.

103. Nuala Costello, *John McHale, Archbishop of Tuam* (Dublin: Talbot Press, 1939), 114.

104. *Hogan MP*, 302.

105. Gerald Fitzgibbon, *Ireland in 1868* (London: Longmans, Green, Reader and Dyer, 1868), 54.

106. Hoppen, *Elections, Politics and Society in Ireland*, 236.

107. Emmet J. Larkin, *The Roman Catholic Church and the Home Rule Movement in Ireland* (Dublin: Gill and Macmillan, 1990), 247. Also see O'Shea, *Priest, Politics and Society*, 240–47.

108. O'Shea, *Priest, Politics and Society*, 47. "Money given after an election was not deemed as bribery."

109. Anon. review of *Hogan MP, Spectator*, 12 August 1876, 1013.

110. Ibid., 1012.

Chapter 4: Class, Identity and Education in *Miss Ferrard*

1.   John Sutherland, "The Saturday Review," in *The Stanford Companion to Victorian Fiction* (Stanford: Stanford University Press, 1989), 553.

2.   Anon., Review of *The Honorable Miss Ferrard,* in *Saturday Review,* 29 September 1877.

3.   Rosa Mulholland, *Gianetta: A Girl's Story of Herself* (London: Blackie & Sons, 1889). Katherine Cecil Thurston, *The Gambler* (London: Hutchinson & Co., 1900). Anthony Trollope, *The Macdermots of Ballycloran* (London: Thomas Cautley Newby, 1847).

4.   Lady Morgan (Sidney Owenson), *The Wild Irish Girl* (London: R. Phillips, 1806).

5.   James M. Cahalan, *The Irish Novel* (Dublin: Gill and Macmillan, 1988), xxii, 73, 76–77. OE Somerville and Martin Ross, *The Big House at Inver* (London: William Heinemann Ltd., 1925). "The Big House," in *The Oxford Companion to Irish Literature*, Robert Welch, ed. (Oxford: Oxford University Press 1996), 45.

6.   Poteen (or Poitin) is a home-made illicit spirit, once distilled from potatoes, and made in a cast-iron pot (hence the name). Irish.

7.   John Coolahan, "National Schools," *Irish Education: Its History and Structure* (Dublin: Institute of Public Administration, 1981), 3–27.

8.   Retrousse—Upturned (of a nose). French.

9.   May Laffan, *The Honorable Miss Ferrard* (London: Macmillan, 1881), 21.

10. Tawney—Yellow-skinned, or sallow.

11. Kish of Brogues—Literally, "basket of shoes," this insulting comparison indicates that the speaker considers Helena Ferrard to be unusually ignorant. Irish.

12. *The Honorable Miss Ferrard*, 59.

13. Ibid., 98.

14. Ibid., 99.

15. Ibid., 127.

16. Solicitor—A lawyer.

17. David Thornley, "Dissolution of Parliament by Gladstone 24 January 1874" in *Isaac Butt and Home Rule* (London: MacGibbon & Kee, 1964), 175.

18. *The Honorable Miss Ferrard*, 145.

19. Ibid., 187.

20. Ibid., 368.

21. Ibid., 243.

22. Ibid., 229.

23. Ibid., 234.

24. Ibid., 367.

25. Ibid., 369.

26. Ibid., 401.

27. Ibid., 417.

28. Ibid., 1.

29. William Allingham, *Laurence Bloomfield in Ireland* (London: Macmillan and Co., 1864). Maria Edgeworth, *The Absentee,* (Washington D. C.: William Cooper, 1812).

30. Irish Poplins—Poplin is a woven fabric of wool mixed with linen or silk. Its manufacture is said to have been started in Ireland by the Huguenots, mainly in Belfast and Dublin. Poplin was widely used as a dress fabric in the nineteenth century.

31. *The Honorable Miss Ferrard*, 246–47.

32. The Miss Persses—The reference is to the daughters of an actual ascendancy family living in County Galway, the future Lady Augusta Gregory (1852–1925)and her sisters.

33. *The Honorable Miss Ferrard*, 50.

34. Ibid., 40.

35. Ibid., 76.

36. Ibid., 399.

37. John Sutherland, "Newgate Novels," in *The Stanford Companion to Victorian Fiction* (Stanford: Stanford University Press, 1989), 389.

38. "The moss couch I brought thee today from the mountain / Has drank the last drop of thy young heart's red fountain, / For this good *skian* beside me struck deep and rang hollow / In thy bosom of treason, Mairgread Ni Cheallead." Edward Walsh, "Mairgread Ni Cheallead" in *Irish Poets of the Nineteenth Century,* Geoffrey Taylor, ed. (London: Routledge & Keegan Paul, 1947), 382.

39. May Laffan, "Convent Boarding-Schools for Young Ladies" in *Frazer's Magazine,* June 1874, 778–86.

40. *The Honorable Miss Ferrard*, 28.

41. Dorothea Herbert, *Retrospections 1770–1806* (Dublin: Town House, 1988). 308, 353.Gives instances of Protestant children reared in convents.

42. *The Honorable Miss Ferrard*, 28.

43. Huguenots—See notes for chapter two.

44. Judge William O'Connor Morris, *Memories & Thoughts of a Life* (London: G. Allen, 1895), 275.

45. Gerald Fitzgibbon (I), *Ireland in 1868* (London: Longmans, Green, Reader & Dyer, 1868), 225. George Sigerson, *Modern Ireland* (London: Longmans, Green, Reader & Dyer, 1869), 86.

46. *The Honorable Miss Ferrard*, 364–65.

47. Ibid., 28.

48. The Claddagh was the settlement near Galway City where fishermen and their families lived.

49. *The Honorable Miss Ferrard*, 28.

50. Wild Geese—The name given to Irish soldiers who fought in the armies of France, Spain and Austria during the seventeenth, eighteenth and early nineteenth centuries.

51. Wolfgang Menzel, *History of Germany Vol. III* (London: George Bell & Sons, 1890), 10, 17, 52. Outline of the history of Maurice de Saxe, Duke of Courland. A romantic figure, he was later to appear as a major character in novels, for example M. Alexander's *The Ripple* (1913) and in operas, for example Francesco Cilea's *Adriana Lecouvreur* (1902).

52. *The Honorable Miss Ferrard*, 383.

53. Ibid., 348.

54. Ibid., 396.

55. Cassandra. In Greek mythology, she was the daughter of Hecuba and the hero Priam. The gods conferred on Cassandra the gift of prophecy but later punished her by arranging that when she truly foretold the future, none would believe her. The nickname Cassandra is sometimes applied to a person whose predictions are ignored as too depressing.

56. *The Honorable Miss Ferrard*, 259.

57. Butter-factor. Until the late 1880s butter was one of Ireland's principal food exports. Butter production took place mainly in Munster, and centred on Cork. The character "Mr. Really," a Corkman, is a butter-factor, or exporter.

58. *The Honorable Miss Ferrard*, 335.

59. Ibid., 259.

60. Thomas Carlyle (1795–1881). A Scottish historian and philosopher, his "personal statement," *Sartor Resartus* (The Tailor Re-Tailored) and his dramatic account of the French Revolution were immensely popular and made him famous. His belief in a superior master-race which should alone be permitted to rule others was admired once but was later seen to resemble National Socialism.

61. Ultramontanism was a centrist movement in the Catholic Church, favouring Papal over national or diocesan authority. In nineteenth-century Ireland, where its chief exponent was Cardinal Paul Cullen, it helped to unite Catholics and to confirm their identity, but since the second Vatican Council has received less emphasis.

62. *The Honorable Miss Ferrard*, 262–63.

63. John Nicholas Murphy, *Terra Incognita, or the Convents of the United Kingdom* (London: Longmans & Co., 1873), 371–74. T. J. McElligott, *Secondary Education in Ireland, 1870–1921* (Dublin: Irish Academic Press, 1981), 490–501.

64. John Coolahan, *Irish Education: Its History and Structure* (Dublin: Institute of Public Administration, 1981), 6.

65. Sister Mercedes Lillis, *Two Hundred Years A' Growing: The Story of the Ursulines in Thurles* (Roscrea Co Tipperary: J. F. Walsh & Co., 1987). John Nicholas Murphy, *Terra Incognita, or the Convents of the United Kingdom* (London: Longmans & Co., 1873), 390–91.

66. Pat Jalland, *Women, Marriage & Politics, 1860–1914* (Oxford: Oxford University Press, 1988), 1–17.

67. Patricia Phillips, "The Queen's Institute, Dublin (1861–1881)," in *Prometheus's Fire: A History of Scientific and Technological Education in Ireland*, Norman McMillan ed. (Kilkenny: Tyndall, 1999), 446–63.

68. *The Honorable Miss Ferrard*, 187.

69. Hedge-schools—These were illicit pay-schools set up to educate the Irish Catholic population during the eighteenth and early nineteenth centuries. Teaching sessions took place in private houses, sheds, or even sheltered hedge corners, hence the name. Curricula varied considerably, some schools offering classics and mathematics whereas others aimed only to teach literacy. Pupils were of all ages and attended irregularly; English was the language of instruction.

70. Alison Jordan, *Margaret Byers* (Belfast: Institute of Irish Studies, Queen's University, 1990), 4, 7–30.

71. *The Honorable Miss Ferrard*, 275.

72. Michael J. McCarthy, *Gallowglass: Life in the Land of the Priests* (London: Simpkin, Marshall, Hamilton, Kent & Co. Ltd., 1904), 539.

73. *The Honorable Miss Ferrard*, 332.

74. Ibid., 152

75. Escritoire—a small writing-desk. French.

76. *The Honorable Miss Ferrard*, 397.

77. Anon., review of *The Honorable Miss Ferrard*, in *Academy*, 22 October 1881.

78. Francis Ledwidge (1891–1917) was born at Slane, Co. Kildare, Ireland. Largely self-educated, he left school at thirteen and worked as a labourer, then as a shop assistant in Dublin. He published mainly nature poetry of which the poem "Twilight in Middle March," from which the lines quoted are taken, is a fair example. Ledwidge was active both in trade union and republican organizations, but he did not foresee the Easter Rising (1916) and enlisted in the British Army before it took place. He was killed on active service at Ypres, France. Although he saw several years of army service, Ledwidge is not counted as a "war poet" because he did not write about his war experiences, preferring to remain a

lyricist in the classical tradition of John Keats. Also see *Complete Poems*, ed. Alice Curtayne (London: Martin Brian and O'Keefe, 1964).

Chapter 5: Conflicting Values, Class and Religion in *Christy Carew*

1.   Anon., "Miss Laffan" in *The Cabinet of Irish Literature: Selections from the Works of the Chief Poets, Orators, and Prose Writers of Ireland, with Biographical Sketches and Literary Notices, Vol. IV,* T. P. O'Connor and C. A. Reade, eds. (London: Blackie & Sons, 1880), 296–300.

2.   Emmet J. Larkin, *The Roman Catholic Church & the Home Rule Movement in Ireland, 1870–1874* (Chapel Hill: University of North Carolina Press, 1990), 150.

3.   Ultramontanism—see references to chapter four.

4.   James Joyce, *Dubliners* (1914; London: Penguin Books, 1961). Regarding "Colonial Systems." The existing colonial system of the 1870s was one in which Ireland had no legislative assembly of its own and was politically and economically dependant on England. The emergence of an Irish Catholic middle class put pressure on this already inadequate system and led to agitation for some degree of self-government which would give the Irish a measure of control, for instance, over secondary and higher education and technical training. The Home Rule movement which developed in 1870 envisaged Ireland achieving a status rather like that of Canada, still part of the Empire but semi-independent. It would still leave Ireland in a colonial system, but an easier one.

5.   "The Liberties" is the name still given to an area in the city near Dublin Castle. This was a suburb during the medieval period in Irish history when Dublin and its environs were English possessions. In the Liberties, however, the Rule of the local territorial lord replaced the Rule of the King, thereby giving inhabitants some specific rights. By the nineteenth century, the area had become a slum, but it is now being reclaimed.

6.   May Laffan, *Christy Carew* (London: George Macmillan & Co, 1882), 156–57.

7.   Ibid., 265.

8.   Ibid., 10.

9.   Ibid., 111–12.

10. Ibid., 383.

11. Papal Infallibility. The First Vatican Council (December 1869–July 1870) defined Papal Infallibility as a dogmatic truth of the Catholic Church, as follows: When the Pope acts as pastor and teacher of all Christians and defines a doctrine concerning faith or morals to be held by the whole Church, he is preserved from error by the guidance of the Holy Spirit. Controversy arising about this pronouncement seems to have been mainly to do with the timing, which some held to be inopportune, rather than the content, which most Catholics already accepted. *The Roman Catholic Church & the Home Rule Movement in Ireland, 1870–1874,* 3–26. The mention of the announcement of the Papal In-

fallibility dogma as a recent event dates the period of the opening chapter of *Christy Carew* to August 1870.

12. *Christy Carew,* 87–88.

13. Ibid., 152.

14. *Christy Carew,* 40.

15. Ibid., 47.

16. Ibid., 175.

17. Ibid., 22. Regarding phrenology. This once popular study originated with the belief of a Viennese physician Franz-Joseph Gall (1758–1828) that the mental capacity of an individual could be known from the outer configuration of their skull. Gall's claims to be able to deduce, for example, violent tendencies by examination of irregularities on the patient's skull were found to have no real scientific foundation.

18. Patrick J. Corish, *The Irish Catholic Experience* (Dublin: Gill & Macmillan, 1985), 220.

19. William O'Connor Morris, *Memories and Thoughts of a Life* (London: George Allen, 1895), 174. Regarding Scotch Marriage and similar irregular marriages.

20. My source for this information is a photocopied report on a judgement delivered in the House of Lords on 13 January 1860 on the Longworth/Yelverton Case, obtained from: The Honorable Society of King's Inns, Henrietta Street, Dublin 1.

21. Linda May Ballard, *Forgetting Frolic: Marriage Traditions in Ireland,* (Belfast: Institute of Irish Studies, Queen's University of Belfast in association with the Folklore Society, London, 1998), 54–56.

22. Anon., "Therese Longworth," in *The Feminist Companion to Literature in English,* Virginia Blain, Isobel Grundy, Patricia Clements, eds. (New Haven: Yale University Press, 1990), 668.

23. For example: Mary Elizabeth Braddon, *Lady Audley's Secret* (London: William Tinsley, 1862). Gerald Griffin, *The Collegians* (London: Saunders and Otley, 1829). Samuel Lover, *Handy Andy: A Tale of Irish Life* (London: Frederick Lover and Richard Groombridge, 1842).

24. *Christy Carew,* 37.

25. Ibid., 51.

26. Kevin Haddick-Flynn, *Orangeism: The Making of a Tradition* (Dublin: Wolfhound Press, 1999), 272–87. Jocelyn was the family name of the Earls of Roden, notorious for their alleged involvement on 12 July 1849 at Dolly's Brae, Co. Down, in a sectarian affray in which thirty Catholics were killed.

27. *Christy Carew,* 237.

28. Ibid., 340.

29. Ibid., 341.

30. Anon., "Father Charles. P. Meehan" in *The Oxford Companion to Irish Literature*, Robert Welch and Bruce Stewart, eds. (Oxford: Clarendon, 1996), 362.

31. Anne Devlin (1780–1851), niece of the Wicklow guerrilla fighter Michael Dwyer, helped Robert Emmet in his preparations for insurrection. Destitute in later life, she was supported by a group of nationalist sympathisers which included Fr. Meehan.

32. James Clarence Mangan (1803–1849), poet and translator, was addicted to drugs and alcohol and relied on a group of friends including Fr. Meehan for accommodation, care and emotional support.

33. Bride Street was part of the Liberties.

34. Patrick J. Corish, *The Irish Catholic Experience* (Dublin: Gill & Macmillan, 1985), 221.

35. *Christy Carew*, 330–31.

36. Ibid., 348.

37. Ibid., 368.

38. William Makepeace Thackeray, *Vanity Fair* (London: Bradbury & Evans, 1846). Becky Sharpe is the "daemonic" heroine of Thackeray's famous novel contrasting with its "angelic" heroine, Amelia Sedley.

39. Hedda is the restless, individualistic "new woman" heroine of Henrik Ibsen's play *Hedda Gabler*, Una Ellis Fermor, trans. (London: Penguin Books, 1950).

40. *Christy Carew*, 16.

41. Ibid., 17.

42. Holland was a light-weight linen fabric much used in Victorian times for summer clothes. In earlier days, its unbleached form was used for shrouds.

43. *Christy Carew*, 7.

44. Ibid., 41.

45. Ibid., 116.

46. Ibid., 148. Esther sings *The Coulin*, a difficult traditional song originally with Irish words. It does not fit naturally into the English setting devised by Thomas Moore. The effect on some listeners is to make them feel a sense of unease, and Laffan seems to be aware of this. See note 48 for details of *Moore's Melodies*.

47. James Joyce, "The Dead," *Dubliners* (1914; London: Penguin Books, 1961).

48. Thomas Moore, *Irish Melodies* (London: Longman, Brown, Green & Longmans, 1850), 9–10. Also on p. 9, see footnote quoting from Walker's *Historical Memoirs of Irish Bards*.

49. *Christy Carew*, 237.

50. Ibid., 410.

51. Ibid., 15.

52. Ibid., 21.

53. *Trompe d'oeil.* This expression (in French, literally "deceive the eye") is generally used to describe a painting technique which presents deceptive reality, for instance, an imitation door, a window view which does not exist, or an open cupboard which appears to have three-dimensional contents until one tries to grasp them. The technique dates back to the fifteenth century at least and was chiefly used in frescoes or still-lifes; it has some affinity to modern abstract painting. I have used the term to describe a technique employed by some writers, and in this case by May Laffan, of presenting an apparent reality and then quietly demonstrating its untruth.

54. *Christy Carew,* 116.

55. Ibid., 418–19.

56. Julian Moynahan, *Anglo-Irish: The Literary Imagination in a Hyphenated Culture* (Princeton: Princeton University Press, 1995), 190.

57. *Christy Carew,* 409.

58. Ibid., 89.

59. James Joyce, "Eveline" in *Dubliners* (1914; London: Penguin Books, 1961).

60. *Christy Carew,* 262.

61. Ibid., 259.

62. Daniel O'Connell (1775–1847) was elected Lord Mayor of Dublin in 1841, the first Catholic to hold that office since the sixteenth century.

63. *Christy Carew,* 426.

64. Ibid., 428.

65. Ibid., 428.

66. Ibid., 61.

67. Frank Hugh O'Donnell (1848–1916). A professional journalist, he was elected M. P. for Dungarvan, Waterford from 1877–1885 when a dispute with Parnell led to the end of his party political career. He was celebrated for his polemical writings, not least his *History of the Irish Parliamentary Party* (1910).

68. John O'Connor Power (1848–1919). A nationalist and member of the IRB, he was elected M. P. for Mayo in 1874 and attempted to integrate political activists with the constitutional Irish Party. Disagreement with Parnell led to the end of his political career.

69. *Christy Carew,* 51.

70. *The Irish Catholic Experience,* 223.

71. *Christy Carew,* 269.

72. Ibid., 277.

73. Frank Hugh O'Donnell, *A History of the Irish Parliamentary Party, Volumes I and II* (Port Washington, N.Y.: Kennikat Press, 1970), I: 104–105, II: 423.

74. *Christy Carew,* 270.

75. David Thornley, *Isaac Butt & Home Rule* (London: McGibbon & Kee, 1964), 161–63.

76. K. Theodore Hoppen, *Elections, Politics & Society in Ireland, 1832–1885* (New York: Oxford University Press, 1984), 236–37.

77. *The Roman Catholic Church and the Home Rule Movement in Ireland.* Regarding political involvement of senior clergy: 278–81 (Patrick Moran), 281–82 (Benjamin Woodlock).

78. *Christy Carew,* 263.

79. Samuel Richardson, *Clarissa Harlowe,* ed. Harriet Ward (London: George Routledge and Sons, 1868). *Clarissa Harlowe* is a novel told in the form of a diary and letters. Clarissa, a headstrong girl at odds with greedy relatives, is being forced by them into an arranged marriage. She wants to get away from home to give herself time to think, and so involves an acquaintance, Lovelace, in her flight, without knowing that he has sworn revenge for past injury on all the Harlowes, herself included. She has now put herself in his power. Richardson, a bookseller who began writing in his fifties, resisted pressure to create a happy ending, but produced instead one of the first psychological novels in English.

Chapter 6: Stories of Poverty and Hope

1. Thomas Carlyle, *Reminiscences of my Irish Journey in 1849,* ed. J. A. Froude (London: Sampson Low, Marston, Searle, and Rivington, 1882), 76: "Never saw such begging in this world; often get into a rage at it." Charles Kingsley, *His Letters & Memories of His Life,* cabinet edition, in one volume, ed. Frances Kingsley (London: K. Paul, Trench, and Co., 1884), chapter XIX, 236: "I am haunted by the human chimpanzees I saw along the hundreds of miles of horrible country [Ireland] . . . . It is a land of ruins and of the dead." Mr. & Mrs. Samuel Carter Hall, *Hall's Ireland: Mr. and Mrs. Hall's Tour of 1840, Vol. I,* condensed edition, ed. Michael Scott, (London: Sphere, 1984), 1–3: they remarked on the very great numbers of Irish beggars, and their persistence. William Makepeace Thackeray, *The Irish Sketchbook* (London: Smith, Elder & Co., no date but c. 1890), 13, 33–34, 48: he liked the Irish but found the sight of such abject poverty as theirs distressing.

2. Anon. review of "Flitters, Tatters and the Counsellor," *Spectator,* 29 March 1879, 410, 411.

3. Joseph Robins, *The Lost Children: A Study of Charity Children in Ireland 1700–1900* (Dublin: Institute of Public Administration, 1980).

4. Ibid., 311–13.

5. Ibid., 299.

6. Frances Hays, *Women of the Day* (London: Chatto & Windus, 1895), 111, 112.

7. Anon. review of "Flitters, Tatters, and the Counsellor," *Scotsman,* January 1881. page no. illegible.

8.   Great Ormond Street Hospital for Sick Children, London, founded 1864.

9.   Some examples: Louise Marston, *Cripple Jess: The Hop-picker's Daughter* (London: John F. Shaw, 1896). Hesba Stretton, *Alone in London* (London: Religious Tract Society, no date, c. 1880). Julia Horatia Ewing, *Lob Lie-by-the-Fire* (London: Society for the Promotion of Christian Knowledge, no date , probably c. 1890).

10.   May Laffan, "Flitters, Tatters & the Counsellor" (1879) (London: Macmillan, 1895) 1–3.

11.   Anthony Ashley Cooper, Lord Shaftsbury (1801–1885), based his pioneering social reforms on the need to compel the governing classes in England to accept responsibility for the welfare of industrial workers. He introduced the Factory Act of 1833 which regulated (and inspected) the employment of children in textile mills, and he went on to support legislation affecting such vulnerable groups as farm labourers and boy chimney sweeps. A quotation from his speech in Parliament of 6 June 1848 appears to be the first recorded use of the term "arab" to describe a street child: "City Arabs . . . are like tribes of lawless freebooters, bound by no obligations, and utterly ignorant or utterly regardless of social duties." *Oxford English Dictionary,* compact edition, complete text reproduced micrographically (London: Book Club Associates, by arrangement with Oxford University Press, 1979), Vol. I, A–O, 106, para. 3.

12.   "Flitters," 59.

13.   Ibid., 26.

14.   Ibid., 6–7.

15.   Ibid., 4–5.

16.   John Ruskin, *Fors Clavigera: Letters to the Workmen & Laborers of Great Britain* (London: Smith, Elder & Co., c. 1883), 161: "Extremely good girls . . . usually die young." John Ruskin (1819–1900), a celebrated art critic, also wrote on social and philosophical themes. *Fors Clavigera* was a collection of his articles, some in letter form, published by instalment between 1871 and 1884. The title is from the Latin and can be taken to mean Fortune's Keybearer. Also see John Sutherland's entry on John Ruskin in *The Stanford Companion to Victorian Fiction* (Stanford: Stanford University Press, 1989), 570.

17.   John Ruskin, review of May Laffan's stories, *Fors Clavigera*, 169–72.

18.   John Ruskin, *The King of the Golden River* (London: Smith, Elder & Co., 1851). Illustrated by Richard Doyle.

19.   Victoria Glendinning, *Trollope* (London: Pimlico, 1993), 332–34. An account of Anthony Trollope's difficulties with the publication of *Rachel Ray* (1863) as a serial in an evangelical magazine.

20.   May Laffan, "Baubie Clarke" (1881) (London: Macmillan, 1895), 177.

21.   Ibid., 226.

22.   Ibid., 216.

23.   Ibid., 225.

24. Anon. review of "Baubie Clarke," *Aberdeen Free Press,* January 1881, page no. illegible.

25. May Laffan, letter to John Ruskin, date not given, quoted by Ruskin in *Fors Clavigera,* 169.

26. Victor Hugo, *Les Miserables,* Norman Denny, trans. (London: Penguin, 1976), 495–511.

27. Anon. review of "The Game Hen" *Warder and Weekly Mail,* 23 October 1880, ". . . the pugilistic encounters read like an imitation of M. Zola in *L'Assomoir.*"

28. May Laffan, "The Game Hen," (1881) (London: Macmillan, 1895), 102.

29. Ibid., 130.

30. Ibid., 129.

31. Huckster. Name given in Ireland to a dealer in cheap household goods.

32. Game Hen. Feminine of Gamecock or Fighting-cock, a fowl bred for fighting.

33. May Laffan, "The Game Hen," 158–59.

34. George Moore, *A Drama in Muslin,* Belfast edition (Vizetelly, 1886; Belfast: Appletree, 1992), 63–64.

35. Fictional examples of women who "atone by dying": Oliver's unnamed mother, and Nancy, Bill Sykes's "moll" in Charles Dickens's *Oliver Twist* (1838); Lady Dedlock in Dickens's *Bleak House* (1852); Ruth in Elizabeth Gaskell's *Ruth* (1853); Lydia Gwilt in Wilkie Collins's *Armadale* (1866).

36. "The Game Hen," 143.

37. *Christy Carew,* 159–60.

38. Joseph Robins, *The Lost Children,* 294.

39. Ibid. 274–78.

40. "Flitters, Tatters & the Counsellor," 72.

41. "The Game Hen," 164–69.

42. Patrick Touher, *Fear of the Collar: Artane Industrial School* (Dublin: O'Brien, 1991), 172.

43. Erving Goffman, "On the Characteristics of Total Institutions," *Asylums: Essays on the Social Situation of Mental Patients and Other Inmates* (New York: Anchor Books, Doubleday, 1961), 1–24.

44. Harriet Martineau, see chapter three, note 55.

45. Touher, *Fear of the Collar,* 23.

46. Jane Barnes, *Irish Industrial Schools, 1868–1908* (Dublin: Irish Academic Press, 1989), 26, 43, 86–87.

47. Jacobite. A term relating to James II, King of England 1685–1688. (James = Jacobus in Latin). He was superseded by Prince William of Orange, but still regarded as

rightful king by Irish and Scots who supported the House of Stewart to which he belonged. Followers of James were called Jacobites.

48. Barnes, *Irish Industrial Schools,* 32.

49. May Laffan, "Convent Boarding-schools for Young Ladies," *Frazer's Magazine,* June 1874, 778–86. Also see May Laffan, *Ismay's Children* (London: Macmillan, 1887); Hannah Lynch, *The Autobiography of a Child* (New York: Dodd, Mead, and Co., 1899); Frank Hugh O'Donnell, *The Ruin of Education in Ireland* (London: D. Nutt, 1903)

50. James S. Donnelly, Jr., *The Land and the People of Nineteenth-Century Cork: The Rurual Economy and the Land Question* (Boston: Routledge and Kegan Paul, 1975), 251–307.

51. May Laffan, letter to George Grove, editor of Macmillan's Magazine, 5 August 1881. Unnumbered letter from Macmillan Archive at Reading University Library; Reading, Berks, England.

52. 11 Montagu Place, Russell Square was evidently the London address of one of May Laffan's friends, with whom she was staying. George Macmillan refers to the possibility of Laffan ending up in a less comfortable place, for instance, prison if she is not careful.

53. George A Macmillan, letter to May Laffan, 24 October 1881. British Library Macmillan Archive, no. 61.

54. The Ladies' Land League was set up in 1881 by Michael Davitt, under the leadership of Anna Parnell, sister of the leader of the Irish Party. The members were women with nationalist convictions, coming mainly from middle-class families, and mostly politically active for the first time. May Laffan knew the Davitts well but we do not know if she was a member of the LLL. Its purpose was to take over Land League activities if the leaders of the main organization were imprisoned, as they were. Unfortunately Charles and Anna Parnell disagreed about the level of responsibility and autonomy allowed to the LLL, and it was wound up a year later at Anna's insistence. A history of the organization remains to be written, but see Anna Parnell, *The Tale of a Great Sham,* Dana Hearn, ed. (Dublin: Arlen House, 1986).

55. Donnelly, *The Land and the People of Nineteenth-Century Cork,* 286–88.

56. May Laffan, "Weeds" in *Flitters, Tatters and the Counsellor and other sketches* (1881), (London: Macmillan, 1895), 282–283.

57. Ibid., 289–90.

58. Ibid., 292.

59. Ibid., 312–13.

60. Ibid., 313.

61. Ibid., 340.

62. May Laffan, letter to George Grove, 5 August 1881, 5 August 1881. Unnumbered letter from Macmillan Archive at Reading University Library; Reading, Berks, England.

63. James O'Shea, *Prince of Swindlers* (Dublin: Geography Publications, 1999), 399–423.

64. Resident Magistrate. These local magistrates were appointed by the Lord Lieutenant (Viceroy). They were not required to have any legal training, and their appointments were seen as political favours.

65. Nancy Murphy, *Guilty or Innocent: The Cormack Brothers* (Tyone, Nenagh: Relay, 1998), 152–54.

66. Ibid., 1–101.

67. Laurence M. Geary, "The Land War on the Kingston Estate 1879–1886." Unpublished PhD Thesis. University College, Cork, 1979, 7.

68. Ibid., 13.

69. Ibid., 13–17.

70. Ibid., 29. Also see Donnelly, *The Land and the People of Nineteenth-Century Cork,* 198.

71. James S. Donnelly, Jr., *The Land and the People of Nineteenth-Century Cork,* 199.

72. Personal communication from Mairead Maume, grand-niece of John Sarsefield Casey.

73. *Full & revised report of the Eight Day's Trial in the Court of Queen's Bench on criminal information against John Sarsefield Casey at the prosecution of Patten Smith Bridge; from Nov. 27th to Dec. 5th.1877.* E. Dwyer Gray, ed. (Dublin, 1877). *Report of the Arguments in the Court of Queen's Bench on Shewing Cause against the Conditional Order for a Criminal Information against John Sarsefield Casey at the prosecution of Patten Smith Bridge, with the Judgements of the Judges, with an Appendix of the Affadavits and documents used on the motion.* E. Dwyer Gray, ed. (Dublin, 1878), p. ix.

74. "Weeds," 257.

75. *Miss Ferrard,* 269.

76. "One of our Own." This is not a quotation, but a colloquial phrase, meaning "one of us," as opposed to "one of them."

77. "Weeds," 314.

78. "Flitters," 26–27.

79. The Ladies' Land League paid tenants' legal costs, but was credited with damaging landlord/tenant relations on the Kingston estate. Laurence M. Geary, *The Land War on the Kingston Estate,* 28, 41, 49.

80. *Report of the Arguments in the Court of Queen's Bench on Shewing Cause against the Conditional Order for a Criminal Information against John Sarsefield Casey at the Prosecution of*

Patten Smith Bridge, with the Judgements of the Judges, with an Appendix of the Affadavits and documents used on the motion, E. Dwyer Gray, ed. (Dublin, 1878), 53–57.

81. Whiteboys. A secret society which originated in North Tipperary and County Waterford in the 1760s to obtain redress for local grievances. The members met at night and disguised themselves by wearing white shirts over ordinary clothes.

80. "Weeds," 309.

Chapter 7: A Political Allegory of Fenian Ireland?

1. May Laffan, letter to George Grove, ed. of *Macmillan's Magazine,* 5 August 1881.

2. George A. Macmillan, letter to May Laffan, 3 March 1882. Macmillan refers to Laffan's news that *Beyond the Back Gates* is being published as a serial.

3. May Laffan, *A Singer's Story* (London: Chapman & Hall, 1885).

4. *Collins English Gem Dictionary,* J.B.Foreman ed. (London: Collins, 1974), 13.

5. Thomas Moore, *Captain Rock,* a description of the origins of terrorism, in the form of a family history; Moore's *An Irish Gentleman in Search of a Religion,* an attack on proselytism, in the form of an autobiography.

6. R. F. Foster, *Modern Ireland,1600–1972* (London: Penguin, 1988) 282–83.

7. Lady Morgan, *The Wild Irish Girl* (Oxford: Oxford University Press, 1999.)

8. Forster, *Modern Ireland,* 280–81.

9. R. F. Foster, *Paddy & Mr. Punch: Connections in Irish and English History* (London: A. Lane, 1993), 184–94.

10. Kathyrn Kilpatrick, introduction to *The Wild Irish Girl* (Oxford: Oxford University Press, 1999), vii–viii.

11. Lady Morgan, *The Wild Irish Girl,* 191.

12. Ibid., 190–91.

13. Tom Dunne, "Fiction as 'The Best History of Nations,'" *The Writer as Witness,* Tom Dunne, ed. (Cork: Cork University Press, 1987). 133, 137, 148, 150–51.

14. Jean-Jacques Rousseau, *LaNouvelle Heloise.* Rousseau believed that nature educated better than nurture could.

15. May Laffan, *Ismay's Children* (London: Macmillan, 1887), 87.

16. R. F. Foster, *Modern Ireland,* 396. W. J. McCormack, *Sheridan LeFanu and Victorian Ireland* (Oxford: Clarendon, 1980), 224.

17. W. J. McCormack, *Sheridan Lefanu and Victorian Ireland,* 12.

18. Andrew J. Kettle and Laurence J. Kettle, *The Material for Victory: Being the Memoirs of Andrew J. Kettle* (Dublin: C. J. Fallon, 1958) 116–17. See appendix to *Memoirs.*

19. R. V. Comerford, *The Fenians in Context* (Dublin: Wolfhound Press, 1985), 144–45.

20. Ibid., 142–43. "While revolution appeared to threaten, normal political activity was impossible."

21. Ibid., 109. The IRB presented a perpetual threat.

22. T. D. Sullivan, *Recollections of Troubled Times in Irish Politics* (Dublin: Gill, 1905) 210. Regarding "Union of Hearts."

23. Gerald Fitzgibbon, *Ireland in 1868: The Battlefield for English Party Strife; its Grievances, Real and Factitious; and Remedies, Abortive or Mischievous* (London: Longmans, Green, Reader, and Dyer, 1868), 5–13.

24. Louisa Murray, "Little Dorinn: A Fenian Story" in the *Canadian Monthly* (Toronto 1873), 291, 515.

25. Jeremiah O'Donovan Rossa, *O'Donovan Rossa's Prison Life: Six Years in Six English Prisons* (New York: Kenedy, 1874).

26. Anon. review of *Ismay's Children*, *Athenaeum*, no. 3129, 15 October 1887, 501.

27. Laffan's readiness to tackle political issues struck reviewers as highly unusual. The following tribute to her qualities comes from an anonymous reviewer in the *Warden & Weekly Mail*, a Dublin paper strongly Unionist and Conservative: "We must in fairness admit that we know of no novelist of our time who has a better grasp of her subject, or a more keen awareness of her country's deficiencies. Miss Laffan indeed is one of the very few writers of the day who seems to write for a purpose" (4 February 1882, 3).

28. By "Barrettstown" seems to be meant Mitchelstown, in North Cork. The surname Barrett is very common in Mitchelstown, and at the time Laffan was writing *Ismay's Children*, there were serious agrarian problems there connected to the Kingston estate. There was also a castle, so called. In fact, it was an immense early nineteenth-century house.

29. Demesne or domain. A term commonly used in nineteenth-century Ireland for an estate surrounding a mansion and belonging to it. Norman-French.

30. *Ismay's Children*, 385.

31. James Joyce, *A Portrait of the Artist as a Young Man* (Oxford: Oxford University Press, 2000), 74. The missing verse is as follows: "Oh, turn around, you wheel of fortune / Turn around, love, and smile on me, / For surely there must be a place of torment, / For those who treat others as you treated me." The song, "Love is Pleasing," is traditional, and the author is unknown.

32. A Diocesan College was a boarding school founded by the Bishop of the diocese, to educate boys to university level. The assumption was that some of them would go on to a seminary to become priests, so fees were low and there were always some free places. The education was based on classical and religious studies, and its quality varied. The physical care of the boys was sometimes very poor.

33. Trinity College, Dublin, was founded in Elizabethan days to educate the Ascendancy, that is, upper-class members of the Church of Ireland. Catholics who could afford to do so had to seek higher education abroad. By the 1860s, the time when events in

Ismay's Children are supposed to be taking place, Trinity would take Catholic students but would not confer degrees on them. The Irish Catholic Church discouraged Catholics from attending Trinity, preferring to press for a university which would acknowledge their religion.

34. *Ismay's Children,* 104.

35. Ibid., 96.

36. Ibid., 423.

37. For example: Charlotte Grace O'Brien, *Light and Shade* (1878). Charles Kickham, *For the Old Land* (1886). William O'Brien, *When We Were Boys* (London: Longmans, Green & Co., 1890). Hannah Lynch, *The Prince of the Glades* (1891). Edna Lyall, *Doreen* (London: Longmans, Green & Co. 1894). Patrick Sheehan, *The Graves at Kilmorna* (1915).

38. Examples of first-hand accounts by IRB members: Joseph C. Clarke, *My Life and Memories* (New York: Dodd, Mead & Co., 1926). Joseph Denieffe, *A Personal Narrative of the Irish Revolutionary Brotherhood* (Shannon: Irish University Press, 1969). John Devoy, *Recollections of an Irish Rebel* (1929). John Denvir, *The Life Story of an Old Rebel* (1910). John O'Leary, *Recollections of Fenians and Fenianism* (1896). Richard Pigott, *Recollections of an Irish National Journalist* (1882).

39. For a typical example, see Joseph Denieffe, *A Personal Narrative,* 151–55.

40. Whiteboys. See chapter six, reference number 81.

41. *Ismay's Children,* 117.

42. Maria Edgeworth, *The Absentee* (London: Penguin, 1999), 125–26. Regrading "Mr. Bourke, the Agent."

43. *Ismay's Children,* 140.

44. Ibid., 174–75.

45. Ibid., 281–82.

46. Ibid., 323–24.

47. Ibid., 362.

48. R. V. Comerford, *The Fenians in Context,* 98, 99, 134.

49. *Ismay's Children,* 464.

50. Ibid., 417.

51. Ibid., 495.

52. Ibid., 117. Blanche's maiden name, MacAnalley, identifies her as being from Ulster.

53. Charles Dickens, *Bleak House* (London: Collins Pocket Classics, 1900), 22.

54. Anthony Trollope, *Doctor Thorne* (Oxford: Oxford University Press, 1934), 162.

55. Patrick Corish, *The Irish Catholic Experience* (Dublin: Gill and Macmillan, 1985), 220.

56. Edith Somerville, *The Big House of Inver* (London: Heinemann, 1927), 22–23. Regarding "Pindys" (Prendevilles).

57. William O'Connor Morris, *Memories and Thoughts of a Life* (London: George Allen, 1895), 174. Regarding marriages of doubtful legality.

58. Matthew McDonnell Bodkin, *Famous Irish Trials* (Dublin: Duffy, 1928), 44–78. Regarding the Yelverton case.

59. Anon., "Therese Longworth,"*The Feminist Companion to Literature in English,* Virginia Blain, Isobel Grundy, Patricia Clements, eds. (New Haven: Yale University Press, 1990), 668–69.

60. Maria Edgeworth, *Ennui* (London: Penguin Classics, 1992), 192–93.

61. *Ismay's Children,* 136, 146.

62. W. M. Thackeray, *The Memoirs of Barry Lyndon* (Oxford: Oxford University Press, 1984).

63. *Ismay's Children,* 460.

64. *The Irish Catholic Experience,* 62.

65. Declan Kiberd, *Inventing Ireland: The Literature of the Modern Nation* (London: Vintage, 1996), 9–25.

66. Emmet Larkin, *The Consolidation of the Roman Catholic Church in Ireland, 1860–1870* (Dublin: Gill and Macmillan, 1987), 113–80.

67. F. S. L. Lyons, *Ireland Since the Famine* (Glasgow: Collins/Fontana,1973), 90–98.

68. Father Paul's brother seems to have been a member of Young Ireland (1844–1848), an offshoot of the political movement working for repeal of the Act of Union between England and Ireland. Following an abortive insurrection, members were transported or permanently exiled from Ireland.

69. *Ismay's Children,* 206–07.

70. Ibid., 207.

71. John F. Fleetwood, *The History of Medicine in Ireland* (Dublin: Skellig, 1983), 250. Peter Froggatt, "Competing Philosophies," *Medicine, Disease and the State in Ireland, 1650-1940,* Elizabeth Malcolm and Greta Jones, eds. (Cork: Cork University Press, 1999), 75.

72. John F. Fleetwood, *The History of Medicine in Ireland,* 247.

73. Emmet Larkin, *The Consolidation of the Roman Catholic Church in Ireland, 1860–1870,* 167, 310.

74. St. Catherine's, Dominican Convent, Blackrock, Co. Dublin.

75. Church of Ireland schools received extra income from legacies and charitable funds; Catholic schools did not. Church of Ireland schools were also more influenced by the English public school system

76. *Recess Committee Notes,* see chapter two, reference 62.

77. Seán P. Farragher, Père Leman: Educator and Missionary Founder of Blackrock College (Dublin: Paraclete, 1988), 258–59.

78. John Nicholas Murphy, *Terra Incognita* (London: Longmans, Green, 1873), 496.

79. Some examples: Dean Farrar, *Eric, or Little by Little* (1858); Thomas Hughes, *Tom Brown's Schooldays* (1857); Harriet Martineau, *The Crofton Boys* (c. 1840); Talbot Baines Reed, *The Fifth Form at Saint Dominics* (1887).

80. According to Laffan's correspondence with Dr. William Walsh, Archbishop of Dublin (see chapter two, reference 58), a number of Dublin families sent children to be educated in England or to Protestant schools in Dublin.

81. Paul Bew, *Land and the National Question in Ireland, 1858–1882* (Dublin: Gill & Macmillan, 1978), 47. R. V. Comerford, *The Fenians in Context*, 180–81.

82. Emmet Larkin, *The Consolidation of the Roman Catholic Church in Ireland, 1860–1870*, 50–54.

83. R. V. Comerford, *The Fenians in Context*, 98–99.

84. Ibid., 119.

85. *Ismay's Children*, 129–30.

86. Ibid., 102.

87. Ibid., 370.

88. Ibid., 105.

89. Ibid., 110.

90. Ibid., 102–103.

91. Ibid., 230.

92. Ibid., 306.

Conclusion

1. W. B. Yeats, "Title of Article" in the *Bookman*, October 1895.

2. Kevin Whelan, "An Underground Gentry? Catholic Middlemen in Eighteenth-Century Ireland" in *Irish Popular Culture: 1650–1850*, J.S. Donnelly and Kerby A. Miller eds. (Dublin: Irish Academic Press, 1998), 118–164.

3. One of these, Hannah Ryan (1872–1928), became the mother of Brendan Bracken, founder of the Financial Times (London), and Winston Churchill's Private Secretary and Minister of Information during the Second World War.

4. William O'Brien (1852–1928) was first a journalist, then a novelist and a politician. The best-known of his novels, *When We Were Boys*, is a fictionalised account of his own early life, written during his 1880–1881 prison sentence mentioned in chapter six.

5. Charles Joseph Kickham (1828–1882). Fenian, journalist, novelist and poet, he wrote the best-selling and still widely read nostalgic story *Knocknagow: or, The Homes of Tipperary*, which tells of the destruction of a rural community.

6.   George Augustus Moore (1852–1933). Born into an Irish landowning family, Moore lived mainly in France and in England, where he became a successful novelist after his failure to engage with the literary renaissance in Ireland. Deeply influenced by Balzac and Zola, Moore developed an elegant and effective literary style, which he exercised in his Irish novels *A Drama in Muslin* and *The Lake,* and which anticipated literary techniques used by Joyce.

7.   James Aloysius Joyce (1882–1941), novelist and poet, and one of the most celebrated innovative writers of the twentieth century.

8.   "Somerville and Ross." This term refers to the literary collaboration of two cousins, Edith Oenone Somerville (1858–1949) and Violet Martin (1862–1915), whose pseudonym was "Martin Ross." Together they successfully produced five novels and three collections of humorous short stories; following Martin's death Somerville continued to publish under their joint names. The cousins came from an Irish Ascendancy background and their work reflects this. The short stories depict cunning peasants and bewildered gentry, but attempts, in the novels, to portray middle-class Irish Catholics are unconvincing. Acknowledged to be the finest of their novels is *The Real Charlotte* (1894) which has overtones of Balzac.

9.   The Honorable Emily Lawless (1845–1913) was a daughter of the Anglo-Irish Lord Cloncurry. Brought up partly in England, she began her career as novelist in London, but soon gravitated to writing novels set mainly in the West of Ireland, the best known of which is *Hurrish* (1886). This novel deals with the effects of the "Land War" on a peasant family and is told from an Ascendancy standpoint, since Lawless did not believe the Irish to be capable of self-determination.

10.   May Laffan, *Hogan MP* (London: Macmillan, 1881), 52.

11.   Charles Stewart Parnell (1846–1891), Irish nationalist leader, in 1889 during attempts to get Home Rule for Ireland, was cited as co-respondent in the O'Shea divorce case. The case followed a period of ten years during which his relationship with Kitty O'Shea, the wife of a colleague, was concealed from the public at large, although Irish politicians knew about it. The Liberal Party in Parliament, strongly anti-divorce, promptly threatened to withdraw support from the Irish Party unless Parnell resigned as leader. (The Liberals had earlier in the 1880s ejected Sir Charles Dilke, a prominent Radical politician, from their own party because he was involved in a divorce case.) The Irish Party, the Catholic Hierarchy, and the country split on the question of whether to support Parnell or not. The majority decided not to support him, and this aroused strong feelings for a considerable time even after Parnell died in 1891. But it is difficult , in view of Dilke's experience, not to consider that Parnell in this case overplayed his hand.

ᴊꙙᴘ INDEX

A

Aberdeen Free Press 176, 177

Aberdeen Journal 51, 177

Academy 135

Act of Union (1800) 13, 199

Alexandria College 26–27, 46, 57, 62

Allingham, Helen (née Paterson) 56

Allingham, William, 56

    Laurence Bloomfield in Ireland 118

American Civil War 223

Andersen, Hans Christian
    "The Little Match Girl" 171

Arnold, Thomas 52

Athenaeum 51, 55, 203, 205

Austen, Jane 82

B

Balzac, Honoré 79, 86, 110

    Pere Goriot 83

Barry, Father Gerald 5

Bayard, Emile 50

Bentley, George 45, 46, 49, 50

Bentley, Richard 72, 111, 171

Black, William 51

Blackrock College (French College) 19, 22, 23

Bloomfield Institution 67, 68

Bridge, Patton Smith 192

Brophy, Ann 190, 191

Broughton, Rhoda 45, 52, 54

Butt, Isaac 4, 89, 99, 101, 106, 164, 165, 166

C

The Cabinet of Irish Literature 48, 49, 95, 137

Carleton, William 95

The Black Prophet 154

    Fardorougha the Miser, 145

Campbell, Sir George 165

Carlyle, Thomas 31, 225

Carroll, Lewis 51

Casey, John Sarsefield 191, 192

Catholic Emancipation (1829) 30, 32, 95, 122, 129, 199

Catholic University 98, 99, 105, 130–31, 221, 224

Cecilia Street Medical School 221

Celtic Revival 44, 94

Charter Schools 34

Church Act of 1869 78, 98

Collins, Wilkie 213

    No Name 213

Conroy, Father Paul 5

Cork Examiner 192

Corkran, Father Jim 47

Corlett, Barbara 44

Cormack, William and Daniel 189, 190, 191

Cullen, Cardinal 166

Cullen, Paul 62

D

Davitt, Michael 64, 104, 185

Davoren, Dicky 37

Davoren, Nellie 20, 43, 69

Devlin, Anne 147

Dickens, Charles 27, 172

    Bleak House 173, 213

    Little Dorrit 83

    Little Nell 170

    Oliver Twist 213

    Paul Dombey 170

Dilke, Sir Charles 52

Dillon, John 104

Disestablishment of the Church of Ireland 32, 103, 122, 148, 201

W

Y

Z